FREUD—HIS DREAM AND SEX THEORIES

Other Books by Joseph Jastrow

FREUD

HIS DREAM

AND

SEX THEORIES

BY

JOSEPH JASTROW

Ph.D., LL.D.

THE WORLD PUBLISHING CO.

CLEVELAND, OHIO   NEW YORK, N. Y.

PRINTED IN THE UNITED STATES OF AMERICA

WBC

To the
NEW SCHOOL FOR SOCIAL RESEARCH
In Recognition of its Services
in the Cause of Intellectual Stimulation.

CONTENTS

CONTENTS

FOREWORD

The project of subjecting the vast body of doctrine known as psychoanalysis to a critical scrutiny must find its justification in the execution of the task. For reader and reviewer alike it may be well to indicate that the appraisal of the Freudian structure is largely confined to the latter portion of the book, to the concluding chapter particularly. My reflections upon the endless, repetitious, befuddling and irritating hours that I have spent over Freudian literature are of mixed character. There is so much dross, so little precious ore. Yet my faith in its value when refined remains. It has been my task to separate the one from the other, often trusting to the balance of my own judgments. I have conferred with psychologists and psychiatrists of every persuasion and psychoanalysts of each denomination. I have listened and have been enlightened; I have objected and have been listened to and consigned to unpleasant places.

The dogmatic tone of confirmed psychoanalysts and the cumbersome and assumptive verbiage in which they have swathed and glorified their doctrines, are as unfortunate for the reader as they were burdensome to me. I have reduced citation to the essential documentation. The architecture of the house of Freud is so largely an afterthought, and the liberties taken by his disciples in building their huts and mansions upon similar plans so many, that I have often had to interpret the design as best I could. In my personally conducted tour I could not spare the reader the intricacies of the tortuous passages and underground connections of the edifice. I have relieved the expedition by dwelling upon the more engaging if less convincing features of what remains a significant if amazing production. I have met frankness with frankness and left the reader in no uncertainty as to my views.

JOSEPH JASTROW

ACKNOWLEDGMENTS

The painstaking compilation of Healy, Bronner and Bowers: *The Structure and Meaning of Psychoanalysis* —a veritable Talmud with text and commentary—has saved me so many hours of toil and has proved so convenient a reference-book, that I gratefully record my appreciation. At every stage of preparation from title to finis, the manuscript has had the valuable criticism of my associate, Miss Elsie Junghans—an acknowledgment, personal and professional.

PART ONE

FREUD—HIS DREAM AND SEX THEORIES

INTRODUCTION

When this book was issued, a menacingly paranoid personality was rising to dictatorial power. In the intervening years this psychopathic mind has imposed its delusions upon an aggrieved, goose-stepping people, prone to be misled by doctrinaire phrases, sanctioning the ruthless methods of terrorizing the peace of Europe. Pronouncements, threats, exiles, confiscations, degradation camps, broken pledges, invasions and destruction generally followed thick and fast. A year ago, a Prime Minister of Great Britain, returning from a mission of appeasement, confidently displayed a memorandum bearing his own signature and that of Adolph Hitler, assuring the amicable solution of possible difference between the two empires which they represented. To a competent psychiatrist, that document would have carried no greater value than attaches to the word or the mood of an irresponsible paranoiac, as insensitive to pledges as to compassions. The lesson, extending to the present ominous times, is that on occasion the clue to history may be offered by psychiatry.

A far-seeing psychiatrist would concede that one paranoid dictator with a sufficient following might wreck the stability of civilization. For the direction of national no less than of an individual life, rests basically upon the

3

sanity of emotion, judgment and control. Among the havocs and horrors consummated by the Hitlerian psychopathic motivation was the rape of Austria, and the consequent exile of the founder of psychoanalysis to England, where he was invited to inscribe his name upon the honor roll of the Royal Society. So subversive of the dictatorial tenets were the views of this aged and ailing "non-Aryan," that his release from Nazi captors required a ransom of 250,000 shillings, offered by a princess of Greece. Dispossessed of home, property, books and papers, Sigmund Freud died in London on September 23rd, 1939 at the age of 83. His momentous contribution to a novel interpretation of human motivation remains, whatever may be the measure of one's assent to or dissent from the psychoanalytic structure. A brilliantly creative mind has left its impress upon an era. We have traveled far in thought from pre-Freudian days.

This book presents a critical epitome of the definitive system of Freud and his followers—its underlying premises and far-flung applications. It may stand, as when originally issued, upon its merits and appeal; nor in the seven years between has a comparable project been attempted. The interest in the Freudian contributions continues through the turbulent times of a troubled world. Recently a thousand-page compilation of *The Basic Writings of Sigmund Freud** achieved an extraordinary popu-

* The compilation is edited with an Introduction by Dr. A. A. Brill, the most active leader of the Freudian movement in America. It contains *The Psychopathology of Everyday Life, The Interpretation of Dreams, Three Contributions to the Theory of Sex, Wit and Its Relation to the Unconscious, Totem and Taboo,* and the *History of the Psychoanalytic Movement.* (The Modern Library 1938.)

In 1939 appeared a psychoanalytic interpretation of *Moses and Monotheism,* a work begun in Vienna and completed in London. In

lar circulation. Freud, more than any other modern thinker, requires a critical comment; without it the layman is lost, and even the professional needs a map. For the entire thought sequence of Freud moves in an abstruce domain, which after decades of various and violent opposition, has obtained a public hearing. The question remains pertinent and insistent: What is sound and stimulating and what unscientific and misleading in the house that Freud built and furnished. A fair position upon the value of his conclusions is vital to those who would understand the problems of wholesome, intelligent living, and no less the disagreements upon their foundation and technique. One can no longer be just for or against Freud, but must place his contributions somewhere in the total view of the psychic life.

My critique concludes with the forecast of a trend; the prospect there indicated seems to me to have moved toward fulfillment. The camps remain and display their banners; but the great majority of psychologists and psy-

this thesis Freud returns to the cultural problem in which legend, the cult of the hero, the inhibitions of taboo, symbolic rites converge upon a religion and a people, wandering for centuries from exodus to exile, and shaping history in all their habitats, from Egypt to the New World. His interest is centered upon the light which psychoanalysis sheds upon the origin of the Mosaic dispensation. It is avowedly speculative at every stage of the interpretation.

In 1933, Freud issued a revision, which is also a continuation of his *General Introduction to Psychoanalysis*. It offers little that affects the presentation of his leading principles. It is franker, more discursive, and somewhat more personal than the lectures of 1916 (in the English translation by G. Stanley Hall, issued in 1920). Since the logic remains the same, the modifications in statement result from further interpretation of the reports of the analyzees.

(In the English version by W. J. H. Sprott, published by W. W. Norton, it is entitled *New Introductory Lectures on Psycho-analysis*.) These "lectures" were written for his readers; a serious operation upon his throat deprived Freud of the ability to address an audience. The academic habit suits his type of exposition.

chiatrists and of the informed public, would agree in the
intent to salvage the significant products of psychoanalytic thought—very much restated—and to allow the
extravagances of a movement that has entered signifi-
cantly into the making of the modern outlook, to recede
into the alcoves of history.

Today, the followers of Freud assume far greater lati-
tude in accepting the doctrines of the founder; the perspective of principles and the technique of practice
present a divergent front. Freud himself veered very little
from his original position. In the revised *Autobiography*
(1935), he admits the sexual assaults reported in analytic
confessions may have been fantasy rather than fact, but
remain as authentic in the one origin as in the other;
likewise that the energy of libido radiates from sex to
ego-assertion, which in turn varies from Narcissism to
object libido. But the dominance of the first five years of
life with its infantile sexuality and the ubiquity of "Oedipus" must stand; or there can be no psychoanalysis.
Equally indispensable to the Freudian practice is "transference"—an intensive emotional relation, which may be
love and hate in turn between patient and analyst—and
that because this relation re-enacts some phases of the
original Oedipus situation or similar attachments. So
completely proprietary is psychoanalysis that it determines the details of practice no less than the psychological
theory. Even the common interest of his first foreign
champion Carl Jung of Zurich, in the analytical interpretation of myth and fantasy and his addition of a collective
unconscious, does not save him from exclusion from the
fold. From the neutral position of an adherent and an
innovator, Jung like Freud has moved his interests from

the clinical to the cultural aspects of "depth psychology."

More and more those who remain Freudian in trend, especially in their views of the neuroses, are moving toward the position of the Neo-Freudians in the agreement that principles and applications must make terms with accredited psychological fundamentals interpreted on a naturalistic basis—a position which is set forth in several connections in the present critique.*

The liberalization of Freudian adherence brought a wide popularity, especially in the United States, to the views of Alfred Adler. His long residence in America, his genial personality, the ready comprehension of this common-sense—and somewhat evangelical—approach made his formula of "a way of life" acceptable to the American psychiatric tradition.

That position looks upon a neurosis as a failure in a balanced life, commonly founded upon a predisposition, often precipitated by outrageous fortune. It recognizes the existence of conflicts—and indeed between primary instincts and social enforcements,—both Freudian contributions—but gives them their setting in the cultural environment. Its therapeutic aim is to normalize the disturbed emotions, by reinstatement of energies, interests and natural releases. Clearly this formula applies most directly to the neurasthenias, the most common of all neuroses, which Freud (apart from their share in the anxieties) exempts from psychoanalysis. As many have said—and Freud quotes it with a touch of disdain—the "analysis" concepts, and no less the clinical revelations, are in the Teutonic temper, which is in contrast with the *genie latin*, and equally with the American or Anglo-

* As for instance from page 163 on.

Saxon loyalty to a common sense logic and a factual (biological) basis. It is not an unexpected conclusion that depth psychology should reflect the national cultural trends.

Adler died in the fullness of his powers, while lecturing at Aberdeen, in 1938. His active sponsor and translator, Dr. W. Beran Wolfe, was killed in an automobile accident about a year before. "Individual psychology," as it was rather meaninglessly called, continues as a trend but without a leader. Adler, no less than Freud had a single-track thesis, which made character defects and their issue in the psychoneuroses a face-saving assumption of superiority to mask a hampering sense of inferiority. Yet Beran Wolfe had set forth the illuminating interpretation that a "nervous breakdown" was a knock-out blow in the neuropsychic mechanism, arranged by nature to prevent more complete disaster. How it can be that and as well a face-saving device and to the Freudian a long-distance reincarnation of an infantile complex, is not easy for a biologically minded psychologist to conceive. Clearly the "depth psychologists," who may all reaffirm their debt to Freud, have not reached a wholesome relation with the fundamental doctrines of psychology and psychiatry.

With the more peaceful penetration of Freudian concepts, it appears with increasing definition that the two issues center about the nature of the psychoneuroses and the scheme of motivation of "depth psychology."* Freud

* Academic orthodox psychologists, with few exceptions, have been completely occupied with the mental mechanisms, mostly with an intellectual emphasis. In all this Freud had no interest. But the biological foundations of the total psychic life affect every chapter of the story; the ignoring of these was a serious Freudian neglect. The naturalistic view reinstates the joint sovereignty of the physical and psychical components of our wonderful being.

staked his all on the hysterical complex, which in all truth, from Mesmer to Coue, furnishes one clue to psychic distortion; but those who view the neuroses broadly in all their diversity realize that the keys are many and cannot be forced into one matrix.

The turn to depth psychology through the problems of the psychoneuroses is a Freudian insight; it might have been reached otherwise; it came through the challenge of psychology by psychoanalysis.

JOSEPH JASTROW

CHAPTER I

PLANS AND SPECIFICATIONS

FOUNDATIONS

Psychoanalysis was born in Vienna just fifty years ago. The germinal idea was suggested by a case of hysteria treated by Dr. Joseph Breuer, fourteen years the senior of Dr. Sigmund Freud, his associate. Freud delicately gives the credit to Breuer, and the tribute is deserved, by noting that "America is not named after Columbus." The idea will ever be known as Freud's "discovery"; it reads that a bodily symptom in a neurotic patient may have a psychic origin of a peculiar type. Innocent as that announcement may appear, its consequences proved to be a shock that was heard around the world.

It was this idea that in 1885 took Freud, on a medical scholarship, to Paris, to the leading neurologist of Europe, Jean Marie Charcot, some of whose writings he later translated into German. In Charcot's clinic he witnessed the disappearance of hysterical impairments under hypnosis. Charcot, Freud records twenty-five years later, had no bent for psychological theories. Indeed, he was thinking in quite other terms. He distinguished three stages of *"le grand hypnotisme"* found in hysterics and hystero-epilepsy: catalepsy, lethargy, and somnambulism, each characterized by distinct physio-

10

logical symptoms. This tenet of the "School of Paris," despite its prestige, was superseded by the position of the "School of Nancy" under Bernheim, which referred the hypnotic phenomena to suggestion, thus moving toward the psychic origin of "bodily" symptoms in hysteria, but with no definite clue as to the mechanisms involved. There could be but one conclusion: that Charcot had been misled by the suggestibility of his subjects. The three states were an artefact; they appeared in Paris, not in Nancy. Freud's interest was not in hypnosis, but in neurosis. To account for these elusive symptoms—which appeared as strangely as they disappeared—that, and not merely to observe and record them, was the question. Freud wished to penetrate below the surface and explain why just these particular symptoms occurred, and why so variously in different cases. On a second visit to France, that insistent search took Freud to Nancy. At the age of thirty, he embarked, a lone pioneer, on what proved to be a life-long expedition.

Janet, associated with Charcot, regarded the essence of the hysterical condition to be the tendency to lapse into a dissociated state—a split in consciousness—which in turn was referred to a congenital weakness in the complex (psycho-neural) integration by which personalities are formed. Most of us develop normal, if not quite harmonious, personalities; in hysteria, the personality is invaded by an alien disturbance. Janet suggested a subconscious origin for the invasion, spoke of a disturbance of "psychic tensions," but made no deeper search for the why and wherefore. By admitting that his phrase *idées inconscientes* was just a convenient phrase and not a new conception, he "needlessly deprived himself of high credit" (Freud). Both factors —a state of trance and a psychically induced symptom

—were present in the first "Freudian" observation; the symptoms which furnished the clue were traced and in turn relieved in a state of "absence" or mild dissociation.

When Freud asked *why* hysterics behave as they do, declining to accept their symptoms at their face value, his approach implied a dynamic view of the human psyche. The approach of Charcot and Janet was descriptive and expository, analytic only so far as all diagnosis must be so, but with no effective curiosity as to the source and meaning of clinical symptoms. They observed the varying tides of the ebb and flow of psychic disturbance. Breuer initiated the search which Freud pursued, as to the causes of the psychic tides, alike for their regularity and their variations. They asked the question because they glimpsed the answer; and that answer was not, as in the oceanic tides, a force outside set in a solar cosmos, but was determined within the urgings and strivings of the organism itself. That is the nuclear concept named for English readers by E. B. Holt: "The Freudian Wish." Dissociation was a rather static and descriptive term; it labelled a state which brought on disqualification, anaesthesia, paralysis.

This issue has since become familiar in the "shell-shock" of war. Under the dynamic Freudian "wish," there was both a cause and a motive. Freud "has given us a key to the explanation of mind. It was the first key which psychology ever had which fitted" (Holt). At once the entire possibilty of explanation was lifted to a different plane. There loomed a new plan and new specifications for the house of psyche; it was no longer merely a formal structure but became a living habitation.

The First Case of Psychoanalysis

Breuer's case of Anna O., aged 21, as the virginal instance of a psychoanalytic diagnosis, has a place in the history of psychology. This young woman had developed a paralysis of the right arm, a blurred vision, a difficulty in swallowing, and also a group of other perplexing symptoms. Hysteria is as versatile as the *varium et mutabile semper femina,* being characteristically of the same gender. The symptoms, variable from case to case, were both mutable and stubborn in their persistence while they held the field, in time displaced by others. But why just those incapacities? That was the puzzle, and this was the Breuer-Freud solution: They arise under emotionally tense situations; they may be compulsions, tics, spasms, gestures, rituals, muttered words, if they are positive bits of behavior; or pseudo-paralyses and selective anaesthesias if they are negative disqualifications. They impose and they impair; they intrude upon normal behavior. They are, in effect, situation-scars. When Freud said: "Let us trace the hysterical vagaries to their source in personal, intimate, emotionalized situations, and these in turn to whatever motivations may lie behind them," his Columbian voyage was inaugurated.

Like the caravels of Columbus, the principles with which Freud set out, were three: First, *determinism.* These symptoms were not haphazard or meaningless; they had a cause, a psychic one. Second, the *subconscious.* The origin of the symptoms was hidden from the patient, and operated underground. Third, the reason for the *suppression* was that the memories concerned were unpleasant, or at least were heavily loaded with conflicting emotion, which played havoc with a normal peace of mind.

Anna's story was this: She had been in attendance at the bedside of her father in a long illness which proved fatal. She had fallen asleep with her arm hanging over the back of the chair; when she awoke, startled, the arm had become numb; she could not feel it or move it. The momentary incapacity was accepted as real. What a constricted circulation started was fixed by her emotional agitation; such is the hysterical mechanism, converting a psychic idea into a bodily symptom. Believing herself paralyzed, she was paralyzed. Next, the tears in her eyes prevented her from seeing clearly the face of her watch when her father asked for the time; her vision, blurred first by tears, later continued so by fears. Her fatigue longed for relief; she was impelled by a sense of duty to keep on. The numbness and blurred vision were not accepted for what they were, as they would have been under normal conditions, but became hysterically fixed afflictions, the plot thickening as the sequence of hysterical impairments developed.

Breuer and Freud were well aware that these issues closely paralleled those produced by hypnotic suggestions; they were in a sense products of self-suggestion, which persisted because the agitation which imposed them continued, and there was no force to nullify them. They might be likewise—this a later "discovery"—not merely recent wounds but the flaring up of older injuries, dating from disturbed childhood experiences or deeply emotionalized relations. The neurotic constitution was such because it was susceptible to such shock. Breuer's part in the "discovery" was not alone in suggesting this peculiar psychic origin and mechanism of bodily symptoms, but also in developing the technique of relief of "psychogenic" maladies by the "talking

cure" of explanation, a variety of catharsis. He also
recognized the intense emotional quality of the disturbing memory (cathexis). The "three contributions to hysteria" by Breuer are the germinal ones. The first stone
for the house that Sigmund Freud built was laid by
Joseph Breuer. Beyond this, psychoanalysis is substantially the product of Freud's mind.

It was by following the clues from the words mum-
bled in this state of "absence," or secondary condition
of Anna (which Breuer induced by hypnosis), that the
explanation of the symptoms was found. The case is
thus complicated by hysterical episodes in a serial development. Bodily symptoms, reveries, hallucinations
enter. Thus, the right arm was not only "asleep" as the
result of hanging over the back of the chair, but the
patient had dreamt or reveried a black snake, which
frightened her, and threatened her father; the attempt
to drive away the snake intensified the helpless feeling;
the same anguish drove away her power of speech also.
Finally, she thought of, and recited, an English nursery
song, and then for a long time spoke only English. It
was by reviving the memory of this scene that the
symptoms were aroused and in turn dispelled. So
tangled a tale may be variously interpreted, especially
in the light of later Freudian hypotheses, as will duly appear (see p. 242). For the present purpose the simplified interpretation, though incomplete, and without
precise reference to the sequence of the symptoms, will
answer; for the hysterical picture changes kaleido-
scopically, as each symptom is summoned from the unconscious breeding-ground and by its rationalization
rendered harmless. Had the original "case" been one
of compulsion (see p. 21), the principles would have
appeared somewhat differently. Yet it is precisely the
generalized application of this mechanism, applicable

to several types of neurosis, that constitutes the Freudian formulation of the "discovery" of Breuer.* Prompting the memories under hypnosis brought forth the
story of a governess in her childhood whom she dis-
liked and of her disgust when this governess permitted
her pet dog to drink from a family glass. After relating
this incident, Anna woke from hypnosis with the glass
at her lips and had no further difficulty in drinking.
That symptom was *abreacted,* dispelled by *catharsis.*
Thus was "discovered" or conjectured the childhood
situational origin of symptoms appearing in mature life.
This remote connection, supplying the psychological
missing-link, was destined to play a commanding part
in psychoanalysis. It led Freud to the thesis that "hys-
tericals suffer from their reminiscences"; their subconscious cannot forget.

A different interpretation is favored by Jung, psychoanalyst of another school: that the same hysterical
liability which made the child Anna react so violently
to the "disgust" incident, was reinstated under the general emotional upset of her present situation. She is reviving older impairments. To Freud this is *regression;*
Anna's psyche is regressing to an infantile stage. To
Jung this means partly that, and mainly that she is
again in a susceptible, vulnerable state of mind; her
neurotic susceptibility appeared in childhood and reappeared in later stresses.

* It is well to explain that in the interests of focusing upon the
essentials of the psychoanalytical discovery, I have simplified this
"case," and follow the account of it given by Freud at the maturer
stage of his interpretation, in the American lectures (1909); in which,
however, he cites in part from the earlier joint report by Breuer
and himself (1893–95) of the original "case" observed a dozen years
earlier (1880–82). It should be noted also that this patient displayed
the typical hysterical states of "absence," amounting to an altered
personality. This, as observed in hysterical cases, may vary from light
trance to disorientation, to stupor.

A still more remote or indirect psychogenic impairment was also noted. In her distress at the bedside of her stricken father, Anna tried to pray, and was able to recall only an English prayer, presumably taught to her by her governess. Out of this momentary limitation, her hysterical self elaborated the conviction that she could speak only English, which impairment continued, the record says, for one-and-a-half years. The ways of hysteria are strange indeed! When, by explaining and talking to the patient, Breuer uncovered the sources of these impairments, Anna regained her native German, which loss, of course, was as unreal as the impairment of sight or movement, but of a higher type of psychic organization. Let me repeat that other interpretations * in the light of later emendations are possible; yet the first fruits of the psychoanalytic method contain the seed for all later blossoms.

The Freudian analysis concludes: that the normal state knows not, is amnesic to, the sources of the symptoms; that these can be recalled in hypnosis. or by any technique that will tap the subconscious which elaborates the impairments and stores them; that the connection may be remote in relation and in time, going back typically to a childhood shock or trauma; that the entire psycho-neurotic drama, is set in an intensely disturbing emotional atmosphere; that resurrecting the buried sources of the impairments and ventilating them by free discussion, dissipates them. Anna was relieved, and psychoanalysis scored its first success. Thus did hysterical impairment suggest to the fertile mind of Freud, reacting to the original suggestion of Breuer, the first principles of psychoanalysis—the groundplan of the house that Freud alone was to build. For

* See p. 242.

Breuer, for various reasons, was disinclined to pursue the matter further.

HYSTERICAL IMPAIRMENT

Since it is possible that we should never have heard of Freud as a founder of a momentous movement but for this original interpretation of hysterical impairment of function, the nature of that strange constellation of psychic disturbances becomes part of the Freudian story. The hysterical impairment appears as a symptom real in its disturbing power, yet unreal in organic basis—an incapacity neither assumed as in the malingerer, the *malade imaginaire* of either sex—nor yet the issue of an actual lesion within. Stated bluntly, the neurotic invalid is not a neuronic invalid; hence the search for some other mechanism; hence the proposed solution, first announced in 1892, the "1492" of the Freudian era!

The peculiar unreality of hypnotic and hysterical symptoms was known before Freud. The hysterical Sphinx is an ancient enigma. Its prevalence was broadcasted by cases of "shell-shock" impairments of war, when able-bodied soldiers in the prime of life went suddenly blind with no real defect of vision, deaf with the hearing structure unaffected, paralyzed in limb with the motor apparatus intact. All that is psychogenic, a term which may be applied to any effect imposed upon the physiological organism by way of ideas and feelings.

All suggestion is psychogenic; but the psychogenic procedure operates at many levels. It may be as extraneous and as temporary an illusion as that by which the soldiers saw the Angels at Mons, or the civilians reported the presence of Russian soldiers on English soil. It is far more pervasive and disturbing in shell-shock; it then strikes much deeper into the psychic integrity which we call a normal state of mind. Hysterical cures, no less than hysterical afflictions, were well known in older days—crutches left at shrines, sight restored by a healing touch. When a patient is suddenly stricken, not by an apoplectic but by an emotional stroke, and when he is as suddenly cured by a like emotional mechanism—mind cure or relief by exorcising or dismissing a "demon" fear—the mechanism is psychogenic on the intimate level of bodily sensation. But conversely, that impairment may be relieved when its inducing cause is removed; many a shell-shocked soldier was, in that sense, cured by the Armistice. This statement does not mean that there is no physiological mechanism underlying the psychic effect. Presumably there is; at present we do not know what it is and must proceed as best we can with what knowledge we have.

Breuer and Freud were interested in both problems: how the symptoms were induced; how they might be removed, not by a healing miracle, nor yet by a drastic hypnotic suggestion, but by a more natural and controllable psychotherapy. They found the solution in the *abreaction* or talking cure, or, more generally catharsis. Psychoanalytic probing, like religious confession, is a psychic cathartic—a way of getting disturbing products out of one's system.

The Breuer-Freudian insight recognized behind the symptom-inducing situation an emotional stress, and specifically a *conflict*. That, and not the situation under which the powerful affect operated—which was but its setting—created the hysterical affliction; the emotion was the powder, the situation the spark. Anna's conflict lay between fatigue and filial duty, the soldier's between loyalty and the self-protecting instinct projected as fear. Whatever makes an assault on the vital urges may precipitate the hysterical impairment; there is no essential difference in *Lebenswund*, in emotional assault, between the trials and ordeals of peace and of war.

Before dismissing this basic pattern of a psychoneurotic symptom, that suggested the idea, that started the practice, that developed the system that furnished the plans of the house that Freud built, it should be noted that the connection between symptom and "cause" is in these instances close, by reason of the relation of the symptom to situation; presently we shall see how it may become puzzlingly remote, indeed, by ardent theorists made so remote, indirect and hypothetical as to lose the warrant of its function. A rather simple stress-situation is that of an attendant in the women's room of a noisy railway-station, who developed an hysterical deafness; she too broke down under the wear and tear of a nerve-wracking occupation. The "shell" as a situation could deafen or blind or maim; the incessant bustle and noise could only deafen. The impairment is either a persistence or an escape from further stress, perhaps both. Symptom and the occasion that sets it off are in some sort of causal relation, and there is always a profound emotional disturbance; if we remain calm, we are not "shocked." Such is the Freudian "discovery," yet not all of it by any means. This diagnosis discovers the first stratum of "depth psychology." The turn of psychology in such direction will be permanently associated with psychoanalysis.

It is simpler and conforms to the historical sequence, to present the Freudian view of psychogenic action in terms of the clinical picture of hysteria. There are other varieties of psycho-neuroses; just how they are classified and described varies with the approaches and conceptions of psychiatrists.

The psychoanalysts regard them all as psychogenic in origin and amenable to the same treatment as hysterical impairments. The experience of modern life has made painfully clear that a large number of otherwise normal persons suffer from conflict situations, in type psycho-neurotic. It is toward the hope of relieving these, that the central mission of psychiatry is directed. What has been illustrated in terms of hysteria was step by step extended to the psycho-neuroses generally. In the sequel the conflict situation, of whatever nature, will be the central consideration; the question whether all psycho-neuroses so arise may be held in reserve.

For clarity of exposition, I have focussed upon hysterical impairment. Equally important for the basis of psychoanalysis is another order of neurotic symptom. This is not an impairment by default of normal function, but an invasion of normal behavior by impulsive intrusions, equally "unconscious," but compelling. Such is the *compulsion neurosis* which imposes laborious and repetitive rituals. Only when these are dispelled will peace of mind be (temporarily) restored. The psychoanalytic problem is the same: why just these compulsions and rituals? The solution is the same: the fixation of a deep-seated uneasiness, possibly dating from childhood, or symbolically elaborated by way of a set of ideas deeply emotionalized, often with a sexual content or reference. The further course of exposition will give opportunity to recount "cases" of compulsion neurosis and of their psychoanalytic interpretation. These form as important data for the Freudian structure as do the hysterical impairments.

What is common to the neurotic symptoms which it is the purpose of psychoanalysis to discover and to release, is their paradoxical unreality. They are in one aspect self-imposed, whether appearing as impairment, compulsion, anxiety, dread or other handicap—all impediments to leading the normal life. The most generic, inclusive name for that status is hysteria; though when distinctions are in order, the several types of symptoms should not be indiscriminatingly so grouped. They are authentic in the hysterical sense. But let the term pass, and a further rather amusing example be added, free from any direct Freudian implications.

A young woman suffered from a common hysterical symptom—globus—a feeling of a lump in her throat, moving up and down and inducing abortive swallowing movements. Later she reported that the lump had moved down to her stomach and that she was sure "it" was a frog. A mock operation was performed and a lively frog in a bottle shown her upon recovery. She believed that she had been surgically relieved of her "frog," and her feelings were justified. All was peaceful for a time until she reported to the doctor that again she felt a frog in her stomach. When assured that the frog had been removed and shown to her, she replied: "Yes doctor; but there's another. You see the first was a female frog." The tale may be apocryphal, though it appears in a medical statement; but it is in point to make clear that hysteria may appear at any level of intelligence, and that many of its symptoms are not of the "complex" order, but fairly superficial and by the same token fairly conscious. The psychoanalytic procedure is often unnecessary. Not all hysteria operates in the deep "unconscious" level. That reminder is important for judging the validity of the theory and the pertinence of the explanations. The hysterical symptoms, then the hysterical mechanisms occupied Freud; from these he generalised to universal types of relations in all sorts and conditions of human behavior, normal and abnormal. Psychoanalysis became far more than a theory of explanation and treatment of neurotic disorders, hysterical in type. The story begins there, but extends to many strange chapters in depth psychology.

EN ROUTE TO THE COMPLEX

I have no intention of losing myself or the reader in the caverns and labyrinths of darkest Freud, at least not until it becomes inevitable. I shall follow the direct clinical trail and others branching from it, always on the concrete purpose bent of explaining significant phenomena of the mental, including the abnormal mental life. In due course, we shall consider the psychological theses which these findings seem to demand or to justify. For psychoanalysis, as it developed, proposed a universal solvent of the elements of personality and an exegesis of the careers and entanglements of human, all too human, selves on happiness and salvation bent, to misery inclined.

Psychoanalysis was born in a clinic, perhaps an unfortunate origin for prospects of a normal career. Early in Freud's epoch-making clinical approach appeared the prospect of a general application to normal minds. His concepts of the subconscious, of the suppression into its sheltering recesses, and the determining factors in the process, were conceived as constantly operative in normal lives. The hysterical impairments and neurotic compulsions were regarded as exceptional and dramatic issues of the same mechanisms, which were psychopathic in so far as the neurotic constitution of the individual disposed thereto. The clinician is interested in cure; a correct diagnosis is the first step to that end. The novel element of the Freudian diagnosis was the recognition of the psychic mechanisms, in terms of *situation* on the surface level, of occasion in terms of *motive* on the deeper level of vital urges and personal relations developing from them. As his construction progressed, the psychologist in Freud shared the direction with the clinician, and later took the lead.

The curative procedure furnished a clue to further understanding. Hypnosis had shown that the stranglehold of these hysterical and related impairments and distresses could be released by disengaging the subconscious tentacles. The procedure of hypnosis was uncertain and limited the relation of physician and patient. Breuer and Freud sought and found the effective release of subconscious secrets by inducing their patients to assume a passive attitude and talk about themselves freely and intimately; this was the "talking cure," or "chimney sweeping," or psychic housecleaning or catharsis. This "discovery," that symptoms could be banished by giving free vocal play to the affect, came upon them "with the greatest surprise." It raises an important question for later consideration: why consciousness cures, why talking things out helps, why confession is good for the soul.

In Breuer's catharsis we recognize the first stage of the protracted confessional technique which today supports the profession of psychoanalysts. This free-lance probing became in Freud's hands a divining-rod, and eventually uncovered the underground currents that issued in nervous handicaps and the conflicts behind them—what by way of anticipation may at once be called the "complex." Once discovered, its very acknowledgment, the recognition of the need of its dissolution, its *abreaction* by such skill of persuasion and authority as the analyst possessed, determined the course of release, and paved the way for the patient's readaptation to his circumstance and the attainment of normality—all this potentially for normal as well as neurotic case-histories.

It is well to point out that in the first psychoanalytic case there is slight suggestion of the leading parts of the developed Freudian drama, particularly no dominance of sex. There is little more than the normal mourning of a devoted daughter for the loss of a father, hysterically expressed. There is likewise no "sex" factor in shell-shock. There is an assault on some of the fundamental life urges, original or derived. That sex occupies a unique and within its domain supreme place in the vital urges is supremely plain; that it is a fertile source of intense conflict, no less so. As clinical experience increased, hysterical impairments formed but one order of psychoanalytic cases; anxiety neuroses, compulsion neuroses, obsessions, were frequently met with; general instability, unrest, maladjustment predominated. With the free inquiry into personal history, with longer and more detailed interviews, the psycho-neuroses were revealed as arising uniformly from conflict situations; these, traced to their source, disclosed difficulties of some order in the sexual relation, often traceable to a childhood shock. These findings are stages on the way to the "discovery" of the complex.

We have next to bring into the picture the compulsion neuroses, which are active impairments, and impose upon the victim not incapacities or deprivations of function, but intrusive bits of behavior, tics and habit-spasms, wayward impulses or obsessive thoughts, as fully disturbing to the normal even tenor of the individual's behavior patterns, as many forms of impairment of sense or limb. There are also the anxiety neuroses, constant and troubling fears and doubts and hesitations, and unrests and feelings of frustration, and losses of zest, and exhaustion states, and panicky moments, at times punctuated by marked bodily symptoms. All disqualify for a calm, normal occupation and smoothly adjusted pursuits. They twist the cogs in the wheels of life; they gum the works. They set the same problems: what discharges them as occasion and motive, why they assume the particular forms, why an anxiety or a compulsion rather than an impairment? Such issues, we may assume—since so many exposed to comparable shocks never show them—occur only in those constitutionally disposed. Yet, be it repeated, the same order of mechanism is at work in ordinary reactions and in normal individuals, who either find successful solutions, or find themselves slightly maladapted and troubled, scarred but not maimed. The clues found in the abnormal illuminate the normal. Psychoanalysis offers a "depth" psychology for all, as well as a therapy for the psychically crippled.

To follow an hysterical or compulsion neurosis along the Freudian way becomes an excursion into the highways and byways of sex. How far this is justified is a later consideration. Without further ado we read the motto above the portal: "All hope of reticence abandon, ye who enter here!" and proceed.

Symptoms: A nervous girl of nineteen, discontented, depressed, hesitant, is afflicted with a dread of open places—the well-known agoraphobia—and with a compulsion neuroses that leads her to adopt a rigid "sleep" ritual, not such a mild habit-routine as most of us observe, but an elaborate and fanciful series of actions for which the reasons professed seem insufficient. The performance is necessary to her peace

of mind. She desires quiet and to that end stops the
clock and removes her wrist-watch; vases are placed
on the desk lest they fall and break and disturb,
though she admits that this is not in the least likely.
She demands that the door between her room and
the bedroom of her parents remain half open. The
bed ritual requires that the large pillow at the head
of the bed shall not touch the wooden-back-rest of
the bed; the small head-pillow must be placed diag-
onally. These and other minute details are repeated,
to ensure their precise observance. These neurotic
precautions may take an hour or two; until completed, neither she nor her parents venture to go to
sleep.

As the result of months of analysis, with constant
protest and resistance on the part of the patient, Freud
was able to convince her of the correctness of his interpretation of these symptoms and to relieve her compulsion; she abandoned the ritual.

Interpretation: The patient was made to understand that the clock, associated also with the regularity of a periodic function, is the symbol of the
female genital, and the ticking comparable to the
throbbing of sexual excitement. "Flower pots and
vases are, as are all vessels, also female symbols."
The precaution against breaking is part of a "virgin-
ity complex." By way of confirmation, Freud cites
the custom of breaking a dish at an engagement or
wedding, symbolic of the renunciation by each guest
of any claim upon the bride.

An additional reminiscence: As a child she had
slipped and fallen with a glass dish in her hand and
cut her finger so that it bled; this in due course was

associated with vaginal bleeding. "One day she guessed the central idea" of her pillow ritual. "The pillow always had seemed a woman to her, the erect back of the bed a man. By means of magic, we may say, she wished to keep apart man and wife,"—her parents. In earlier years she had in fear, real or feigned, induced her parents to leave ajar the communicating door between their rooms, and sometimes induced them to let her sleep between them, thus separating "pillow" and the "wooden back," and in so far displacing her mother. The diamond position of the smaller pillow is explained as an additional female symbol. "Wild ideas, you will say, to run riot in the head of a virgin girl. I admit it, but do not forget that I have not created these ideas, but merely interpreted them."

The fantasies associated with childhood incidents, recalled in analysis are made responsible for elaborating the ritual, all in the subconscious. A deeper source of the fantasies is an "erotic attachment to her father" dating from early childhood, and an unfriendly attitude toward her mother. Such is the psychoanalytic explanation of a compulsion neurosis. Comment is reserved. The immediate purpose is to set before the reader how symptom and interpretation proceed in the Freudian exegesis.

The second of the two cases by which Freud chooses to expound to a general audience the nature and psychoanalytic decipherment of a compulsion neurosis turns upon a similar theme.

"A lady, about thirty years old, suffered from the most severe compulsions. I might indeed have helped her if caprice of fortune had not destroyed my

work." . . . In the course of each day, the patient
often executed, among others, the following strange
compulsive act: "She ran from one room to the ad-
joining one, rang for her maid, gave her a trivial
order, dismissed her, and returned to the other room.
The explanation, Freud insists, came without his aid
or suggestion. When asked why she went through
this senseless performance, she answered: 'I don't
know.' " . . .

Interpretation: "But one day after I had succeeded
in surmounting a grave ethical doubt of hers, she suddenly saw the light." . . . "More than ten years
prior she had married a man far older than herself,
who had proved impotent on the bridal night. In the
morning he poured red ink upon the sheets saying
petulantly: 'It is enough to make one ashamed before the maid who does the beds.' " "The patient led
me to the table in the second room and let me discover a large spot on the table-cover. She explained
also that she placed herself in such a position that
the maid could not miss seeing the stain." She identifies herself with her husband who went from his
room to hers repeatedly in that night. It is true that
she shields him in actual life while yet seeking a divorce.

"I shall be glad to have you dwell upon this instance"
Freud tells his audience, "as the experience does not,
as usual, belong to the half-forgotten period of childhood, but to the mature life. All the objections which
critics ordinarily offer to our interpretation of symptoms fail in this case. Of course, we are not always so
fortunate." He further explains that the ritual replaces
the bed and the sheet by a table and a table-cloth. "Bed
and Board" constitute marriage, so a table may repre-

sent a bed. The spot "shields her husband from malicious gossip." As we are merely describing Freud's clinical methods, comment may again be postponed.

We continue the excursion; for we have still to consider obsessions and troubled doubts and harassing concerns, whatever their cause. They are of the same order of handicap to normality. To relieve them is the great hope. Psychoanalysis offers first aid by tracing baffling symptoms to hidden causes. I again cite Freud to give the reader direct contact with the authentic script of psychoanalysis:

"A young officer, home on a short leave of absence, asked me to see his mother-in-law who, in spite of the happiest circumstances, was embittering her own and her people's existence by a senseless idea." The patient proved to be a pleasant lady aged fifty-three, married for thirty years to a kind, thoughtful husband, with never a quarrel between them. There were two children, now married.

A year ago she had received and given credence to an anonymous letter "accusing her excellent husband of having an affair with a young girl, and since then her happiness is destroyed." It appears that this estimable lady had the not quite so estimable habit of gossiping with her maid. They had been speaking of an elderly gentleman visiting at the house, of whom it was known that he did not live with his wife, but sought the consolation of a mistress. In a thoughtless moment the remark slipped the patient's tongue: "It would be dreadful to learn *that* of my good husband."

Next day came the letter which despite its disguised handwriting she suspected had been written by her maid; for the "woman" in the case was one

against whom the maid had a grudge, in that, starting from the same station in life as herself, she had
advanced socially and was now a trusted employee
in the factory belonging to the head of the house.
The maid was dismissed; but the patient, despite her
rational conviction of the baselessness of the charge,
was emotionally troubled by it; it rankled and would
not subside. After two hours of analysis, she reached
the stage of having nothing more to say; she was
prepared to drop the procedure. She declared that
she already felt cured and was confident that the
obsession would vanish.

"In these two hours, however, she had let fall certain remarks which made possible definite interpretation, indeed made it incontestable; and this interpretation throws a clear light on the origin of her
obsession of jealousy. Namely, she herself was very
much infatuated with a certain young man, the very
same son-in-law upon whose urging she had come to
consult me professionally. She knew nothing of this
infatuation, or at least only a very little. Because of
the existing relationship, it was very easy for this
infatuation to masquerade under the guise of harmless tenderness. With all our further experience, it is
not difficult to feel our way toward an understanding
of the psychic life of this honest woman and good
mother. Such an infatuation, a monstrous, impossible
thing, could not be allowed to become conscious. But
it continued to exist and unconsciously exerted a
heavy pressure. Something had to happen, some sort
of relief had to be found, and the mechanism of displacement which so constantly takes part in the
origin of obsessional jealousy, offered the most immediate mitigation. If not only she, old woman that
she was, was in love with a young man, but if also

her old husband had an affair with a young girl, then she would be freed from the voice of her conscience which accused her of infidelity. The phantasy of her husband's infidelity was thus like a cooling salve on her burning wound."

Let this explanation carry what conviction it may. With these examples of diagnosis and treatment, the case may rest. With increasing self-restraint, I reserve comment.

Before dismissing compulsive symptoms, it may be well to illustrate that they too may be simple persistences, such as the tremors of shell-shocked soldiers. The following case is suggestive.

A girl of sixteen was subject to violent spasms of the muscles of the arm and neck. These gestures were traced to her frantic exertions to duck under the water while bathing in a brook and suddenly surprised by the appearance of a man at the roadside. The cure in this case was neither by hypnosis nor by analysis, but by a strategic form of suggestion. She was given a whiff of ether and her arm bandaged; on awakening, she was assured that a successful operation had been performed.

It is uncertain how far she may have been aware of the origin of her compulsive movements which her companions regarded as somewhat shammed. The mock operation served to justify her contention that her illness was real. She was vindicated and thereby cured. Psychoanalysis might have done as well; but it was unnecessary.

Psychoanalytic symptoms may present fixations or persistences or an obsessed action or impairment due to fears, shocks or anxieties. The impairment, which constitutes the neurosis, may be imposed, or more or less accepted, or even sought; if the last, it becomes a solution of a conflict by an "escape into illness"—a formula frequently applied by Freud and Freudians. In the light of such cases, Freud pronounced neuroses to be universally the issues of deep-lying conflicts, often associated with a psychic shock in childhood, and predominantly sexual in plot or incident, the mechanism subconscious and psychogenic in this new Freudian sense. Gradually there were recognized certain constant emotional and situational factors in the case-histories, which gave rise to the concept of the complex, and more specifically to definite, typical orders of complexes. The psychoanalyst discovered not only complexes but psychopathic dramas of the unconscious as the common fate of humanity.

The stage is thus set, and the curtain rises upon the central drama of the Freudian "family romance." It is evolved from what goes on behind the scenes in the psychoanalyst's clinic, and by him called discoveries. To the sceptical critic they resemble the cryptic procedures of Faust's chamber or the arcana of the occultist's retreat; for no more than these divinational adept discoveries, are the Freudian findings available to laboratory methods. Their truth must be otherwise tested. The theory arises from precisely the same order of scientific interest that supports psychology and psychiatry, and directs their progress. The failure to recognize this is responsible for the attitude of hostile disdain which Freud met for long and lonely years. His theories may be all wrong, his data forced or unreal and their significance overstated; but the intention is of the same order as that of other solutions accredited in medical practice. Ridicule and contempt were hardly the appropriate weapons to meet the in-

novations, though there was much that was ridiculous
and suspicious in the mode of their presentation.

"Kobold im Keller"

Such is the disdainful name given by Dunlap to the
complex, to indicate that the creature is an imaginary
habitant in the subterranean house of mind—one is
almost tempted to say, the house of sex. For whatever
the ailment, when traced back to its source, in shock,
in frustrated urge, in conflict, in situation, in motive,
the plot hinges increasingly on sex. Whatever story the
patient brought as to the causes or occasions of the
symptoms as he or she experienced them, there was always beneath the tale, the submerged, distorted features of a disguised, incarcerated skeleton in the family
closet, a goblin in the cellar. The task of analysis was
much the same whether the patient had or had not a
knowledge or opinion—possibly a false one as to the
cause of the neurosis. To bring the Kobold from his
hiding place into the ventilated air of consciousness was
to make him vanish like the ghost at daybreak; and if
he proved to be a ghost, a figment in part of the imagination, he needed exorcising none the less.

The Freudian complexes are disturbances of behavior through desires, fears, anxieties, concerns strongly
emotionalized, suppressed into the subconscious, center-
ing about sex, and often traceable to an initial shock in
early childhood. They grow with general growth; childhood shocks, often of a sexual nature, childhood attitudes toward sex, appear in the neuroses of adults con-
fessing in the Freudian clinics. When primary urges
run their course smoothly, Freud concluded, there are
no neuroses. The inclusive urge of urges is *libido*. In
libido with its dominant sex-component lies the

fountain-source of complexes. Psychoanalysis invaded
the nursery; to speak more academically, it became
genetic. Its problem was to trace the genetic course of
libido. Libido is lust, and "libidinal" and "sexual" are
almost interchangeable in the Freudian vocabulary. We
readily grant that Freud may develop the course of
libido as he sees fit. But it will avail him not at all to
repeat scores of times, and his followers hundreds of
times, that "sexual" is not used in a literal sense but is
expanded to include all varieties of erotic susceptibil-
ities and love relations. The reader who reads his Freud,
and the genitalized scripts of his followers unexpurgated, will be perfectly competent to judge how refined
and remote are the ramifications of sex relations, and
how delicate the garb they assume in the complexes,
as interpreted by the analysts.

We may as well aerate this Kobold at once. That
sexual means psychosexual was known long before
Freud. We are all well aware of how much of what
makes life worth living irradiates from the sex relation,
nor have we added more than a name when we speak
of sublimation. The more adequate recognition of sex
as sex in the motivation scheme and in mental therapy, Freudians may duly claim. That emancipation,
was at work in the modern temper. The question is
whether the rôle of sex is correctly indicated in the
Freudian scheme; it is not whether other psychologies
have considered sex too little. We shall judge not by
statements and definitions and manifestos of intention,
but solely by the actual use made of sex-incidents in
the presentation.

In deciding what part sex plays in complexes, we
are fortunate in having the comparison of other psychoanalytic systems. While to the "central wing" of
psychoanalysts, the Freudian view of sex is focal, vital,

and indispensable, it is not so to the "right wing" of Jung, where, however, it receives no less extreme an interpretation, but in a setting more considerate of other urges; and it is decidedly not so to the "left" wing of Adler, whose disposition of the life urges proclaims a different sovereignty. The place of sex varies with the psychoanalytic theory and practice.

Since, in Freud's view, the nuclear complexes are considered to be libidinal in content and sway, and since libido is a growth, psychoanalysis becomes genetic; which means that the circumstances leading to complexes are more or less common to the growth-stages of the human psyche. We are all subject to complexes as we are to birth, growth, shock, stress and strain. Symptoms will continue to reflect circumstances; but the emotional relations which breed conflicts, will be generically inherent in all sensitive lives. We all have the problem of maturing; and maturity involves sex maturing quite centrally, though personality maturing no less.

Complexes, as they are met clinically, will accordingly be individualized according to the personal experience, yet will follow type-patterns. In passing from persistence of shocks to conflicting urges, and from these to type-forms of complexes, the psychology developed by psychoanalysis becomes the depth psychology of the life-drama. It goes beyond the explanation of specific symptoms to the formulation of the intimately personal relations which engender such symptoms; it invades the inner sanctum of personality.

We have reached the controversial core of the psychoanalytical system: not the existence of complexes alone, but more definitely and controversially just what are the orders and specific natures of the major complexes. The patient tells his story, directed, prompted, encouraged, readily or reluctantly, according to the temperament of the patient and the skill of the analyst. The issue, the verdict, the plot, is the complex, which the analyst uncovers or discovers, and which the patient is to accept. It is in the uncertainty of this relation between the tangles of symptoms and the specific solution offered by the "complex" that the issue lies.

The time has come, indeed, to talk of many things as obvious and unrelated as cabbages and kings, as contradictory as why the sea is boiling hot, as plausible as whether pigs have wings; for on first acquaintance the Freudian system seems a medley of improbabilities ingeniously rationalized, and with a sequence of ideas as paradoxical as those of the walrus and the carpenter. Yet it is presented as a series of objective findings of an intrepid discoverer who for the first time has the temerity to describe man as he is. Consequently the time has come to make clear that the principles of psychoanalysis are not any such order of realities, but are conjectures, schemes, constructions of Freud's fertile imagination. Their *reality* rests upon the case-histories of his patients, supplemented, as will appear, by a variety of evidence from other sources. Their *validity* depends upon the plausibility of such assumptions. Do they aid in accounting for the deeper psychic life? Do these interpretations extend and correct current insights into the mechanisms and dynamisms of the mind? Do they fit in with the basic concepts of the sciences dealing with man? Are they necessary, correct, logical?

It is a judgment in terms of such criteria that will determine the fate of psychoanalysis in general, and of any special variety of it, such as Freud's version, which remains, despite his many thousand pages of contribution, a constellation of suppositions. That criterion does not exclude other and more objective tests. While following Freud's course in developing such concepts as complexes, libido, the unconscious, conversion, regression, identification, transference, sublimation, and a score of similar postulates, we must have constantly in mind that they are not "discoveries" in the sense that Freud came upon them, with all the features and garbs which he describes, in the jungles of the land of psyche; or that had Freud not entered upon his Columbian voyage, they would have been similarly reported by any other qualified observer entering the same terrain and underbrush of an unexplored mental continent. The *"discoveries" are hypotheses*—and they are nothing more—which he finds necessary and convincing, and which others may find neither, or even contradictory and absurd. Though set forth as pronouncements of fact, they are only *his* solutions, *his* total interpretation of the introspective recollections of patients under the provocation of free association (which may be far from free), of dream incidents and childhood fantasies, to bring them into a related scheme. Such is the logical framework of the entire construction, called by reason of its source and application, psychoanalysis.

Are there complexes? Do they account for the psychoneuroses and the allied difficulties of adjustment? Do the complexes fall into type-forms, and have Freud and his followers determined what they are, how they arise, how they are to be relieved? And how far, in the process of discovering complexes, have they come upon the true nature of the human psyche and the understanding of its processes and products? These are momentous questions which justify the attention that the house of Freud commands. In a pragmatic sense there *are* complexes; for we can agree that this is altogether the best and most convenient name for the psychic factor in the varieties of mental and emotional difficulties which appear as clinical realities, as common impediments to right thinking, right feeling, right living. Psychology welcomes the "complex" as a long needed, fundamental concept, and offers a vote of thanks to psychoanalysis for the contribution. But psychoanalysis goes much farther; it sets forth that there are specific complexes which Freud has identified, such as the Oedipus, the castration, the death complex, which others can recognize—like the egg of Columbus—after he has shown them the trick. Are critics who take no stock in the enterprise right in holding that he, Freud, and we who, though not of the crew, are interested in following the voyage, are setting out on so fantastic an expedition as the hunting of the snark, which may prove to be a boojum? I have indicated that, as I see it, the Freudian quest is important and not vain, that the results of the expedition warrant critical examination. The quest is scientific; whether his report will meet the requirements of the logic of science is an open question. It is on that expedition of inquiry that I am inviting the reader's company.

In presenting the philosophy of *"As If,"* Vaihinger offers a formula for many a hypothetical scheme. Neuroses and dreams and lapses occur "as if" there were complexes, repressions, and the rest. Psychoanalysis is in so far an "as if" construction. With equal aptness, William James called the tendency to reduce one set of phenomena to another, simpler or better known, as a *"nothing but"* explanation. Excessive irritability, the "glandular" psychologists tell us, is "nothing but" hyper-thyroidism. Similarly, the Freudian concludes that the urge to explore is "nothing but" a deviate of sexual curiosity; that the trait of cruelty is "nothing but" an outlet of sadism; that the passion of the martyr is "nothing but" a religious variety of masochism; and that many another activity that men live by is "nothing but" a variant of the libido. The "nothing but" psychology of reduction frequently proceeds upon an ounce of truth alloyed with a pound of fallacy. Psychoanalysis in Freud's hand combines an equal confidence in the validity of "as if" and of "nothing but." That faith, at times naïve in its expression, is precisely what is to be questioned.

We have no reason to believe, despite the specific claim of at least one disciple, that Freud has access to a form of knowledge denied to the rest of us. The decalogue of psychoanalysis is not a Mosaic revelation, nor the inspiration of a mystic communion. The Freudian house is as strong as its foundations; these must be judged by logical criteria no differently than any other views that bid for scientific sanction. One may freely grant to an innovator the right to construct his edifice upon such concepts as he finds justifiable, while recognizing their problematic character. It is in that attitude that we shall proceed to follow the constructions of Freud. The house that Freud built is a project submitted in competition on the theme: "the human psyche," to a qualified jury of scientifically minded critics and the larger lay jury of intelligent men and women, who have sufficient interest in the same inquiry, since by chance or choice they live in a world of views influenced by Freud. Such is the issue raised by this "Kobold im Keller," which to Dunlap is not only the status of the complex, but of Freud and all his works—an imaginary Frankenstein of the psychoanalytic studio.

Psychoanalysis is not a discovery like that of a virgin forest untouched by the hand of man, but a speculation suggested by findings elaborated to explain other findings, but subject through and through to the uncertainties attaching to the most complex phenomena in human experience. There is indeed a hidden machinery in our psychic life; that is why psychology arises. Whether Freud has found the hidden springs of behavior, is an intensely controversial matter.

COURSE OF LIBIDO

In the Freudian web of life the supporting thread is libido, a sexualized *élan vital*. A prominent tenet of Freudianism is infant sexuality. The infant is his own sex-object; he is auto-erotic. Fondling, tickling, are (in part) gratifications, kissing still more closely so, which later belong to the sex pleasures. There are erogenous zones in various parts of the child's body. These excitations compose infant sexuality, including stimulation of the genital areas. Every child is born with an organically determined sexual excitability. Infantile sexuality "is the most novel and important of the psychoanalytical contributions" (Ernest Jones). The *Infancy period* extends from birth to about five years. The sexual life of infancy is rich and extensive, with great influence upon the future development of libido.

The second stage of libido is the *Latency period*, from about five to twelve years. Sex "by no means ceases at this period." The crude infantile interests fall away; the broadening activities and attitudes of the "school-boy" age still derive their energies from libidinal sources. But there is a relative lull of sex before the storm and stress of the third age: the *Pubertal or Adolescent* period, from about twelve to eighteen years. These early stages are likewise characterized by the *direction* of libido, at first toward self, then toward individuals of the same sex, or bisexually, indifferently to either sex; while with the advent of puberty, libido becomes heterosexual. By virtue of the fact that in childhood there is an acceptance of sex-objects which, if continued in later life, becomes a perversion, and by virtue of the diffuse distribution of child libido, what was formerly described (when psychology was innocent of psychoanalysis) as the age of innocence, now bears the formidable name: "polymorphous perverse." That is what children are by nature; it represents a stage of their development. The radiations of sex at this critical period are many. Being in love with one's self represents the narcissism of childhood. There is also the tendency to exhibit the body, exhibitionism; and an interest in the bodies of others, especially of the opposite sex, voyeurism or inspectionism, *à la* peeping Tom. Sex perversions, homosexuality particularly, are fixations or regressions in the development of libido. Volumes have been written on the Freudian theme of the aberrations of sexual love in children.

It is as though by an unfortunate arrangement of nature, children were afflicted with parents which, like other children's diseases, they must outgrow. Libido has a family setting, for which Freud develops a "family romance." The Freudianized family appears to be not a pleasantly domestic circle, but a seething and somewhat vulgarian center of strife. The typical complex is a parental one. Freud gives it a dignity by calling it classically the *Oedipus Complex*. The boy's libido is directed toward the mother, his envy toward the father, whose place he wishes to usurp. As the story of Oedipus is that of the royal son doomed to kill his father and marry his mother, all unwittingly, in unconscious obedience to the decrees of fate, the source of the title-role is in so far located. Though the Greek drama does not at all follow the Freudian sequence, yet it is held that the Greek dramatist intuitively projected the plot of which Freud discovered the generic application. The tragedy of libido is that we all have the heritage that sets desire in this forbidden direction; we must all dissolve and resolve the Oedipus complex before attaining a normal sexual life. The Oedipus stage has no limits of age. Normally it is accredited with a set period of ascendance in early life, yet by reason of the long endurance and imposing figure of the parent, it stands as a menace and a persistent problem. One has an "Oedipus" as inevitably as one has a "Binet" or "I. Q." It is "a general human characteristic decreed by fate." Psychoanalytic paternity is a formidable, even an ominous, liability.

There are other liabilities incident to the perilous wanderings of libido, steering between the menaces of one and another Scylla and Charybdis. Foreshadowing the course of true love, the course of the libido rarely runs smooth. The "Oedipus" tie hovers threateningly over every son of man born of woman. This is "such an important thing that the manner in which one enters and leaves it cannot be without its effects." Not only libido, but Freud's presentation of it goes through developmental stages. In the later analyses appears a monster-complex whose hideous mien seems the reason for its being cherished and embraced. As gradually the adolescent libido is directed towards independent gratification, the hostile attitude toward the father—always tinged with fear, for the father is authority—develops a "castration complex," a fear of sexual failure or deprivation. This successor or descendant of the Oedipus complex plays a variable part in development.

From the outset the egocentric infantile attitude affects libido. The infant is a cruel tyrant, demanding omnipotence. This trait in later life, when sexually expressed, presents the quality of "sadism," combining cruelty with desire in behavior toward the sex-object, and a mingled pleasure in both. Cruelty, even teasing, is actually or embryonically sadism. With this as Scylla, the Charybdis is its converse, "masochism"—combining a perverted joy in suffering with sex gratification. It is in this stage or episode of libidinal development that the divergences of the masculine and feminine version become marked. Psychoanalysis, being a masculine discovery, derives its libidinal concepts from the rôle of the male, although it owes so much of its clinical material to women. To balance the Oedipus there is the Electra complex, the analogy not complete, but going far enough to satisfy Freud in maintaining that there is an inherent tendency toward incest, affecting both sexes. The cultural incest taboo is regarded as a confirmation of a strong native trend in the forbidden direction.

The contrast in external conspicuousness of the genitals of the two sexes, he maintains, gives rise in girls to an envy complex, which is the equivalent of castration. These paired opposites—impressively called "polarities": pleasure and pain, love and hate, the masculine and feminine—and likewise "ambivalence," or simultaneous yet contradictory emotional attitudes: fearing and hating while yet loving, creating and destroying—all enter into the conflict of rival urges, for the most part libidinized. To present even in barest outline an epitome of the Freudian "Scylla-Charybdis" sexology would require a chapter for which I have neither taste nor talent. I am content to indicate how Freudian psychoanalysis strongly and strangely sexualizes the human career.

Emerging from the Ulyssean wanderings of libido, we reach the haven which we all, whatever our psychological allegiances, readily recognize as the prime of life in every sense, recognizing also that in attaining it we come upon a concept as familiar as acceptable—renamed "sublimation." The source of motive power by which men maintain their interests and direct their energies is libido. *Ego-libido* is the energy expended in self-expression and in securing station, income and social recognition. In later writings the ego-urge is given a companion place beside the sex-urge, yet still derives both the manner of its expression and its driving force from that central fount. Expended upon problems, acquisitions, activities, it becomes *object-libido,* combining qualities from the ego completion and from the authentically libidinal stream. When we are in a self-congratulatory mood or pleased with our mirrored reflection, libido is directed from sex to ego; and when we get interested in a job, libido goes into objects.

Such transference in the mature expressions of libido involve some measure of sublimation; but that term applies more directly to the issues of libido in creative ability, which remains closer to the sex-motive and its radiations. Poetry, drama, romance, chivalry, are sublimated products of libido and would have no existence in a libido-less world. The affective element of attachment, devotion and loyalty, derived from sex desire and its passionate intensity, when thus redirected, is responsible for relations in every field of human activity, and for the personal and cultural products of "psyche." Libido in this broader sense, favored in Freud's later writings, approaches and fuses with *Eros,* or love generally, yet retaining—as in the usual use of "erotic"— the stamp of its origin. None the less "Eros" redeems libido as an essential step to the complete maturing of psycho-sexual and affective development.

The genetic wanderings of libido lead to its implications. As applied to the neuroses, Freud regards them specifically and universally as the expressions of failure in the sex life; with a normal sex life neurosis is impossible. Such a sweeping and momentous conclusion requires careful consideration, to be duly accorded.

Life in the Freudian manner is exposed to fixation or arrest, and to regression, which means lapsing back to an earlier stage of libido. Libido is conceived in quantitative terms, as a reservoir of energy, which so far as it is not absorbed in sexual expression, is available for other life-purposes. As libido bears throughout life the impress of its early vicissitudes, a portion of it remains fixed on self. That trait is termed *Narcissism*, a typically Freudian concept, derived from the myth of the youth who saw the reflection of his shapely body in the water and fell in love with his own image. Narcissism is ego-libido and reappears in later stages of character development; the Narcisstic component of libido is universal. Self-admiration is Narcisstic; it is a persistence of, or regression to, infantilism.

Similarly there is a homosexual component in libido that continues to operate, for we have all passed through it; intensive friendships and "crushes" between adolescents of the same sex are regarded with suspicion. Those in whom this trend dominates, largely determining the course of their emotional lives, are fixated at the homosexual stage. Their abnormality sets them apart; theirs is the "well of loneliness." Fixations at the Oedipus stage shape character variously, as the dependence on the mother or the envy and resentment against the father plays the major part. From Narcissus to Oedipus, the course of libido leaves its dire impress on later life; it brings woe to those who do not run the libidinal gauntlet successfully. The heavy hand of sex threatens human fate.

Assuming that the development of libido has in major part achieved a mature expression, there still remains the danger that under stress, which is typically a frustration or obstacle or difficulty in expression, there will be a regression to earlier stages and expression levels of libido. Masturbation is a widely prevalent example of fixation or regression. The possibility of reassertion of partially outgrown trends depends upon their original strength when dominant. It may not be easy to determine how far libidinal complications indicate fixation, how far they represent regression. Regression is likewise a general psychological concept corresponding unquestionably to a reality; the concept was current before the Freudian era. It is applicable to libidinal or to non-libidinal urges and to instincts and the character-trends deriving from them. Genetic psychology requires the concept of regression; psychiatry employs it. Dr. Core regards hysteria as the typical regressive neurosis.

But of all the Freudian libidinal concepts arising from developmental stages, those derived from the direction of libido to bodily zones lead to the most unexpected views of the sources of mature character-traits—again by the way of fixation, arrest, over-development, or regression. The three erogenous zones are oral, anal, and the completing genital, with a urethral component associated with the anal activities. The rest of our visceral anatomy is excluded from a share in character formation by lack of libidinal association; otherwise we might have "hepatic" and "pulmonary" and "cardiac" character-traits. Our characters are to be read not in cranial bumps but in visceral attachments.

Freud "discovered" the "anal character," by reducing traits prominent in adults to "nothing but" their infantile source when body habits were in their pre-genital stage. He concluded that in persons in whom the anal-erotic libido was strong, that portion of it which did not pass on to a genital stage is "absorbed by transformation" into character-traits—a strange psycho-alchemy indeed. The transformation proceeds by way of habit-reactions, symbols, identification and sublimation. This bizarre chapter in Freudianism will be considered in illustrating the mood and method of Freudian logic.* Other analysts brought to light "oral" characters and "urethral" character-traits. This body of doctrine is advanced as an integral part of psychoanalysis, and affects technique in ways that pass ordinary understanding.

The story of the implications of libido by no means ends here. Clearly, however modified by later concessions, Freudian psychoanalysis is sexual psychoanalysis. The fate of Freudianism depends largely on the fate of the sexology incorporated in it.

* See pp. 212 to 221.

CHAPTER II

BUILDING MATERIAL

Repressed Desires

The house that Freud built stage by stage was destined to become an impressive mansion. Its clinical foundations were the mechanisms of hysteria, a matter of interest mainly to physicians, yet with important implications for psychology and a promise for the relief of neurotics. Freud's altogether heterodox views met with professional ridicule and neglect, Teutonically expressed. While his problem was clinical, his approach was psychological. That approach was gaining favor among the psychiatrists; abnormal psychology was in the making. The meeting of these two interests made clear that symptoms of mental disorder required a large measure of psychological interpretation; that neurotic and psychopathic fixed ideas, strange states of mind, queer varieties of behavior of minds astray, appeared among the normal on a minor scale, with their oddities toned down. All this is well recognized today; it was not so when Freud began his exploration in a no-man's land of medicine. Psychoanalysis helped to build the bridge between the normal and abnormal.

Seeking quite properly more worlds to conquer, Freud looked for other psychic processes in which the same mechanisms were at work as appeared in the subconscious undertow of the neuroses. This neglected psychic underworld fascinated his attention. There emotion ruled; urges pressed forward; in its recesses the unpleasant, incompletely suppressed, took shelter. In the interests of conscious peace of mind, that suppression was a protective barrier, yet an unwise defense when it resulted in neurotic symptoms with their disturbing consequences. The neurosis he regarded as an escape into illness, a false compensation—again indicating how subtly unconscious motivation laid its plans. Neurotics were at war, one phase of the personality in conflict with another; but conflicts are of one order in the normal and in the abnormal life. The same mechanisms must be sought in expressions of the psyche, more common and more normal than neuroses, in the everyday thought and behavior of everyday people. Having discovered the universality of repressed desires, Freud's next step was to discover the several avenues of their revelation; the neurosis was one disastrous evidence of the tragic side of their operation.

Where else may one find evidence of the same forces differently at work? Freud had the insight both to ask the question and to recognize in dreams the very embodiment of his quest. Dreams likewise were a product of the "subconscious," breaking through the repression of conscious control. If in daylight waking thought, consciousness and all its works have their innings, sleep, which is the dismissal of that censorious activity, gives the subconscious its turn. Here was further building material, another story of the Freudian house.

For the repressive forces, Freud adopted the convenient name of the *censor*. Nobody does as he feels like; we are all more or less inhibited. We are policed from without, and we police ourselves. When is the censor off guard? Regularly in sleep; and in sleep we dream. But instead of that being the rub, "in that sleep what dreams may come when we have shuffled off" this logical and social coil—that was the golden Freudian opportunity. Dreams were a godsend. Dream-analysis would supply hints to psychoanalysis, would extend the gospel of Freudian determinism.

That dreams might have meaning was known to Joseph; but Joseph was not a Freudian, though a symbolist, nor was Pharaoh a neurotic patient. Freud had in mind a deeper, more vital dream-interpretation. It became an important instrument in his technique. The neurotic repressed the unpleasant; the dreamer under similar stress expressed the pleasant. In dreams the "Freudian wish" escaped; the repressed desire became the wish fulfillment; the subconscious was set free in a world of its own making. Far more was involved in this "discovery." It suggested a principle in psychology of large moment, not wholly new but set in a novel light. For what is dreaming? It is romancing in the wake of desire. "If wishes were horses, beggars would ride." In dreams, wishes produce horses as readily as fairies produce chariots to take Cinderella to the ball and to her prince. Fairy-tales are folk-dreams set to narrative; myth is racial dream-thought. Dream thinking and wish thinking are one; each was a variety of a common tendency. Freud thus arrived at his fertile suggestion of "two orders of thinking." Dreaming as romancing is older and more universal than so-called (logical) thinking; we are inveterate dreamers all. By the Freudian route, day-dreaming has come to its own as a recognized procedure and a symptom in mental behavior. There are thus two principles guiding our mental procedures awake or asleep: the pleasure principle which directs our urges awake or asleep; when unconstrained we wish and day-dream and romance. There is the reality principle to which we must adjust in this rigid, codified, censored world. When released, our minds naturally drift as we stroll and muse; during office-hours we are bent on errands and keep our minds on the job.

Whether or not we follow Freud partly or wholly, with reservation or with protest, in his psychoanalytic interpretation of dreams, his concept of dreaming is a valuable contribution to the illumination of the psychic stream. The critical question remains: What will Freud do with his nugget?

The first employment of the dream was to aid psychoanalysis. Despite ample encouragement to the analysee to talk on and on, the course of revelation halted; it could often be revived by the simple invitation: "Tell me some of your dreams." Dream analysis became a subsidiary psychoanalytic art. It revealed not only the personality of the dreamer and the focus of his conflicts, but the mechanisms of disguise by which the subconscious reached expression. It revealed the primitive force of the urges in their nearer-to-nature setting. It revealed also the rich variety of mechanisms by which the motive and bent of the dream accomplished its purpose. A dream was an autobiographical interview, the dreamer a subconscious journalist, or rather nocturnalist. Dreams supplied supplementary and important building material for psychoanalysis, and for the comprehension of the deep inner life of the waking and the sleeping psyche alike.

What is often said of language artfully employed—that it conceals as well as reveals thought—is still truer of the language of neurotic symptoms. There is a conflict of two pressures: the urge to expression of primary instinctual drives, and the necessity of suppression in the interests of social acceptability. We dream at all because of the first order of pressure; we dream as we do, with all the disguises and transformations, because of the second order of pressure, and for the additional reason that this symbolic, fantasy language of disguise is close to the primary service of the thinking process following the clue of pleasure. So there is ample reason for the distortions of dreams from the point of view of the world of reality, and for their reference to the system of desires with all the repression upon action to which we are subject. In all these respects the Freudian additions and corrections of the dream process find a welcome niche in the general psychology of dreams. Even more: that aspect of dream life is the very one most necessary to furnish the general motivation clue to the entire procedure; but not the sole clue, for fantasy has other moods and vagrant purposes. The ultimate acceptability of the Freudian theory of dreams depends upon the mode of its application; its principles command assent.

THE STUFF OF DREAMS

With the recognition of the significance of dreams, the principles of psychoanalysis were not only generalized, but popularized. *The Interpretation of Dreams*, which appeared in 1900, may be said to date the Freudian century. According to enthusiastic disciples it "has come to occupy the same central and important place for abnormal psychology as the *Origin of Species* did for biology." Freud attempts a definite naturalization of the dream in the mental domain. In that effort he has succeeded, but so had others, though only partially, before him. The Freudian "dream-book" does not replace the study of dreams as states of dissociation; it enriches the topic by the introduction of a motive factor. Dreaming is not quite idle, nor is it in either plot or detail so chaotic and capricious as it seems. The dreamer fantasies, and since he also sets the stage, he presents as real and accomplished, what to the waking self seems too unreal to be plausible, or what he hesitates to admit. The Freudian elements in dreams are readily recognized, once they are looked for. The dream trait of a motive with a string of suppression is as real as the reality of conflicts. Dreams at times carry and reveal motives.

To Freud, a dream is a "bootleg" traffic in repressed desires. Its method of evading the internal-revenue-officers of the moral and social world are interesting. It smuggles its wares by wrapping them in camouflaged packages and employing ingenious dramatic disguises, at times with as little regard for the moral as for the logical proprieties. The tale as dreamed and as told by the dreamer forms its superficial or patent content. Its below-surface, naked meaning is its latent content. That is what it really "means," intends, serves and expresses. To derive the one from the other is the task of dream analysis. It is not strictly a decipherment, in that a cipher is invented as an intentionally artificial code, while Freud insists that the dream-script, though to our conscious intelligence trained in waking thought-language not readily intelligible, is a natural psychic language, indeed, a more authentic prototype of the original thought-processes. Fantasy is nearer to the mind's vernacular. If its use tends to the crude, the selfish, the dramatic, the vulgar, the wily, the playful, the fantastic, it displays this medley of tendencies by right of psychic primacy, as indigenous as the trends of childhood, as autochthonous as the myths of the race, to both of which cultural products, the dream is compared and assimilated in matter and manner of composition. They are of an imagination all compact—lunatic, lover, poet, child, primitive, and dreamer.

The "dream-work" proceeds from a subconscious craftsman, laboring at once under his imposed restrictions, and enjoying the liberties and licenses which he takes without asking; he delivers the product when completed to the dreaming understudy of the conscious psyche. Upon awakening, the conscious master may regard the dream as a foundling deposited on his doorstep, failing to recognize the identifying features of his own paternity; this the dream analyst supplies, possibly imposes. But the identification is by no means as certain as that of finger-prints, for both the waking and dreaming self use alibis and aliases. Unravelling the dream-work, guessing the process from the product, tracing the primitive paternity and genealogy of the dream-relations, is part of the art that Freud inaugurated.

Viewing the Freudian version of the dream more critically, we must bear in mind that the study of dreams belongs to psychology. If the dream as it emerges in the psychoanalytic clinic suggests that dreams are repressed desires; that they disguise the desire as they project it into the dream; that they employ symbolism; that the symbolism uses preferred patterns of relation between the symbol which it selects and the thing, person, relation, emotion, thought symbolized: all these points become matters of investigation for students of dreams in general. The evidence supplied by psychoanalysis is in itself far from complete. Psychology cannot turn over the study of dreams to psychoanalysts. Pierce has studied several thousand dreams of several hundred persons. He found that not fifty per cent of his material could be interpreted as

wish-fulfillment or compensation "except by ingenious
and arbitrary assumptions or distortions." Using a
method of encouraging free associations similar to that
of Freud, he fully supports Freud's contention that
dreams have a latent meaning, that they wear disguises and employ a great variety of symbolisms. A
dream is often a pictorial rendering of a deeper group
of ideas and emotions, a cinema projection of a bit of
life filmed by and for the dreamer—who is actor and
spectator in one.

The issue is not so simple a one as whether Freud's
theory of dreams is true or false. Admitting its pertinence, we are left to judge how far it applies and
whether Freud's manner of applying his principles is
warranted. It still remains well established that dreams
are many-sided products, with several theories to account for them. These Freud reviews, and it is almost
the only instance in which he proceeds by considering
the contributions of his predecessors. He finds these
theories partial, and lacking the dynamic motive central
to his interpretation. Freud's theory leaves many questions open. Have all dreams a patent and a latent
meaning? Does the latent meaning always predomi-
nate? Are there no dreams that tell their story well
enough in the dream narrative itself? Do dreams always speak in parables?

The methods by which the dreamer, whatever his
relations to the waking self, prepares the dream material, including its disguises, has given rise to a considerable vocabulary, much of which labels familiar
processes conveniently, if at times pedantically. The
dream *condenses;* it flashes scenes and pictures; it
chooses dramatic moments readily "filmed," all of
which is familiar. Next, it *symbolizes,* as we do likewise

when we paint pictures and tell stories in words. Language uses metaphors, similes, analogies, no less than do dreams. The dream is even verbal-minded enough to pun and play on words. That the dream is not literal, but richly and fantastically figurative, has long been known and abundantly recognized by psychologists before Freud. The dreamer more or less *identifies* himself with the personages of his dream; he *transfers* an actual situation to another setting; he *introjects* one item from one source to another scene; he *rationalizes;* he *idealizes;* he *elaborates* and embellishes; in brief he fantasies as he does in day-dreaming, and in all, more or less discloses what manner of personality he is. He may reveal in dreams phases of his personality and motivation-scheme which he is unwilling, or unable to discover by conscious intention. One may agree with every one of these "discoveries" of dream mechanisms, and yet reject almost in toto the detailed psychoanalytic interpretation of the dream-material. The principle may be valid, but the application questionable or even absurd.

In including under the generic formula of repressed desires or unfulfilled wishes, the terror and catastrophy dreams, even the night-mares, Freud but recognizes the common emotional sources of hope and fear, which explains well enough what slight measure of truth there may be in the traditional dream-book statement that dreams go by contraries. If, in danger at sea, one man dreams of a rescue and another of a wreck, they both express the same hope and the same fear. And if under no danger at all, either dream occurs, it indicates a relative tendency to imagine such possibilities and dream them, either in terms of hopes or of fears. As there are conflicting trends in emotion, at once loving and hating, altruistic and self interested, the dream may express just that part of the contradictory state of feeling which the conscious censor inclines to disown.

What Freud does not sufficiently recognize is that dreams do not all follow similar courses because dreamers have different psychologies. That factor is the central goal of Pierce's investigation. According to one's temperament one may be rather decidedly the same person in one's dreaming as in one's waking life, or appear quite differently as the person one is not, but privately thinks oneself to be, or would like to be. Of eighteen dreamers, nine men and nine women, Pierce finds ten who are different waking and dreaming, and eight who are the same personalities in the two worlds. It may be suggestive that of the eight who are much the same personalities dreaming and waking, six are women and only two men. Whether this indicates a greater consistency in women, or a larger satisfaction with their actual lot, or a duller imagination, is an open question. At all events, dreams are highly individualized products of the entire personality. They represent under-cover escapes of the fear-wish-fantasy phase of the psychic life. There is hardly a statement or an incident, an inference, a process that the Freudian dream interpreters employ to support their thesis, which is not readily substantiated here, there and elsewhere, frequently or occasionally, in a fair and sufficient sample of average dreams. So much is readily conceded. But when the principles thus suggested are generalized far beyond their warrant, are constricted and contorted into remote meanings, and summarized in formulae that are but prepossessions ingeniously twisted, and when the entire significance of dreams is exaggerated to an importance far beyond its worth, a sceptical attitude toward the entire construction is justified.

Dreams in Analysis

That primitive urges repressed by moral restraints may come to expression in dreams, is an ancient knowledge. Freud cites from Plato's "Republic" that the virtuous man "contents himself with dreaming that which the wicked man does in actual life." In the same dialogue, there is a more explicit anticipation. Speaking of unlawful "pleasures and appetites," which are "an original part of every man," controlled in the rational but strong in others, it is explained that these appetites "bestir themselves in sleep; when, during the slumbers of that other part of the soul, which is rational and tamed and master of the former, the wild animal part, sated with meat and drink, becomes rampant, and, pushing sleep away, endeavours to set out after the gratification of its own proper character." Plato recognizes urges, repressed desires, the censor, the wish fulfillment in dreams. With this sanction "the Freudian view becomes at once distinctly more respectable"; it is equally pertinent that it reveals its familiarity. The current protest when an objectionable procedure is proposed: "I shouldn't dream of doing that," is based on a like conviction. It might be truer to say that only in dreaming would the lapse be possible. We have always recognized a partial responsibility for our dreams, and that they may reveal what we prefer to conceal.

The thesis that what appears in dreams meets with resistance is vital to the Freudian use of dreams. Yet not all dream-material is of this nature; and Freud admits that simpler dreams are rather freely flowing, undisguised wish-fulfillments. This *leit-motif* appears in children and simpler order of human beings, who have no complicated organization of their repressions. Dreaming is then close to conscious wish or fantasy. Freud relates of his own children, that they dreamed of accomplishing such portions of their holiday excursions and enjoying such treats as they were denied in reality. It is related of sailors on Arctic cruises, lonely and on scant monotonous rations, that a common dream is of feasts and meeting ships and friends; all of which is familiar and requires slight emphasis. The wish is father to the thought both in waking and in dreaming; so much so that we tend to merge the two in wish-thinking which Bleuler named *autistic*, and recognized as an important factor in the formation of delusions in the eccentric and unbalanced. The wish-fulfilling dream falls in well with the general concept of wish-thinking generally, which has become a well-recognized principle of psychology and psychiatry. Our opinions, our sentiments, our prejudices are bent to desire. It is only the determination of the Freudians by hook or crook to make *all* dreaming repressed wish fulfillment, that runs contrary to the findings of a wide and neutral survey of dreams among all sorts and conditions of men, women and children, and is responsible for many a fantastic page in Freudiana.

To bring the dream within the wish formula involves what Freud calls distortion. Unquestionably dreams distort; the dreaming eye sees astigmatically and out of focus. But what impresses the "neutral" reader of psychoanalytic dreams is not the distortion in presentation but of interpretation, for which (one suspects) that the analyst is responsible. So once again, while the principle is acceptable, the strained processes of interpretation to bring the dream within the formula, are not.

Unquestionably, what seems remote to the reader

may seem less so to the dreamer when the connections are revealed. What makes corroboration difficult, if not impossible, is Freud's insistence that the connections are sunk deep in the "unconscious," are lost to the dreamer; that furthermore the laws of "unconscious" logic are quite different from those of the logic we use while awake. With or without psychoanalysis, it is plain that typical dreams are concerned with common desires, individually expressed. Most dreams are as individual as the person's experience; he alone can supply the clues. The analyst claims to have developed a technique—a legitimate project—to aid the dreamer in recovering lost clues between the superficial incident and the deeper motive.

He asks the dreamer to take one by one the items of the dream and describe freely what the word, the name, the place, the episode calls up in his mind. By following one clue and another, the latent meaning is eventually arrived at. If the solution is satisfactory to the analyst and accepted by the analysee, the dream is said to be interpreted. It is so entirely obvious that this process is a mingled product of the dreamer's contributions and the analyst's interpretation, that the method is inevitably subject to large uncertainty. (I am well aware that the Freudians deny this categorically; so I must for the moment meet denial with denial.) By that method one can prove anything or nothing, far too much or much too little. The mechanisms of dream-construction thus revealed, are real enough in the sense that they sometimes, more or less loosely, and now and then rather strikingly, apply. Let the reader consider some examples and judge of the cogency of the bond between the substance of the dream and its interpretation, and how far its discovery is due to the dreamer or to the interpreter.

Dream: A young man is on a brief visit in a household which he finds attractive. He dreams that bulbs recently planted in this house take root and blossom.

Interpretation: He wishes to prolong his visit. It takes time for bulbs to grow; so he dreams himself staying on until they root and blossom. The interpreter adds that "the wish in this dream is perfectly clear."

It may be so, and it may not! A dozen other and equally plausible interpretations are possible.

Another dream: A woman dreams that her brother was about to be hanged. This is hardly a sisterly desire, and the thought is highly repugnant. The "dream work," as shown by the analysis, is rather complex. The brother in the dream is not a real brother, but a composite of one brother who died of tuberculosis eight years before and of another who died of cancer four years ago. The dream occurred shortly after the dreamer had undergone an operation for a small tumor, which proved not to be a malignant growth, but had been a source of worry to her. She had also been concerned about a persistent cough. The one ailment gave rise to the suspicion that she had tuberculosis, the other that she had cancer, both of which she regarded as hereditary.

Interpretation: The real wish is that her brothers had died of some non-hereditary disease, and so relieve her of her worries. "In fact even hanging would be preferable so far as her own peace of mind is concerned."

The interpretation is ingenious, and almost tempts one to invent a better one. Let it be noted that Freud

explains to his patients that their dreams *are* wish fulfillments linked to repressions. When they protest that
they are not, he obtains further associations which he
analyzes into an interpretation to prove his point.

Still another dream: Mrs. A. dreams that she
wishes to give a supper-party but has nothing on
hand but smoked salmon; she cannot market for
other provisions as it is Sunday and the shops are
closed. She tries to telephone to a caterer, but the
telephone is out of order; so the supper must be
given up.

Interpretation: Her husband, Mr. A. had told her
the day before that he was growing too stout, that
he had decided to exercise and diet, and avoid suppers. (Mrs. A. adds that she is fond of her husband
and fond also of teasing him.) Though she would en-
joy a caviar sandwich in the middle of the morning,
she grudged the expense, and had asked her husband
not to send her any caviar, although, as a wholesale
provisioner, he was in a position to indulge her. But
she preferred the flirtatious game of teasing and re-
fusing him, an innocent but intelligible foible.

Deeper interpretation: This explanation seems to
Freud superficial; the motives revealed are not convincing. So he probes more deeply. Mrs. A. reports
that the day before she had visited a friend, Mrs. B.
of whom she is jealous because her own husband is
constantly praising Mrs. B. Mrs. B. is slender, and
remarked that she would like to gain weight. She
asked Mrs. A. when she would invite her again to
one of her abundant suppers. "Now," says Freud,
"the meaning of the dream is clear." As Mrs. A.'s
husband "likes well-rounded figures," it is as though
the dreamer had said to Mrs. B. in friendly (!)

irony: "So you want me to invite you, so you can eat yourself fat at my house and become still more pleasing to my husband. I would rather give no more suppers!" Behold! the dietary tragedy is solved!

The Freudians maintain that all the incidents and properties of the dream drama are determined. To make the interpretation clear, additional clues are inserted. The dream "over-determines," which means that it tells the same story in several ways, reënforcing the theme with corroborative details.

Epilogue: The salmon, is still unaccounted for. Further analysis reveals that smoked salmon is Mrs. B.'s favorite dish; her choice for a morning indulgence would be a salmon sandwich. Freud's ingenuity is not exhausted. He adds yet another explanation: namely that Mrs. A. identifies herself with Mrs. B. and by dream logic dreams that her own wish is not fulfilled in *substitute* for *her real wish that her friend's wish shall not be fulfilled.* Is this Mrs. B.'s subtlety, or Freud's?

These episodes may shed as much unintentional light upon Viennese social habits, culinary and marital, as upon dream interpretation. Freud insists that we never dream of the trivial, only of what deeply matters; so again this dream may indicate the perspective of importance of this order of incident in the dreamers' lives.

A *non-conforming dream:* In another instance one of Freud's patients contested the dictum that dreams are wish fulfillments. She offered as her "non-conforming" *dream* the following: She was travelling with her mother-in-law to a summer resort where (in the dream) both had rented villas. As a fact she had rented an estate intentionally as remote as possible from that of her mother-in-law.

Interpretation: "According to this dream, I was in the wrong. *It was thus her wish that I should be in the wrong, and this wish the dream showed her as fulfilled.*"

Whether or not dreams go by contraries, this dream indicates to Freud how "contrary" persons dream. It is obvious that in this argument the analyst has all the advantage; he has the last word, makes the last move.

Dreams in their rôle of revealing indirectly, distortedly, discreetly or acceptably, the repressed factor of their content, may travel far afield in episodes and in the play of emotions which they arouse. It is difficult to anticipate what subtle and canny or uncanny disguises the subconscious will devise. The Freudians point out that the dream of a death of a beloved person may at times be a suppressed wish in an ambivalent or equivocal situation, one in which the dreamer is beset by the opposed emotions—love and hate—or is in an uncertain frame of mind. Yet they find also that the dream of such a death may be a mask to conceal a forbidden yet cherished emotion.

An equivocal dream: A young girl dreams that her sister's child, Charles, lies dead in his coffin. The candles are lit, just as in the case of his brother Otto's death some years before. Surely she did not wish the death of her sister's only surviving child!

Interpretation: Stimulated by free associations, the dreamer finds the clue to the dream in the fact that she, the dreamer, was early orphaned, and brought up by this older sister. In her sister's house she met a young man with whom she fell in love. The sister, for reasons not given, prevented a possible marriage. This suitor, a man of letters of some distinction, she could not forget. When he spoke in public, she was in the audience. Knowing that he was to attend a concert on the day on which she told the dream, she had planned to go also. One of the occasions on which she had seen him was at the funeral of little Otto. The wish then projects Charles's funeral so that she might see her suitor again. The explanation seemed satisfactory to the dreamer; but how subconscious is it?

Another unnatural dream: In a similar dream, another female patient saw her fifteen-year-old daughter lying dead before her in a box.

Interpretation: In the course of analysis she remembered a discussion concerning the various meanings of the English word box—a "box" at the theatre, a "box" on the ear, as well as a chest—and also had been haunted by "the vulgar meaning of the word, which made it a synonym for the female genital." . . . It was therefore possible, making certain allowances for her notions on the subject of topographical anatomy, to assume that "the child in the box signified a child in the womb of the mother. At this stage of the explanation she no longer denied that the picture of the dream corresponded to one of her wishes"—a wish when pregnant that the child might die before birth. "The dead child was, therefore, really the fulfillment of a wish, but a wish which had been put aside for fifteen years; and it is not surprising that the fulfillment of a wish was no longer recognized after so long an interval. For there had been many changes meanwhile."

The interpreter has the privilege of drawing upon the entire range of the patient's experience to find a fact to fit the theory.

Wish-dreams that go by contraries: "Here is a pretty 'water' dream of a female patient, which was turned to extraordinary account in the course of treatment." At her summer resort at Lake So-and-So, she hurls herself into the dark water at a place where the pale moon is reflected in the water.

Interpretation: Dreams of this sort are parturition dreams; their interpretation is accomplished by reversing the fact reported in the manifest dream content. Thus, instead of " 'throwing one's self into the water,' read 'coming out of the water,' that is, 'being born.' . . . Now what can be the meaning of the patient's wishing to be born at her summer resort? I asked the dreamer this, and she answered without hesitation: 'Hasn't the treatment made me as though I were born again?' Thus the dream becomes an invitation to continue the cure at this summer resort, that is, to visit her there; perhaps it also contains a very bashful allusion to the wish to become a mother herself."

These eclectic instances will serve their purpose, which is to illustrate the Freudian manner of deriving a connection between the dream-data and their interpretation. Freud assures his readers that through just such dream-data he "discovered" the nature of conflicts and complexes of neurotic patients; he is equally confident that he does not prompt or suggest or invite such connections, a confidence which sceptical readers may not share. He finds the same principles applicable to ordinary dreams of normal persons. He emphasizes the frequent almost constant sexual components, the reinstatement of incidents from early childhood with which some emotional shock—again usually of a sexual nature—is associated. He maintains that "that which has actually remained indifferent can never be reproduced in a dream." We do not dream idly or trivially, and everywhere there is determinism; nothing in dreams is indifferent. That is an important, if disputable tenet, of the Freudian oneirologist. Dreaming to the Freudian is not a playful diversion or a restful relaxation. The dream-shift works only at night after the office-hours of the censor. The dream like the burglar, waits for the still of night to steal a march on the conscious self. "Experience teaches us that the road leading from the foreconscious to the conscious is closed to the dream-thoughts during the day by the resistance of the censor."

In spite of the many extravagant and extreme applications, and the contradiction of its own principles, it still may be maintained that dream analysis has led to the discovery of complexes. Freud's theory of dreaming contains important truths; it has advanced our understanding of the dreamy (and possibly of the seamy) side of life.

RECURRENT DREAMS AND SYMBOLISMS

Symbolism has a prominent part in the Freudian drama, even more so in the Jungian version of the psychic life. Freudianism has revived symbolism. Yet it has long been recognized that the process of thinking in symbols is natural and inherent in the mental procedure. Man has a symbol-making mind. We both feel and see resemblances, and in words hear them and play and pun upon them. They please and attract.

They fall in with the more primary order of mental movement. Thinking is imaging; the pictorial antedates the verbal; the imagination realizes and idealizes. When we drift in thought and muse, we are near to the mood of symbolism.

The art of communication makes primitive man a sign-maker; his urge to explain makes him a myth-maker, and a believer in signs; in all he is symbolic. Were it not that he can make one thing stand for another, he could hardly think. Myth and fable derive their appeal from the same source. They set the fancy free and bring the remote together. Myths have been well termed the dreams of the race.

The specific Freudian point that the dream resorts to symbols to disguise socially inhibited purposes, is an added stimulus to symbolizing, which Plato also recognized. As our minds have much in common they may develop similar symbols. Yet, as Heraclitus recognized, we share the waking world in common, while in dreaming each retires to a private world of his own. Our dreams may be poor things, but our own. Still we dream with a common human nature; and that provides some measure of community of dream-experience. We all have had parallel and comparable dreams.

How much of a common theme and manner runs through the symbolism of dreams is an ancient yet engaging question. In so far as dreams recur because of common motives and take on common forms, symbolism becomes a language, a dialect of the imagination. The Freudian interpreter finds both generic and individual dream-symbols; he finds common symbols in dreams, in actions, in mental habits. By the same token there are parallels and types in poetry, in drama, in art generally. They are all manifestations of the metaphorical, somewhat cryptical, mind. For this quality of the Freudian psychology the term *anagogic* has been used. Through psychoanalysis, symbolism, including some novel interpretations of its function, has come into its psychological estate. Dreams proceed upon suggestive resemblance and particularly upon equivalence of emotional values. The very existence of typical dreams, of dreams with a recurrent theme, variable in detail, such as Freud posits in the Oedipus situation, replicas of which he so readily finds in the dream life, depends upon a common symbolism. The pictures vary; the meaning is one; otherwise one could hardly generalize about or interpret dreams. One of the difficulties of interpretation lies in determining how far the dream is generic, how far individual. The symbol is a secondary instrument of Freudian interpretation. We summarize by noting, first that symptoms, incidents in dreams, lapses in daily life have a meaning to be interpreted according to the Freudian code; second, that the code may proceed by way of a symbol; it may be a private symbol with the meaning known only to the individual, or it may be a generic symbol in common use.

The dreams already cited illustrate forms of symbolism; these may be supplemented by others bearing specifically upon that relation. Dreams of flying are common. Some dream interpreters make them symbolize ambition; others a desire for release from social restraint. The symbolism in either view and in half a dozen other interpretations, is apparent enough. But it is well to have in mind that flying, as one dreams of it, is a bodily sensation. Many can describe precisely how it feels to fly and how one manages one's wings; for their dreaming selves are intensely interested in the experience. This raises the question whether flying is not just a fantasy interpretation of physiological changes, possibly a shift in lung action; just as similarly dreams of falling may be due to a bodily feeling of loss of support. Freud does not wholly disregard the bodily component as an excitant but prefers the symbolic interpretation, usually pointing it to a sexual implication. Falling means an emotional or moral descent; dreams of falling follow the thought of a "fallen woman." By the same route objects acquire "symbol" value. We may stay on safe ground and interpret cautiously or go far afield and approach the dream-book stage of oneiromancy. A ladder is a common instance. It may represent ascent, coming up in the world, mounting; but Freud gives it meaning in terms of sexual approach and consummation. A piano, because on it one plays scales similar to steps, likewise becomes sexualized. By reason of the powerful taboo affecting the mention of sex-processes, and by reason of their strong affective value, sex becomes—as the reader has discovered—the favorite symbolic reference. The symbolic disguise gets by the endopsychic censor, the internal "watch and ward" agent. In deference to a more pragmatic censorship and of Freud-unenlightened postal authorities, it may be prudent to follow a neutral zoological symbolism in citing Freud and substitute ♂ —the sign for Mars—for the male element and ♀ —the sign for Venus—for the female, leaving the rest to the reader's uncensored imagination.

"All elongated objects, sticks, tree-trunks, and umbrellas (on account of the stretching-up) . . . all elongated and sharp weapons, knives, daggers and pikes" . . . and for different reasons "a nail file" are ♂. "Little cases, boxes, caskets and stoves" are ♀. The dream of walking through a row of rooms is a brothel or harem dream. Staircases, ladders, and flights of stairs, or climbing on these, either upwards or downward, are symbolic representations of the sexual act. "Smooth walls over which one is climbing, façades of houses upon which one is letting oneself down, frequently under great anxiety, correspond to the erect human body, and probably repeat in the dream reminiscences of the upward climbing of little children on their parents or foster-parents. 'Smooth' walls are men. Often in a dream of anxiety one is holding on firmly to some projection from a house. Tables, set tables, and boards are women, perhaps on account of the opposition which does away with the bodily contours. Since 'bed and board' (*mensa et thorus*) constitute marriage, the former are often put for the latter in the dream, and as far as practicable the sexual complex is transposed to the eating complex. Of articles of dress the woman's hat is ♂. In dreams of men one often finds the cravat as ♂ because cravats hang down long, and are characteristic of the man, but also because one can select them at pleasure, a freedom which is prohibited by nature in the original of the symbol. Persons who make use of this symbol in the dream are very extravagant with cravats, and possess regular collections of them." By way of further elucidation: "In this country (America) where the word 'necktie' is almost exclusively used, the translator has also found it to be the symbol of a burdensome woman from whom the dreamer longs to be freed—'necktie' —something tied to my neck like a heavy weight— my fiancée, are the associations from the dream of a man who eventually broke his marriage engagement."

"All complicated machines and apparatus in dreams

are very probably genitals, in the description of which dream symbolism shows itself to be as tireless as the activity of wit." "Many landscapes in dreams, especially with bridges or with wooded mountains" are also symptoms of the same origin; and a Freudian disciple with the courage of his conviction (or is it a complex?) detects in those who love to wander in forests of erect trees a strong sexual proclivity. If in dreaming of a landscape one has the strong impression of having been there before (a well known phenomenon, in French called *déja vu,* and referred to an illusion of memory), the locality "is always" the womb of one's mother.

The meaning of the "dreams of dental irritation" escaped Freud for a long time because of the great resistance to their analysis. "At last overwhelming evidence convinced me that, in the case of men [they meant] nothing else than the cravings for masturbation." Having teeth pulled may have a similar meaning. Freudians such as Jung and Rank discuss learnedly and at great length the dream symbolism of teeth, Jung holding that in women "dental irritation" refers to child-birth, by reason of the common belief that every child means the loss of a tooth, or as reflecting another folk belief that when a woman with child has a toothache, the child will be a boy; while Rank's reference to teeth lost in childhood when sexual practices begin, are too involved for summary.

Of the making of symbolisms by Freudians there is no end. Let these instances, as eclectic and arbitrary as the interpretations themselves, suffice to suggest the versatile repertory of symbolism in dreams and other Freudian manifestations. We shall approach the problem of symbolism in more critical vein in appraising its logical status; for it raises the fundamental question whether a system that depends upon so variable and tenuous evidence has any claim to scientific consideration. Whether or not symbolism and science are as oil and water, the Freudians find the emulsion palatable. Such is Freudian dream-interpretation; thus is their theory carried out in practice.

SYMPTOMATIC ACTIONS

There is another order of building material in the house that Freud built, stones rejected or neglected by other builders of psychological houses. First a neurosis psychology; then a dream psychology; now an accident psychology. They are all subject to the same order of determinism, the same play of motive. We are all familiar with inadvertent, unpremeditated, half-intentioned actions, transactions and mis-actions, that obtrude into the consciously directed stream. Seemingly accidental, they are suppressed motives breaking through. When done or spoken, one is usually aware of them, at times embarrassingly so, as the things one would like to have said or done differently. The simplest name for this miscellaneous group of bits of behavior, unintentionally revealing motives, is *lapses;* they have also been called errors, slips, mistakes. They form the subject-matter of the *Psychopathology of Everyday Life.* This popular contribution to a new variety of diagnostic mind-reading, traces covert meanings in such overt acts as slips, accidents and forgettings, commissions and omissions. Like dreams, they have a patent (intended and expressed) and a latent (half intended, but to be suppressed) content, which through the strength of the latent urge or the momentary off-duty of the censor, gets by and through to the muscles, including those of speech.

Their formulae of interpretation parallel those of dreams, but usually function closer to the conscious level. In import they may be more trivial, but as illustrating Freudian procedure quite as illuminating, and richly variable in plot and incident. No one questions that there is a frequent wish-element in dreams, or questions the abundant symbolism and interesting tricks of the mind, which Freud's fertile curiosity has discerned in lapses. But the same doubt recurs: how far may one legitimately go in tracing the bridge between what was done and said (or left undone and unsaid) and what was meant?

Let us begin with some simple and fairly acceptable examples from Freud.

Professional lapses: Dr. Freud relates of several fellow-physicians that now and then they absent-mindedly try to open the door to the clinic or office with the key to their residence—never the reverse—thereby indicating a preference for being at leisure at home rather than at the more formal and exacting task.

When Freud himself, on a visit to a patient, takes out his housekey instead of ringing the bell, he interprets the mistake as due to a subconscious symbolic wish to be "at home" there. When in calling on another patient in an apartment-house he walks up to the floor above, lost "in an ambitious day-dream," he regards the lapse as due not to inattention but to the resentment of the criticism then frequently made against him, that he went too far in his views, which in the symptomatic action is replaced by "climbed too high" as a metaphor. This ambition is translated into a Freudian bit of behavior upon an actual flight of stairs.

Some readers may consider that in this very instance he went too far, and more will do so in regard to the next example.

Incident: When about to leave for a visit by train to a patient, Freud by mistake took up from his desk a tuning-fork instead of the "reflex" hammer to test the knee-jerk—both being testing instruments.

Interpretation: For this mis-handling he found a deeper reason, requiring a more elaborate analysis of his subconscious understudy, the Freudian Freud. The fork had recently been used to test the hearing of a feeble-minded child. Could this lapse mean that he, Freud, was an idiot? It may be so, as the German *hammer* and the Hebrew *chamer* (ass) have a similar sound. Why this insinuation? The case he was to attend was that of a patient who had fallen from a balcony and was apparently paralyzed. Freud was summoned in consultation to decide whether there was a spinal injury, or only an hysterical impairment. That brought up another recollection: The railway-station to which he was going was the same to which he went on another occasion when he actually made a partly incorrect diagnosis. So the mistaking of the fork for the hammer meant: "You fool, you ass, don't repeat this mistake."

Thus is an inadvertent slip of the hand made the issue of a subconscious intrusion, a protective warning.

A personal incident: Freud regards himself as by no means awkward, as he rarely breaks anything. On his desk, there is a collection of precious *objets d'art*. A working desk thus equipped would seem to invite accidents; yet they never occurred. However, one day he happened to make an awkward movement with his hand and swept the marble cover of his ink-well to the floor. Why this accident? There *must* be a reason.

Interpretation: Some hours before, he was proudly showing some new acquisitions to his sister. She shared his pleasure, then remarked: "The desk looks very well; only the inkstand does not go well with these things." It was on his return from a walk with his sister that he "performed the execution of the condemned inkstand."

The slight rankling of the criticism subconsciously broke through into a symptomatic act.

Freud confesses to a tendency to impulsive action, an enviable sign of freedom from inhibition.

Incident: In a moment of joy on learning that a member of his family, gravely ill, was on the safe side of recovery, he kicked off his dressing-slipper and with it brought down "a beautiful little marble Venus from its bracket" on the wall.

Interpretation: This "accident" (?) was a thank-offering, the choice of the Venus a "gallant homage to the convalescent."

Incident: On another occasion a glazed Egyptian figurette was broken, while Freud was writing a letter of apology to a friend whom he had offended by going a bit too far in interpreting personal bits of behavior as evidence of undesirable qualities.

Interpretation: That breakage he set down as "a pious offering to avert some evil." . . . "Luckily both the friendship and the figure could be so cemented that the break would not be noticed."

This manner of interpreting the incidents of daily life seems to have both its dangers and its compensations. It may be interesting, but is it scientific, or even warranted as a speculative indoor sport?

Not only what we do seemingly by chance, but what we leave undone, is interpreted as implying a similar semi-intention determined by a subconscious undercurrent. Forgetting has a bit of suppressing about it; things do not so much drop out of mind, as that they are pushed out or kept out as unpleasant. We avoid the unpleasant by forgetting it; or there is some uncertainty as to whether we really do or do not want "it." The conscious *we* is in doubt; the subconscious decides, or makes us aware of our decision. That is a well recognized form of behavior, which Freud has made more interesting. Has he overdone it, and offended rules of logic, as he offended his friend by overstepping the social proprieties?

These lapses are familiar, and the element of motive likewise. With a long list of commissions, one may find at the end of the day that the irksome ones failed to be attended to. Dr. Freud admits that in making a round of professional visits, those that promise little pleasure or slight prospect of fees, may be "forgotten." That this common process may proceed more elaborately and more suppressedly may likewise be admitted, and also that it is capable of more rigid or formal formulation; but that it can be extended indefinitely, and more and more remotely, and attain a high diagnostic value and a secure logical status: that is more than doubtful. Yet that value is assigned to it in psychoanalysis.

A collection of lapses. We may summarize a few additional and miscellaneous instances. A young chemist who remained at the laboratory instead of appearing at the ceremony at which his bride was waiting, wisely took the hint from his subconscious that he was not very seriously inclined to matrimony, and remained a bachelor. As a companion incident for the bride: a young woman who forgot an appointment at the modiste's for her wedding-gown, may well have been expressing subconsciously her hesitation in taking a step which the future proved undesirable, as a separation took place after a few years.

Yet we can hardly conclude that if those contemplating marriage would listen to the still small voice of the subconscious as expressed by symptomatic acts, Reno would find its occupation gone.

That we forget words, proper names particularly, is a common and exasperating experience that may well drive its victim to psychology or even to a stronger stimulant. We are equally and more agreeably puzzled to know how the lost word returns; on this phase Freud is silent.

He thus explains his own forgetting.

Incident: He could not recall the location of an Italian sanitarium which was perfectly familiar to him.

The clue: Why? There must, he reflected, be something unpleasant about it. At last it came to him. The name was "Nervi"; he had enough to do with *nerves* as it was, so "Nervi" escaped his memory for the time. At least there is so much in a name.

Another forgetting: He was disputing with a friend who maintained that there were three hotels at a certain pleasure-resort, while Freud insisted that there were only two. As a fact there were three. The third was called *"Hochwärtner."* For seven summers Freud had lived in its vicinity. Why had he forgotten so familiar a name?

The clue: The name, he found, was similar to that of a Viennese rival specialist; he forgot, or rather repressed, because the name touched his professional complex.

Though Jung differs from Freud in many positions, he also "symptomatizes"; and why not, since we all do it, Freudian or non-Freudian, at our own risk. Jung tells of a Mr. A. who fell in love with a young woman who had the bad taste to marry Mr. B., whom Mr. A. knew fairly well as he had business relations with him. Yet, again and again, Mr. A. would forget Mr. B.'s name, and had to ask his clerks for it when he wished to write to him.

The reason for suppression is obvious if we hold to this theory; yet to others that would be the one name they could *not* forget. It may work either way. Here is a case in which "Jung" figures as the forgotten name.

Forgetting youth: Ferenczi tells of a lady, a patient of his, who could not recall Jung's name. He tried the free association method, asking her to think of the lost name, and to tell what came to mind. She thought of Mr. Kl., then of Mrs. Kl. who was an affected type of person, who did not show her age. Then of Wilde and Nietzsche and Hauptmann. This led to the remark: "I cannot bear Wilde and Nietzsche; I do not understand them. I hear that they were both homosexual. Wilde occupied himself with *young* people." To the name *Hauptmann* (which means captain) she associated *"half"* and *"youth";*

only when the analyist called her attention to the
word "youth," did she think of Jung.

The clue: The lady became a widow at thirty-nine
and at that age seemed to have slight prospect of
marrying again; so she did not want to think of
"youth," which in German is "Jung." The similarity
in method in interpreting dreams and lapses is apparent.

Here is a variation in the practice of the symptomatology of forgetting.

In his doctorate examination a student was asked
what he knew of Epicurus, and who among the modern philosophers held a similar position. He answered
"Gassendi," and volunteered the interesting lie that
he had long been a student of Gassendi, while as a
fact he had only heard him casually mentioned by a
fellow-student as a follower of Epicurus. He passed
his examination with honors, but thereafter had
trouble in recalling the name *Gassendi*.

Thus the subconscious punished him for his prevari-
cation. Yet if all students were similarly affected, what
honeycombed memories they would have!

Negative lapses (forgettings) leave a wider margin
in interpretation than positive ones (mishaps or intrusions); they offer larger possibilities for fanciful
conjecture and remote byways of alleged "reasons."

A "remote" instance to which Freud devotes six pages,
but which, when condensed, is quite as consequential,
is the following.

The incident: While travelling in Italy, Freud became acquainted with a young man who was familiar

with his views and career. As they talked, his companion spoke of the anti-Semitic prejudice which obstructed the career of ambitious young men like himself. In that connection he cited the line from Virgil in which Dido asks posterity to take vengeance upon Æneas. As he recited it; *"Exoriar(e) ex nostris ossibus ultor"* he knew that a word was missing. He appealed to Freud to complete the quotation, which he did: *"Exoriar(e) aliquis nostris ex ossibus ultor."*

Then came a challenge, which Freud accepted, to psychoanalyze why the word *aliquis* could not be recalled. Freud induced his companion to dwell on *aliquis* and report what associations the word aroused. The associations tended to divide the word falsely *a-liquis;* then *reliques, liquidation, liquidity, fluid.* That brought up the memory of the relics of Simon of Trent, seen at Trent; then an article in an Italian journal on "What St. Augustine said concerning Women"; then a handsome old man he met recently called Benedict; then St. Simon, St. Augustine, St. Benedict; after prompting, St. Januarius and the miracle of the liquefaction of the clotted blood at Naples; then (with some hesitation) a lady whom he had visited in Naples, whose possible pregnancy was his intimate concern.

The clue: Then Freud cried "Eureka": he had the clue to the avoided word. "You have elaborated the miracle of St. Januarius into a clever allusion to the courses of a woman." That this is the reason for forgetting *aliquis* "appears to me absolutely certain." The reader may be more impressed with the miracle of the explanation.

"I have more than one reason for valuing this little analysis, for which I am indebted to my travelling companion," among them that he was not a

neurotic, but an intelligent, normal man. The analysis
also reveals a strange contradictory wish that formed
the resistance to the recall: on the one hand he called
upon posterity to redeem the position of the Jews;
on the other hand, the fear of an inconvenient posterity was at the moment his personal concern.

Let the reader supply exclamation-marks or question-
marks by way of comment. The quotation-marks vali-
date the tale. They may point the moral that it is better
to leave many slips unanalyzed. There is no end to
such symptomatologies. Once sensitive to them, one
may develop the habit and even the obsession of ob-
serving them; and generalizations are ready so long as
they are not tested, and in the main cannot be so. Let
me add that when a worried patient forgot to wind his
watch, Freud interpreted the omission as expressing
"symbolically that it was a matter of indifference to him
whether he lived the next day or not." As this is a frequent lapse, the results might be serious if all those to
whom it occurred accepted it as a subconscious indica-
tion of suicidal intention.

One must be careful when a symptomatologist is
present; one must mind one's p's and q's and keep the
subconscious suppressed. Freud tells the story of a
young man relating to a company of friends how at
one time he was employed as secretary to a minister
plenipotentiary, but lost his place when this diplomat
was transferred to another post. As he spoke he happened to be carrying a piece of cake to his mouth and
carelessly let it drop. At this mishap Freud remarked:
"There, you lost a choice morsel!" The implication is
that the thought caused the accident.

Accepting the idea none too seriously, a game of
"Revelations" *à la* Freud might prove a social diver-

sion, provided it was played in good humor with charity
toward all, with malice toward none, and not too intimately. It appears that when Freud and Jung came
to America in 1909, they passed the time on shipboard
by "symptomatizing" one another as a means of testing the system, and with good and friendly results;
which, however, did not prevent a break in their relations a few years later.

Freud gives many examples of tracking the subconscious to its sexual lair by psychoanalytical strategy,
thus confirming the diplomatic motto: *"Cherchez la
femme"* which may equally, in view of the fact that
many of his patients are women, be called *"Cherchez
l'homme."* On this point Heine's observation is more
witty and psychoanalytically quite as consequential.
He remarked of women writers, that they all wrote
with one eye on the manuscript and the other on a
man; yet in candor, he had to make an exception of
the Countess Hahn von Hahn, who had only one eye.

The incident: Freud had for years visited twice
daily a patient over ninety years of age to put eye-
drops in her eyes and administer a hypodermic solution. On one occasion he confused the bottles. "I was
badly frightened and then calmed myself with the
reflection that a few drops of a two per-cent mor-
phine solution can do no harm even in the conjuncti-
val sac. The fright was evidently due to something
else."

The clue: Freud's explanation is that while on
this visit, his mind was busy with a dream told him
the night before by a young man, which was interpreted Oedipus-wise, as the expression of a desire to
possess his mother. "Deep in thoughts of this kind, I
came to my patient of over ninety; I must have been

well on the way to grasp the universal character of
the Oedipus fable as the correlation of the fate which
the oracle pronounces, for I made a blunder in reference to, or on, the old woman." In this instance the
connection is as obscure after explanation as before.
It seems to hang on a German word which may refer
to an assault, or mis-handling, or also just a mistake
in general. However such is the interpretation. In
the course of telling this tale, Freud remarks that
"the Oedipus legend takes no offense at the age of
Queen Jocasta" and congratulates his own subconscious. "Of the two possible errors, taking the mor-
phine solution for the eye or the eye lotion for the
injection, I chose the one by far the least harmful."

The possibility that in cases of more serious confusion a jury versed in Freudian symptomatology might
look for a motive, offers interesting speculation.

Since Freud seems to forget (is this accidental, or is
it also quasi-intentional?) that most of these lapses
have other and simpler explanations, I may, for the
sake of completeness include instances in which this is
fairly obvious. Yet Freud, as is true also of his interpretation of dreams, prefers the remote to the near
at hand. In the search for the latent he disregards the
patent.

Freud (this at a later period when his prestige
was established) records his annoyance when his patients fail to close the door between the waiting-room
and consulting room. "I insist rather gruffly that he
or she go back and rectify the omission, even though
it be an elegant gentleman or a lady in all her finery.
Such a person belongs to the rabble and deserves to
be received in an unfriendly manner."

Interpretation: This action conveys disrespect; it suggests an "ugly" reflection in the patient's mind, that as there is no one in the waiting-room, evidently this doctor's office is not much sought, and the door may as well remain open.

Just how subconscious this mechanism is supposed to be is not clear. Whether this social treatment aids the psychoanalytic treatment is also a question.

Certainly is it true and familiar that in mis-speaking, in slips of tongue or pen, in things that might better be said otherwise, in mis-writing and even in mis-prints, there is often a bit of motive that breaks through and lets the subconscious cat out of the bag. Of this the illustrations are endless and often apt and indisputable. Such is the familiar *arriére pensée,* the thought in the back of one's head that comes to the fore. We frequently carry on a double line of thought and speech, revealing and concealing at once. The Freudian principles properly utilize and extend this chapter in psychology. In carrying it through, Freud recognizes that when the intention—the *double entendre*—is somewhat nearer the conscious surface, it becomes a thrust or a jibe, and approaches the *Psychology of Wit and Humor,* upon which he has written interestingly; but that is more an application than part of the evidence of psychoanalysis.

To call attention to the psychology of the casual incidents of every-day life, the little halts and intrusions, the minor slips and casualties of the mind's operations in the double rôle of revealment and concealment which we all must assume in maintaining the contacts and distances of social relations; to set forth that the mechanism detectable in this lighter movement is of the

same nature as that which appears in the wholly different milieu and conditions of the dream, and in serious
neurotic disabilities: that is a well formed project,
which reflects the fertility of Freud's mind. He has indeed a marked flair for creative insight and the analytic
power of detecting both significance and confirmations
in what others pass by. But to carry out the brilliant
idea in such extreme fashion, with such glaring insensi-
bility to the logic and the quality of the relations involved: that is the reverse of the picture. Both qualities
appear in the citations from the clinical note-books
which have been reviewed. These original chapters in
the text of psychology are exclusively Freudian.

CHAPTER III

THE SUPERSTRUCTURE

Metapsychology

It has been duly set forth that psychoanalysis consists of a clinical contribution out of which a psychology was developed. The clinical trail started in the psycho-neuroses and followed their symptoms and case-histories upstream to their sources in urges and complexes; the trail led to the symbolic cryptic tangles of the dream-life, clinically interpreted through the indiscretions of the subconscious; it led to the by-ways of symptomatic actions, revealing further lapses of the double life and exposures of respectable duplicity; it crossed the trail of personality-traits—all engaging excursions in search of building material for the citadel of psychoanalysis. In a more architectural frame of mind we turn to the psychology that Freud built to enclose psychoanalysis.

Always creative, and never a builder on another's designs, but content to build section by section as one enterprise followed another, there came a turn in his center of interest, many sided in origin. With the maturity of years, there comes to many devotees of the intellectual life the desire to attempt a philosophy, to consider the laboratory less, the cosmos more. Freud had before him the deviations of his followers, of Jung and Adler notably, who found the restrictions of the Freudian principles cramping, and the gaps in the structure the centers of their own interests. They found the Freudian *homo* inadequate. In addition, since ideas are rarely independent of events, there was the violent subversive challenge of many a position, responsible eventually for advancing the Freudian vogue—the disconcerting, reflection-compelling interruption of the War. The post-war Freud is more psychologist and philosopher than clinician.

The most adequate account of the Freudian system as system, is the monumental compendium of Healy, Bronner and Bowers: *The Structure and Meaning of Psychoanalysis*. From it we may derive a picture not only of the Freudian house, but of its inhabitant, the *homo Freudiens*. He appears as a generalization of clinical experience. Having discovered the ways of psyche in the clinic, Freud proceeded to reconstruct psychology in the image of psychoanalysis. The Freudian *homo* is composed of *Id, Ego,* and *Super-ego*. First came the Id, the great "Unconscious"—deep-seated, organic, affective—of greater consequences to the "dance of life" than the *homo sapiens* of the intellectualists. The Id is the revised Unconscious.

The problem of psychical living is to reconcile and merge the pleasure principle and the reality principle; to live out the urges, yet attain a life of reason. In *Beyond the Pleasure Principle*—the turning point of the new dispensation—Freud corrected the original doctrine that pleasure alone is primary and regulative, and recognized the collateral instincts, with a larger place for aims as against drives. By this revision psychoanalytic psychology recognized more adequately that within the human psyche there is an Ego as well as an Id. The doctrine finds expression in *The Ego and the Id,* a further epistle in the New Testament of the Freudian Scriptures.

There is a more biological rendering of the distinction,

The Id

Sketch suggesting topographical relationship of Cs and Ucs; Id, Ego, and Super-ego.

(Elaborated from Freud's diagram in *The Ego and the Id*)

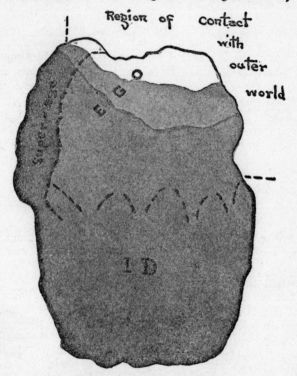

SHADED PORTIONS === THE UNCONSCIOUS—UCS
LIGHTLY SHADED PORTIONS === THE PRECONSCIOUS—PCS
UNSHADED PORTIONS === THE CONSCIOUS—CS

Reproduced, by permission, from Healy, Bronner and Bowers: "The Structure and Meaning of Psychoanalysis"

variously useful, which I shall adopt in the critical discussion. It was introduced by Gross, who speaks of *primary function* and *secondary function* in the psychic realm. All psychic life is primary or secondary or a mingling of the two. The third member of the trinity that shapes our ends, rough hew them as the Id will, is the *Super-ego,* the *Ego Ideal,* created complicatedly by the Ego in its habitat of circumstance, and setting the transformed goal of human endeavor, determining the course of the civilizing process. The Id is all primary, the Super-ego is all secondary function. The Ego partakes of both and in its elaboration is mainly secondary. We cannot live out the primary Id urges and become what we are: complicated Egos living under Super-ego systems and ideals. The more abstract reformulation of Freudianism sets forth how Id became Ego and developed a Super-ego, and how all three rule the world of psyche in normal and neurotic personalities, and in the social and institutional forces shaping the human scene. This large-dimensioned formulation constitutes the Freudian humanism, perhaps forbiddingly formal, but humanistic in intent.

Freud has even reduced to a diagram how the glory of man was shaped out of the void. It seems an uncouth picture of creation; it is offered merely as a memorandum aid to imaginations concretely inclined.

Let me use the pause of its contemplation to caution and console the reader. In this section of our tangled tale, we have before us a speculation, consciously and avowedly such. Those whose tastes care not for such mental exercises may abandon the route and rejoin it later on. There is no recognized bureau of the sciences that issues speculation licenses to competent chauffeurs of the mental highways and byways. As James notes in *The Will to Believe,* we believe, as we travel, at our own risk. There is, however, something in the way of a test or visé with which Freud dispenses when he calls his system a "metapsychology." By frankly calling it such he disarms one phase of criticism; yet just how far this legitimate speculation may be helpful in rendering an account of the psyche, depends upon the manner of its employment.

Though no one has ever seen an Id, wild or in captivity, and some may reflect in terms of the "purple cow" of another yesterday: "I'd rather see than be one," the reader, once reconciled to speculation may approach the Id not as some ungainly Caliban—which in truth "he" at moments resembles—but as a philosopher-psychologist's technical label for a familiar component of human behavior.

> Summarized, the Id is thus described: "It is the source of instinctive energy for the individual; it is unconscious; it forms the great reservoir of libido; it is the region, the hinterland, of the passions and instincts, also of habit tendencies; the pleasure-principle reigns supreme in it; it is unmoral, illogical; it has no unity of purpose; the repressed merges into the Id and is then part of it."

Humanized, the Id is the vital core of our human, including our animal being: it expresses the basic, the ultra primitive, the initial nucleus of psychic life. In Id life begins: the child is all Id, but with the potential Ego gradually emerging. The life of Id is closer to that of primitive man. In the Id reflection, we see ourselves as Adam and Eve, and by aid of the tree of knowledge, serpent and all, recognize libido as the basic life-force that actuates the psyche from its embryonic to its mature stage. Sex thou art, to sex returnest, was decidedly spoken of the Freudian soul. It is true that libido is more than sex, far more; it is the psycho-sexual amplified Freudian psyche; yet the Id is saturated with libido in all its forms and stages.

In re-reading Freud with the metapsychology in mind, it becomes clear enough that the Freudian motivation-scheme is an ego-istic product, that the libidos are all integrated in egos whose total social relation is considered. Thus the father appears as authority as well as procreator, and the mother as protrectress as well as bearer of children; and the Oedipus situation is as much a striving for emancipation and independence as the doom of an infantile bond. But the course of growth is represented as so largely the wanderings of libido that the ego, as self-assertive in a rich and riotous repertory, never comes into his own. Hence Jung's protesting secession emphasizing the collateral sovereignty of Ego-urges, and the will-to-power concentration of the Adlerian position. In the riper formulation the Freudian ego appears in fairer stature and truer perspective. Again we may profit by the key-note summaries of the Healy text.

The Ego

The Ego is a coherent organization of mental life, derived from that more primal structure, the Id, by modifications imposed on it by the external world. Its characteristics are as follows:

It is not sharply differentiated from the Id; its lower portion merges into the Id. Part of it is conscious; part of it is unconscious. From it proceed the repressions, holding in check the superior strength of the Id. Sublimation may take place through the mediation of the Ego; in this way erotic libido is changed into Ego-libido.

Just as instincts play a great rôle in the Id, so perceptions play a great part in the Ego.

It goes to sleep, but exercises censorship in dreams and strives to be moral.

It owes service to three masters and is consequently menaced by three dangers: the external world, the libido of the Id, the severity of the Super-ego.

The Id produces the driving power; the Ego "takes the steering wheel in hand," in order to reach the desired goal.

The Ego has two different censorial duties in respect to the Id: (a) to watch the outer world and seize the most opportune moment for a harmless gratification of Id urges; (b) to induce the Id to modify or renounce its urges, or to substitute or postpone its gratifications. There is no inherent opposition between the Ego and the Id; in the normal person it should not be possible to distinguish between the two.

If the Ego is to exert any real influence on the Id, it must have access to all parts of the Id. If, however, it deals with an Id urge by means of repression, it must pay by losing control of the urge which will attempt in all sorts of disguises to assert its independence. A neurosis is often the result of this Ego-Id conflict; and, in any case, there is bound to be some crippling of the Ego.

While this statement seems to present the issue as a fusion, the warfare of Id and Ego is incessant; without it life, as well as Freudian literature, would be a monotonous prairie. Somewhat in the manner of Hegelian metaphysics, antinomies and contradictions are first laboriously elaborated and then dialectically dissolved; or is it marching the king's men up the hill and marching them down again? Let it not be supposed that the fate of the Ego in psychological systems or in life is a matter of indifference to practice. The present purpose is merely to present (in the impressario sense) the formulations of the Ego in the superstructure of the Freudian house. As indicated, we may arrive at much the same results, more simply and more biologically expressed by considering the evolution and integration of the components of behavior in terms of primary and secondary function.

THE SUPER-EGO

With no further introduction thus speaks the Super-ego in the revised Freudian drama:

The Super-ego is an outgrowth of and is a modification of the Ego; it has a special position in regard to the Ego and has the capacity to rule it. It is to a great extent unconscious; it is independent of the conscious Ego and is largely inaccessible to it. It is always in close touch with the Id and can act as its representative in relation to the Ego. It is a deposit left by earliest object-cathexes of the Id. It is the "heir of the Oedipus Complex"—a precipitate of identifications with the parents "in some way combined together." It is a borrowing by the child's Ego of strength from the father to help in carrying out the repression of the Oedipus complex—a setting up within the self of the obstacle to Oedipus desires— "a most momentous loan." Its chief function is criticism which creates in the Ego an unconscious sense of guilt. It is essentially the same as conscience, and may be hyper-moral and tyrannical towards the Ego. It is amenable to later influences but preserves throughout life the character given to it by its derivation from the parent complex. The mature Ego remains subject to Super-ego domination. The injunctions and prohibitions of other authorities (teachers *et al.*) remain vested in the Super-ego and continue in the form of conscience to exercise the censorship of morals.

The metapsychology of Freud has exercised a marked influence upon his followers. The formulation of far-flung battle lines of propositions has a fascination all its own; it would be irresistible were it not so confusing to attempt to combine these conflicting features into a recognizable portrait. There is no division of psycho-analysis that has developed so much verbal fluency and dialectic subtlety. Its justification or utility is a logical issue to be considered at the proper time. The meta-psychology completes the house that Freud built.

CHAPTER IV

DEVIATIONS

ANALYTICAL PSYCHOLOGY: JUNG

However insistent in defense of his position, Freud does not regard his construction as a closed system. He has modified much and added more to the structure as it grew; he has incorporated the contributions of others so far as they were in line with his major tenets or were developed upon them. But innovators, reformers and dissenters, however ready to acknowledge their indebtedness to his pioneering leadership, have met with short shrift. The dissensions within the psychoanalytical fold reflect the unfortunate temper in which the movement has been conducted. In rivalry to the Freudian citadel, other houses have been built in a similar style of architecture, but with marked deviations in plans and specifications. Among these the contributions of Carl Jung of Zurich are the most notable. Since, with all the efforts of psychoanalysts to resolve others' conflicts, they have not resolved their own, there has come to be an orthodox Freudianism—the most extensive in following and prolific in literature—and also divergent schools, quite as confident and aggressive in presentation, whose contributions are significant in ideas and influence. They have all risen to prominence on the same wave of popularity, and may await a common fate in its decline.

The initial source of dissension was the far reaching sovereignty assigned by Freud to sex in the psychic life, and particularly to the detailed deductions derived from its imperial sway. The protests against the sexualization of the psyche were many and emphatic, and made not by squeamish Puritans, but by responsible scientists and by Freud's own followers. In Jung's "analysis," sex is as strident as in Freud's; but in his survey the urge to live and live the life abundant cannot be confined to the will to live sexually, nor is it derived from it. Libido includes other urges, biologically parallel and equally primary. Libido is life-energy expressed through the psyche. So radical a reshaping of a major doctrine was proclaimed a heresy. Sex was the shibboleth; those who pronounced it differently were of another tribe. They were met by the excommunication of estrangement.

Freud's proprietary claim to the name and practice of psychoanalysis is not a scientifically promising attitude. If psychoanalysis is limited to the Freudian views and practice, it runs the risk of becoming a monument to its founder, and not a contribution to a living science. The public is protectively indifferent to either personally polemical or academic discussions. With no fear of extradition for liberality, I shall include deviations in doctrine as part of the Freudian tale. The names of Jung and Adler *et al.* may be anathema to Freud; but they are Freudians by descent as well as dissent.

Jung's views have strongly influenced the course of psychoanalysis beyond the ranks of his direct disciples. For a number of years—from about 1906 on—he stood closest to Freud personally and in professional position, was, indeed, his chief lieutenant. The frictions within the International Psychoanalytical Association (1911–1913) and the growing differences of point of

view brought it about that—in Freud's diplomatic
phrase—"we took leave from one another, without
feeling the need to meet again." Although Jung was
made the first president of the international congress by
the proposal of Freud, it proved, according to the sponsor, "to have been a most unfortunate step."

Had Freud received hospitably the modifications
proposed by Jung, the story of psychoanalysis might
have read otherwise. The liberalized view of the human
psyche which Jung presents, is headed in the direction
which psychoanalysis must take if it is to survive at
all. The Jungian formulation is but a stage in progress.
To the lay reader, Jung's system may seem as remote
and extreme, as abstract and fantastic, as speculative
and arbitrary, as that of Freud himself. More closely
examined, its many affiliations with accredited psychology become evident. The *Analytical Psychology*
of Jung is a more catholic, more adaptable rendering
of the psychoanalytic dispensation. The point of de-
parture is the treatment of libido.

Libido. Common to Freud, Jung and Adler is their
conviction that deep psychology, the vital sources of
instincts and urges, is *the* psychology of the future,
alike for the understanding of human nature and for
ministration to its ills. To all the feeling is more
fundamental than the thinking self; psyche by affiliation with libido is restored to her authentic stature. The
mission of psychology is not merely to set forth the
intellectual ways of mind, but to explore and bring to
light the depths of personality and serve its right development. Libido is the *Urquelle* of what we, our total
human selves, are and may become; it is "psychic
energy," an all-inclusive life-force. The primal libido
serves nutrition, growth, sexuality and a goodly share of

the vital activities and interests which the ego, as it grows, incorporates.

Libido is innate but set in a cycle of growth; it sets the course of the expanding life. It is sex-infused, and its powers are enlisted in the service of sex; but it is more and other than sex. Freud's error is not only in over-sexualizing the entire scheme of living and in limiting libido, but in falsely reducing to a component in a sexually conceived libido an equally primary, equally distinctive form of psychic energy, which is conveniently summarized as "ego." Freud forgets that there is always a fusion of the instincts, and that we grow in all dimensions integratively. Nor can he save the situation by enlarging the scope of sex until it is paradoxically inclusive; his recognition of the "ego" system of urges is belated and appears more in the superstructure of his system than in the earlier statements; nor has it affected practice appreciably. Jung stakes his claim on an ego psychology; "analytical psychology" aims to re-create the self. That bizarre elaboration of infantile sexuality which makes of it a "polymorphous perverse" sex-expression is to Jung a false rendering of the genetic process; it ascribes to the egg what belongs to the chick or the hen. Growth entails a series of correlated manifestations that precede what later becomes, or is utilized for, a sexual expression. There is a "pre-sexual" stage which extends to the age of three or four years. The early libido is expended in nutrition and growth. In the second, pre-pubertal stage, the inherent mobility of libido expands with increasing outlets of self-expression. With puberty, the sexual component of the urge to ego-expansion asserts its reconstructive sway. Libido is male and female from the outset, but sex awaits its period.

Fixation is accepted by Jung as by Freud, as a source

of disharmony of development, when childish forms of libido persist. The normal course is progressive; the abnormal course is regressive. Such fixations or arrests in the course of libido invite later neuroses and develop character-deficits; they form obstacles in maturing. The manifestations of a neurotic trend reflect the growth-changes of libido. The neurotic child is father to the neurotic man.

Parental Complexes. The parent relation has a parallel place in the two analytic systems. As the child's first satisfactions are intensely fixed upon the parents, these relations exercise a dominant influence on the plastic psyche. The attitudes of the parents, including their complexes, affect the child deeply, including the parental pattern which the child imitates. But Freud's nuclear Oedipus complex is, to Jung, an intensive possession-complex of the child for the mother; it expresses the infantile pleasure-urge and desire for power, bending others to its will; it is also an urge for protection. To think of it as incest, which is an implication of maturity, distorts its meaning. It is quite true that parental relations carry sex implications. An over-fathered daughter may find difficulty in adjusting to a husband. The father image may intrude upon her later adaptation to other types of men in other rôles. A neurosis expresses failure in the libido to meet its task; it returns to a "more primitive way of adaptation." "Therefore I no longer find the cause of a neurosis in the past but in the present. I ask: What is the necessary task that the patient will not accomplish." The infantile fantasies and attitudes are but re-excited by the regressive libido. The practical problem is to secure suitable adaptation to present circumstances, by way of inducing a more adult type of behavior.

Types. There are type differences of temperament which influence the course of libido. The terms "introvert" and "extravert" indicate the chief contrast. Libido is generic, common to all, yet plastic enough to vary notably in its composition according to temperament; and as these temperamental trends are repeated, they may be recognized as types. The introvert, by being such, has his peculiar problems in adapting to reality, which process more congenially and more simply absorbs the extravert's interest and energy. The problem in regression is not the bare tendency to revert to earlier stages of psychic development, but to determine the source in the present situation which induces or invites the regressive trend. Regression may prove to be an introverted liability. Jung's emphasis upon *Psychological Types,* brings into the normal and neurotic picture the basic, hereditary distinctions of personalities, without which all attempts at deep analysis miss their mark. For normal and abnormal alike, the type factor dominates. The trend toward fantasy as well as the phobias and anxieties and Adler's inferiorities, bear the stamp of introversion. Both introversion and extraversion may be expressed on four different levels or segments of behavior; namely, sensation, intuition, feeling and thinking. The combination gives rise to eight varieties of character types, which are rarely pure types, but mixed. Analytical psychology includes "type" psychology.

Experimental. Freud gives Jung credit for building the first bridge between psychoanalysis and experimental psychology. This refers to his experiments upon association. In addition to free association, Jung developed an association test with a selected group of one hundred stimulus words. The principle is simple. He presents a selected and typical array of stimulus-words, to which the subject is asked to respond by the first word which the stimulus-word calls up. A delay or hesitation in response, a failure to arouse any response, or a mere repetition of the stimulus-word, or a remote or very unusual response, may indicate the *resistance* to utterance, which is the index of a complex. The "free association" method probes more successfully among the varied hiding places of complexes; the association test is more objective, yet also more limited. The method has been practically applied. Among a group of three hospital nurses suspected of a theft, the guilty one was found by the "association method." Jung also studied the resemblances of association types in members of the same family, in husband and wife, and in the different forms of mental disorder. But all this is merely interesting confirmation for general psychology; psychoanalytic probing must proceed more directly and with deeper penetration.

The Unconscious. Jung's major explorations were directed to tracing the "subconscious" phases of the psyche to their obscure source. He reports the discovery of a racial or "collective" unconscious in addition to the personal unconscious which shapes the plot and incidents in the Freudian analysis—another heretical finding. By this inclusion, fantasy and all its allied products, symbolism notably, are raised in importance. Fantasy is a racially ancient, comprehensive occupation; it is no less the congenial medium in the mind of childhood and of dreams. Day-dreaming with its clearer intention and its wish-fulfillments and compensations, forms the transition to the creative symbolic fantasies. To Freud, the symbol is mainly a disguised clue to a wish or thought prominent in the complex; to Jung it is a mental product of profound psychoanalytic significance.

Jung's "Unconscious" is more closely assimilated to conscious fantasy; it does not dwell in the inaccessible Freudian nether regions; it may expand and aspire to the heights of ecstasy and mystical absorption, though it roots deep in the urges, including the sexual.

Metapsychology. There is also a Jungian "metapsychology," not so designated. His thought inclines in that direction by reason of his assumption of "the collective" or impersonal unconscious. He assumes "archetypes" of experience, which childish fantasy and dream-imagery and symbolisms draw upon. These are "survivals of archaic modes of thought." That common source accounts for "the universally human symbols" that reappear in mythology.

"The collective Unconscious is the sediment of all the experience of the universe of all time, and is also an image of the universe that has been in process of formation for untried ages." . . . "They have been potentially latent in the structure of the brain. The fact of this inheritance also explains the otherwise incredible phenomenon, that the matter and themes of legends are met with all the world over in identical forms. Further it explains how it is that persons who are mentally deranged are able to produce precisely the same images and associations that are known to us from the study of old manuscripts." . . . "Inasmuch as through our Unconscious we have a share in the historical collective psyche, we naturally dwell unconsciously in a world of werewolves, demons, magicians, etc., these being things which have always affected man most profoundly."

Jung's dream interpretation is affected by this highly questionable hypothesis. He does not hesitate to associate a bull in a dream with the bull symbol of the cult of Mithra and in other cultural products; in these references the symbol retains its strong masculine value. Again Jung finds in the psyche a mask or *Persona* which is that part of the self-conscious personality which we present to the world, and an *Anima* which is part of the collective Unconscious, a submerged personality, like the feminine part of the masculine nature. The anima frequently appears in dreams.

The divergences in the "Analytical Psychology," of Jung and the psychoanalytical psychology of Freud may seem to those who question the basic assumptions of both, as inconsequential as the positions of Tweedle-dum and Tweedledee, with the common tendency in both pairs of disputants to reply to the other: "Contrari-wise." But divergent courses increase their distances of separation as they proceed. The two resultant "psychol-ogies" assume a different stamp; the two resultant prac-tices develop a different procedure. The neuroses in Jung's clinic are referred to a variety of conflicts and maladjustments; the focus of therapy is readaptation. Clearly there is no one inevitable and authentic version of the psychoanalytical approach to the problems of mind.

INDIVIDUAL PSYCHOLOGY: ADLER

Organ Inferiority. The system of "Individual Psy-chology" of Dr. Alfred Adler, like that of Freud, was made in Vienna. Geographically close, its psychologi-cal distance is maintained; it is distinctive and inde-pendent. Its starting point was the observation in gen-eral medical practice that patients handicapped by a bodily defect developed an unfavorable psychic attitude toward their life-problems, which presented many of the ear-marks of a neurosis. This thesis was elaborated in *A Study of Organ Inferiority and its Psychical Compensation* (1907). It led to the consideration of *The Neurotic Constitution*, the second contribution.

This approach is unusual. The observation that organic defect induces psychic disturbance, markedly so in the neurotic, turned a physician into a psychologist, convinced him that psychiatry must look for guidance to psychology. That connection led him to champion the heterodox position of Breuer and Freud in the medical circles of Vienna, where their usual reception was one of disdain and ridicule. He became a member of the first small group associated with Freud as students of psychoanalysis. Adler pursued his independent course of interpretation and treatment. He soon came to be regarded by Freudians as an heretical disciple, if disciple at all. His idea likewise grew into a pretentious system, which has a place of importance in the total movement.

Goals. By contrast to the *urge* psychologies of Freud and Jung, Adler's is a *goal* psychology; all are *depth* psychologies. Instinctive urges drive libido; the goal directs it. All else is subsidiary. The personal goal is always a social one, a striving for recognition and superiority. A phase of the will to prevail, of the ego's desire for power, is the key to the behavior-patterns which each individual develops as his way of life. That explains *his* "individual psychology." There is the normal way, and there is the neurotic way to live. The clue is ever the goal. Analysis proceeds in the reverse direction; not urges first and what they drive to, but goals and what measures are adopted to secure them. Determine first what the individual is seeking to attain, and his behavior is explicable as a means—wise or unwise, normal or neurotic—to that end.

The goal is typically conscious, though in part it is not fully acknowledged, because socially unacceptable; in so far it is private, unacknowledged, masked. For this status Adler uses the term "unconscious," Freud's formula of "escape into illness," which appears as a factor in many cases of hysteria, Adler makes the constant formula of all neuroses. They are subterfuges, more or less deliberate shirkings of responsibility by adopting a protective plan or pattern of action, which ministers to, and safeguards the self-esteem called superiority—the sense of satisfaction in prevailing. In function the Adlerian goal with its secret striving, parallels the Freudian wish with its suppressed desire.

Child and Parent. Goals as ways of life, are set in childhood. This is consistent with organ inferiority, typically present from birth, and with the emphasis on the neurotic constitution, of similar origin. Yet the major part in shaping life-patterns is assigned to the environmental influences, and particularly to the constant intimate environment of the family relation. It is in that milieu that the life-patterns are formed. Freud's tracing of neurotic ailments to infantile trauma confirmed Adler's diagnosis. "Every marked attitude of a man can be traced back to an origin in childhood. In the nursery are formed and prepared all of man's future attitudes."

This turn of the Adlerian psychology proved to be the source of its popularity; it became a guide to character formation, especially in children. Hence the foundation by Adler and his followers of clinics for "problem" children, and the interest of his corrective system to Child Study Associations. The family situation becomes even more critical than in the systems of Freud and Jung, though by a different emphasis. Adler makes the position of the child in the family shape its life-attitudes. The character of the oldest child is likely to be determined by that relation, of the youngest child no less so, and of the only child most of all. The goals and patterns of life repeat and enlarge those of the family.

An Adlerian Analysis. Analysis *à la* Adler, for which he used the term "individual analysis," proceeds upon a quite different assumption than that *à la* Freud. How different is the resulting procedure will appear in the report of a concrete case, whose prolixity I have somewhat mitigated.

"A gifted man became engaged to a girl of high character. He forced upon her his ideal of education. . . . For a time she endured unbearable orders but finally put an end to all further ordeals by breaking off relations. The man then broke down and became a prey to nervous attacks.

"The examination of the case showed that the superiority-goal in the case of this patient—as his domineering demands upon his bride indicated—had long ago pushed from his mind all thought of marriage, and that his object really was to secretly work toward a break, secretly because he did not feel himself equal to the open struggle in which he imagined marriage to consist. *This disbelief in himself* itself dated from his earliest childhood, to a time during which he, an only son, lived with an early widowed mother somewhat cut off from the world. During this period spent in continuous quarrels, he had received the ineradicable impression, one he had never openly admitted to himself, that he was not sufficiently virile and would never be able to cope with a woman. These psychical attitudes are comparable to a permanent inferiority-feeling."

"The patient attained just what his concealed preparations for bachelordom aimed at; he took the same attitude toward both his bride and his mother, namely the wish to conquer. This attitude induced by a longing for victory has been magnificently misinterpreted by the Freudian school as the permanently incestuous condition of being enamoured of the mother. As a matter of fact, this reinforced childhood-feeling of inferiority spurred this man on to providing himself with all kinds of safeguards. Love in this case is simply a *means to an end*, and that end is the final securing of a triumph over some suitable woman. Here we have the reason for the continual tests and orders and for the cancelling of the engagement. This solution had not just 'happened' but had on the contrary been artistically prepared and arranged with the old weapons employed previously in the case of his mother. A defeat in marriage was out of the question because marriage was prevented."

"There remains the less intelligible nervous breakdown. As in the nursery, so here our patient has been worsted by a woman. The neurotic individual strengthens his protections and retires to a fairly great distance from danger. Our patient is utilizing his break-down in order to feed an evil reminiscence, to bring up the question of guilt again, to solve it in an unfavourable sense for the woman. Similarly as a child he had refused to eat, sleep or to do anything, and played the role of a dying person. His fortunes ebb and *his beloved carries all the stigma;* he himself rises superior to her in both culture and character, and lo and behold: he has attained that for which he

longed, for he is the superior person. In this manner
he has consummated what as a child he had already
felt, the duty of demonstrating his superiority over
the female sex."

"Were he aware of his secret plans he would realize
how ill-natured and evil-intentioned all his actions
have been. He would, in that case, not succeed in
attaining his object of elevating himself above women.
But his goal, his life-plan and his life-falsehood demand this prestige! In consequence it so happens that
the *life-plan remains in the unconscious* so that the
patient may believe that an *implacable fate* and not
a long prepared and long meditated plan for which
he alone is responsible, is at work."

The Universal Complex. Such is "individual analysis"
as against "psychoanalysis." The reconstruction of the
life story in terms of a yearning for superiority, mask-
ing an unacknowledged inferiority—such is the universal human complex. In Adler's view that is the only
key we need to explain the alleged complications of
human character and the manner of its failings in the
neuroses and the neurotic.

"Every neurosis can be understood as an attempt
to free oneself from a feeling of inferiority in order
to gain a feeling of superiority." Over self-valuation,
a belief in "uniqueness" and "god-likeness" shapes
the conflict. Illness is an "alibi" and its symptoms
likewise. If there is insomnia, it leads to the excuse:
"What could I not have done, had I been able to
sleep." Symptoms are so many "prestige-mechanisms"
for securing social attention, familiar in the childish
evasions of the nursery. "The symptom is a substitute for the neurotic lust for superiority with its

associated effect." "The neurotic attacks as well as
the choice of neurosis must be able to stand the test
of being utilizable for the life-plan."

Dreams, mannerisms, compulsions, delusions, attitudes, dreads, perversions, moods, hypocrisies, pretensions, ambitions, delinquencies, crimes, passions, superstitions, manias, phobias, human traits in all their
dramatic repertory of comedy and tragedy, of foible
and failure, become variations of the story of vaunted
superiority seeking unworthy compensations to cover
defeat. The house that Adler built is not a house but a
tower from which he observes the human scene in a
monochrome rendering.

The Masculine Protest. A prominent variety of superiority is the "masculine protest." Since superiority
is the theme of the human drama, its urge seems to be
provided for by nature by encouraging half the population to assert its superiority over the other half, iron-
ically and not gallantly termed the better half. The
"masculine protest" means glorying in being a man and
looking down upon women. In the case of the female,
the "masculine protest" expresses itself in wishing to be
a man, acting as one, affecting mannishness. Out of this
doctrine is developed a "psychical hermaphrodism."
This state of affairs poses the pedagogical problem of
"reconciling one half of mankind with an unalterable
condition which it dislikes." Such "male attitudes" appear frequently in "female neurotics" and yield the clue
to the meaning of their symptoms, however cleverly
disguised.

Value. That much of this doctrine, if toned down
to reasonable proportions is in conformity with general

experience, is clear enough. It is easily intelligible and makes a popular appeal. By the same token it leans toward a somewhat commonplace, platitudinous series of reflections on life in general and its manifold difficulties.

Human behavior cannot be adequately interpreted in terms of urges; it needs the complement of aims, purposes, goals. Adler's complementation of psychoanalysis is an essential one. His elaborate contribution shows that by sufficient forcing of concepts, one can build up a system of explanation of human behavior quite as logically on superiority-striving and the compensation-mechanisms arising to cover the inferiority, as upon infantile sexuality and its hypothetical consequences in the later life-relations. It is fortunate for the logical critique of psychoanalysis that it may be directed not invidiously against one solution, but against the general mode of approach which is common to several, all emanating from one parent source.

NEO-FREUDIANS

This convenient name is applied by C. W. Valentine to a group of psychologists and psychiatrists who recognize important truths in the basic principles of psychoanalysis, but do not subscribe to its doctrines *in toto*. They view the structure critically, rejecting many of the conclusions as unsound, speculative and even absurd; they hold that the valuable part of psychoanalysis may and must be brought into relation with accredited psychology and psychiatry; they deplore its extravagance of statement, protest against its loose logic and baseless assumptions, and recognize the dangers inherent in its practice; they point out that much of this "new psychology"—an alternate name for the

Neo-Freudian position—is but a restatement of familiar relations from a new approach; they seek a biological foundation for the concepts and their integration with accepted fundamentals of mental behavior, normal and abnormal; they advocate the conducting of the enterprise in a rational and restrained temper. The Neo-Freudians represent a critical yet sympathetic attitude toward the psychoanalytic construction. There is no one authoritative exposition of their position, nor is there any organization of the adherents of this eclectic movement. Its representatives are not, in the discipleship sense, followers of Freud. The name applies collectively to a fair agreement in statement and conclusions of independent minds. The Neo-Freudians accept as readily and as critically the concepts and methods developed by Jung and Adler as those of Freud; some of the group approach the Freudian position more closely than others.

It is hardly accidental that the Neo-Freudians are mainly British contributors,* who became interested in the house that Freud built at a late period of its construction, after the hostility to its invasion of the medical scene had subsided. They came to Freudianism without the hampering sense of loyalty to a master or a system, and with the clarifying freedom of what I venture to call Anglo-Saxon loyalty to logic—alias, common sense—as opposed to the speculative license and obscuranting theorizing of the Teutonic academic

* This applies to those who have expressed themselves on Freud rather than to the population of psychologists and psychiatrists in general. The moderate Freudians who accept the basic positions of Freud but reject with more or less vehemence the main body of extravagant and illogical conclusions, presumably far outnumber all Freudian followers of all persuasions. American psychologists form a goodly number of this increasing fold; and there is definitely appearing in Germany a group similarly disposed. The matter is resumed in the concluding chapter of this contribution.

tradition. Presumably this movement would have not so quickly come to a head, but for the peremptory experiences of the War. It was a moral shock to British complacency to learn of the large number of "shell-shock" cases and related neurotic break-down in the British army. In the words of Rivers—whose place of leadership among the Neo-Freudians is unquestioned—there was hardly a case with which he had to deal in the War which the Freudian theories did not help him to understand better, "not a day of clinical experience in which Freud's theories may not be of direct practical use in diagnosis and treatment." Yet Rivers rejects far more of Freud's conclusions than he accepts. His acceptances involve important reservations, divergent interpretations, and limited applications. The Neo-Freudian movement is dated substantially from the close of the War, though there were allied acceptances of the Freudian position before that period.

As, in my opinion, the Neo-Freudian contribution is by far the most valuable that has been made to psychoanalysis and indicates the favorable route of its naturalization within the community of the sciences, I shall restrict the present consideration and resume it later as a critique of psychoanalysis. It is equally my opinion that *Instinct and the Unconscious* by the late W. H. R. Rivers is the most significant volume in the entire Freudian literature. It attempts, as its sub-title indicates, a "biological theory of the psycho-neuroses." I do not know what Freud's reaction may have been to this work, which is far more a challenge than a confirmation of Freud's own method of handling the problems common to the two contributions; but I question whether he would recognize Rivers as in any sense one of his fold.

The hope of penetrating more deeply into the aeti-

ology of the psycho-neuroses, which started Freud upon
his notable career, was likewise the incentive for the
Neo-Freudian movement. Psychiatry was well set before and by Freud toward the larger recognition of the
psychological factors in mental disorders. This is well
indicated in Dr. Bernard Hart's *Psychology of Insanity*
(1912)—the title itself significant; this popular little
volume is among the earliest Neo-Freudian contributions.

"A very large number of the general principles
enunciated in this book are due to the genius of
Prof. Freud of Vienna, probably the most original
and fertile thinker who has yet entered the field of
abnormal psychology. . . . Although I cannot easily
express the extent to which I am indebted to him, I
am by no means prepared to embrace the whole of
the vast body of doctrines which Freud and his followers have now laid down. Much of this is in my
opinion unproven, and erected upon an unsubstantial
foundation. On the other hand, many of Freud's
fundamental principles are becoming more and more
widely accepted, and the evidence in their favour
is rapidly increasing."

Citing Valentine:

"We can connect some of Freud's theories, after
they are modified as criticism seems to demand, with
fundamental laws of the mind already familiar to
psychology." The main doctrines of psychoanalysis
may be brought "into line with 'orthodox' psychology, . . . may be regarded as unfamiliar examples
of recognized principles; that, indeed, so far as the
new psychology can be counted true, it is not entirely new."

Citing McDougall:

"I believe that Prof. Freud has done more for the advancement of psychology than any student since Aristotle. At the same time, I by no means accept all of his teachings; I regard much of the current psychoanalytic doctrines as ill-founded and somewhat fantastic. But it would, I hold, be a great service to single out what is sound and true in these doctrines and bring it into harmony with the main body of psychological science."

A number of psychologists, who have not contributed directly to the psychoanalytic movement, but have utilized the Freudian approach, who are impressed with the value of its position as strongly as they are repelled by its extravagant and illogical conclusions, could readily be enlisted as Neo-Freudians. Among them I cite an American psychologist, Daniel B. Leary:

"Psychoanalysis in its original form, is a highly speculative philosophy rather than a science. . . . Psychoanalysis, as a system of practices and theories can be, when revised in accord with the present more scientific knowledge of human nature and human behavior, a dynamic-evolutionary theory of personality, plus a practical therapy of cure and prevention of personality abnormalities. That is, when the claims of psychoanalysis, as fact and as theory, have been critically examined, and some of its main conclusions restated in terms of other and better founded psychological knowledge, it will remain not as a separate and independent psychology, but as a new psychological synthesis, a new psychological approach to some of the current problems of human behavior, and the basis of a new technique."

The position of the Neo-Freudians appears in their cognizance of the need of a critical revision of psychoanalytic principles. It remains to indicate some of the leading concepts as they are accepted and employed by Neo-Freudian psychologists and psychiatrists.

The Neo-Freudian position accepts the doctrine that psychic factors play a leading part in the formation of functional nervous disorders; that they operate in some measure subconsciously; that they center about conflict situations, typically a conflict between strong instinctive trends and the restraints imposed by socially acquired controls; that the instinctive trends thus operative include the self-protective, the sexual, the social, and their many derivatives and interactions; that complexes are an expression of such conflict between instinctive drives and their frustration or imposed control, or between derivative issues related to them; that the manifestations of such conflict-tendencies, and of the mechanisms by which they come to expression, appear in dreams, in character traits, and in many varieties and patterns of human behavior; that this recognition can be assimilated with established knowledge of psychic operations.

They recognize the validity of many of the mechanisms that appear in the course of the analysis by which normal and neurotic expressions may be accounted for; such as rationalization, compensation, projection, sublimation, substitution, symbolism; they recognize that by the inclusion of subconscious operations, by the principles of fantasy and reality thinking, by the detection of the hidden motive, by the emphasis upon the motivation factor including some measure of determinism, a large range of human behavior is illuminated.

They take into account the significance of the early stages in the direction of distinctive trends and the habit formations by which their control is established, recognizing likewise the peculiar importance of the intimate personal contacts within the family relations, and that the entire life cycle is set in a progressive direction, whose normal course is beset with the liabilities of arrested development and regression. They are prepared to apply these principles constructively and correctively to the educational process in all its bearings, to focus the efforts upon the wholesome integration of personality, and to develop the social milieu to the proper satisfaction of normal urges and the provisions for the attainment of the sublimated expressions thus indicated.

These constructive precepts naturally imply rejections. The Neo-Freudian position, upholding a general loyalty to scientific procedure, protests against the constant use of unsupported assumptions, extravagant deductions, and remote and problematical conclusions. They would limit speculation to concepts capable of support by biological considerations. They deplore the irresponsible indulgence in fanciful applications of doubtful principles. They look to the salvaging of the essential principles of psychoanalysis and their scientific formulation. The unfortunate course of the development of psychoanalysis cannot be obliterated; it may be redeemed.

It may prove, after the Neo-Freudian revision has accomplished its purpose, that little will remain of the thousand and one contributions to psychoanalytic literature. The Neo-Freudians view the construction as the result of a true lead, falsely followed. They would strip the house that Freud built of its irrelevant façades and fallacious details and incorporate its legitimate constructions in the all inclusive house of psychology.

CHAPTER V

APPLICATIONS

THE HIDDEN MOTIVE

Freud has told in autobiographical vein the story of psychoanalysis. He does not, so far as I recall, describe the moment when it first occurred to him that a modest innovation in interpreting a neurotic symptom bore the seed of a philosophy. That possibility awaited the expansion and the application of the germinal idea to other products of the psyche, past and present. From volume to volume, Freud's conception of his problem came to be more and more comprehensive. Psychoanalysis envisaged a many-sided enlightenment of how and why we behave like human beings—at times as abnormal ones—and why and how the products of the same psyche, collectively and historically expressed, took form. As an instrument for surveying the human scene, psychoanalysis became a psychic microscope, telescope and X-ray apparatus in turn. The house that Freud built as a new order of clinic for the psychoneuroses was enlarged to an institute of human relations. Psychoanalysis was to be applied to the interpretation of all creations of the psyche, to all the varied expressions of its urges in protection and defense, in constructing roads to the life abundant, and directing the psyche in its pilgrim's progress.

Nothing escaped Freud's psychoanalytic eye, from

the lightest to the most momentous of human employments. The trail of the unconscious led to dreams, for
in sleep we surrender control and the unconscious
shelters the hidden motive. The quest for other escapes
of hidden motive led to the seemingly accidental,
momentary lapses; they afforded parallel revelations.
Further along the same trail, but nearer to the surface
and with increasing conscious intention, was the jest,
still in some of its varieties turning upon the hidden
motive. The result was the volume: *Wit and the Unconscious,* the first and lightest of the applications. The
psychoanalytical treatise is as remote from the conven-
tional joke-book as the *Intrepretation of Dreams* from
the popular dream-book. The argument at times becomes so labored as to suggest that even a joke is no
laughing matter; but it carries the important recognition that the situation that creates a joke may be psychoanalyzed. Jokes and dreams indeed differ widely in
plot and purpose; but they share a range of mechanisms. Both parody as they underwrite reality; both
employ symbols, metaphors, analogies; both touch upon
repressions, deal with the personal and the intimate,
stage a release from the rigid tensions of the literal and
actual. In detail, the double meaning is close to the
hidden motive, as the lapse, betraying what the speaker
prefers to suppress, is a joke upon him; betrayals may
amuse as well as embarrass. In the jest there may be
a challenge, a battle of wits, and a thrust or "slam"
of competing personalities. What we laugh at, we are
superior to. In the unexpected turn or touch, the element of surprise, the distortion and many another
mechanism, there is revealed the same order of process
as in other vein may direct the dream. The sense of
humor makes for sanity; it makes contact with human
foibles; it holds the mirror up to human nature, re-

flecting what psychoanalysis differently discloses, and often as of serious, even tragic moment.

The psychology of wit and humor as a product of the intellect at the disposal of the personality, had engaged other thinkers. Sully, in terms of the modernized yet still Victorian psychology, admitting the Rabelaisian touch, had analyzed it engagingly, bringing laughter and its occasions within the range of the biological emotional expressions. Bergson, in more philosophical vein, dwelling upon such principles as the comic effect of the mechanizations of the vital (of which the amusing "Parade of the Wooden Soldiers" is a recent instance), and upon other incongruities, gives the ludicrous, from slap-stick to repartee, a worthy place. They may have sensed, but they did not formulate, the Freudian motivation underlying several of the varieties of wit; here as elsewhere Freud's creative intelligence comes to the fore. Analyzing situations as ancient as Aristophanes, he formulates the personal motive aspect; the psychology of wit was enriched by a new illumination. He may have carried the principle too far and maladroitly; but the formulation is his.

MYTH, CUSTOM AND FAIRY-TALE

From this prelude we turn abruptly to the most significant of large-scale applications of psychoanalytic principles. It is, indeed, an imposing thought that the ways of mind disclosed by psychoanalysis have been in operation since mind took the helm, and have left their deposits in the products of human culture—mindprints in the sands of time; that institutions, rituals, sagas, bibles, folk-lore were created under the impulse of motives and trends not fully conscious, yet delivering their issues in customs and beliefs, in myths and fairy-tales, and in superstitions no less, in what becomes the conscious medium of tribal tradition, the living expression of a psyche whose immortality is its "unconscious" urge to repetition. The conclusion argues for a primitive psychoanalytic undercurrent accompanying what increasing purpose through the ages runs, and its backwaters also. The thought gives an archaeological turn to psychoanalytic exploration. The idea is not wholly novel; it appears frequently in modern anthropological interpretations of cults and customs and especially in the analysis of survivals in all their imposing variety. The Freudian approach supplements the anthropologist's as well as the sociologist's insight and brings the argument to explicit expression.

In *Totem and Taboo*, Freud's thesis relates the primitive psychic devices of symbolic protection and prohibition to those that give rise to the personal inhibitions, repressions, rituals and compulsions of neurotics and normals. The primitive psyche elaborates and fantasies in patterns of construction similar to dreams, analogous to the conflict-situations of harassed humanity. Certain orders of myths become the dreams of the race; cults seemingly fantastic or meaningless fixations of blind tradition, may be read in psychoanalytic terms. How far such explanation of the anthropological drama is valid, the anthropologists must decide; nor can I take space to indicate just how psychoanalysis proceeds to solve the cultural problems which it raises. Some psychoanalysts, such as Rank, have made this their favorite field of exploration. The hero is the central figure in this domain; the manner of his birth and career become psychoanalytic texts and commentary of the racial psyche, speaking in parables. "Cinderella" presents a common family situation that exists in reality and fantasy. The racial habit persists. We all revel in compensation fantasies, and find congenial the appeal of fairy-tale to the wish-fulfillment indulgences and magic-believing inclinations of childhood. The psyche has its history; it was once racially young, as it is ever in each childhood, and remains so in surviving primitive cultures. Human motives have been modified by human history; civilization invites sophistication and disillusion.

There is a suggestive vein of insight in depth psychology contributing a clue to psychoanalytical anthropology. The great mass of myth, custom, cult, fairy-tale, superstition and the folk-lore habit of mind generally, moves more nearly on the primitive level of primary, child-like, intuitional, diffusely conscious, pleasure and fear motivation, than of conscious, rationalistic reflection. Its plots and content reflect much the same order of data and conclusion as operates in the deeper layers of fantasy and neurotic entanglement. The analogy is sound; it must be soundly followed through.

It is only when the analogies between the course of psychic unfoldment in the individual and in the race are carried too far, and engaging hypotheses are regarded as established fact, that anthropological psychoanalysis exceeds its warrant. The intrinsic idea is valuable. It has been sought as well in biological habit, a more hazardous ground. The theory of recapitulation, once in favor, cannot be revived; for the parallel fails. Children do not take to the water because of palaeozoically remote aquatic ancestors, or to tree-tops because of arboreal anthropoid reminiscences. Unnatural history makes even more questionable genetic psychology. Jung's "collective unconscious" does indeed assume that the concrete experiences of primitive man survive and reappear whenever the primitive psyche, awake or asleep, comes to expression. Such psychic reincarnation makes slight appeal to the biologically minded. Freud is content with the more logical deduction that their similarities express parallel culture-stages.* Both are on safe ground in recognizing in symbolism an early and permanent psychic trend. What Freud presents in *Dream and Delusion*, Varendonck in the varieties of *Day Dreaming*, Jung in his elaborate studies of "unconscious" fantasies in the poetic-mystic mind, shows similar mental movements in diverse expressions. Man is a symbol-making no less than a tool-making animal. He dreams, fantasies, dramatizes, poetizes, symbolizes and deludes himself by authentic warrant of the earlier of the two great orders of thinking which Freud has interestingly formulated. By that insight, myth, custom and fairy-tale considered mainly for their imaginative value, form material for a cultural psychoanalytical survey.

Once again a tribute is in place to the fertility of Freud's mind. The psychoanalytic factor in primitive culture has become a permanent possession. Post-Freudian anthropology, including the vast body of folklore survivals, assumes a different stamp. In more than one sense, it has come of age.

RELIGION

Religion is a comprehensive culture-product, a direct expression of deep psychology. It has likewise the collective status of an institution. The psychology of religion was well established independently of the psychoanalytical illumination; a restatement under the newer approach was inevitable. The application was directed

---

* Unfortunately this caution leaves him completely when he considers the psychosexual development of the human species.

primarily to the content, rites and ceremonies of religious doctrine. Religion became to many a way of life. It developed scruples as a special order of inhibitions; in advanced stages it matured such attitudes as asceticism and Puritanism; it included the sex orbit in its domain, in so far as the religious life, the cloistered life especially, implied a comprehensive renunciation; it embraced the healing mission, becoming at times a medium of psychotherapy, its model in the confessional anticipating the psychoanalytic abreaction. And these are but a few of the communities of religious with allied relations and attitudes which psychoanalysis interprets.

Religion deals with the sacred, the mystic, the intimate, and the primitive. The Freudian emphasis upon sex finds confirmation in the phallic orders of ceremonial that extend from primitive cult to organized mysteries. Compensation projected heavens; the sense of guilt begat hells; the parental relation inspired ancestor worship; the mystery of womanhood fostered a mingled idolatry and avoidance; elaborate symbolisms arose at all stages to embody emotional products too deep for rational comprehension; among these the mysteries of reproduction and creation attain prominence. The very doubts and difficulties that in these enlightened days might take one to a psychoanalyst would in older days have sought resolution in the church; faith, stability, salvation, the courage to carry on, endure, renounce, are common aims. Psychoanalysis itself has been embraced with a religious fervor and hailed as a magic solution. Religious faith invites varieties of abnormal expression, as William James set forth in pre-Freudian days. Psychoanalysis may be applied to religionists as well as to cults and sects.

In the same field of application may be included beliefs with marginal religious trends. Jung has presented a psychoanalytic interpretation of the phenomena of the occult and of the medium, with their large dependence upon subconscious states. Whether the telepathic hypothesis can find support in psychoanalytic findings has been considered, for Jung's "intuition" approaches it in one phase. The broad applicability and unexpected penetration of psychoanalytic doctrine has attracted minds of many interests. The products as well as the processes of the human psyche reveal "psychoanalytic" procedure; it is the skill and wisdom in their application that sets the value of the presentations. Freud's personal reaction may be added. His *Future of an Illusion* regards religion as an elaborate wish-fulfillment, with no deeper warrant than other creations of paradise in retrospect or Utopias in prospect.

EDUCATION

The several applications of psychoanalysis stand each on its own basis; they are as diverse as human interests. To the pragmatic temper of the modern mind, the practical applications of psychoanalysis offer greater attraction. Since the avoidance of neuroses and the wholesome training of character are collateral aims, rooting in a common understanding, psychoanalysis raises the hope of a wiser pedagogy. That possibility has been liberally recognized. A leader in this domain is Dr. Oskar Pfister, a pastor of Zurich, who applies Freudian doctrines in the moral education of children, of "problem" children as well as those with normal problems. The general direction of such social and family difficulties as come within his professional relations are similarly conceived. Crichton Miller interprets the *New Psychology* for the benefit of parents and teachers, and Dexter writes of *Psychoanalysis in the Schoolroom*. I make no comment upon the wisdom of the application, the validity of which is conceded.

To reduce even to bare outlines the modifications of the teaching relation that have been deduced from the reconstructed place of childhood in "depth psychology," would far exceed the limits of this cursory enumeration. Two phases of the movement may be selected. The one centers about the emotional life, including the love-life, in its largest sense. In the Freudian doctrine that is the commanding consideration; education is the safe direction through emotional attitudes and erotic tangles. The other is the special clinical and psychiatric guidance of the child, a movement that would have come to the fore through the ideas of Progressive Education and Child-Study, but has been markedly accentuated by the Freudian approach, including particularly the Adlerian contributions. The vogue of psychoanalysis and the interest in it, are due hardly less to the hope of guiding childhood and safeguarding youth from the hazards besetting the paths of development, than to its promise of aid in the treatment of the psycho-neuroses. The two converge in character development. Obviously a new orientation of the sources of character-traits and a new emphasis upon the critical significance of childhood invites a revision of the total educational relation between the adult and the child. Psychoanalysis does not propose a radically novel program of education; it does alter the perspective of its course; in so far it reconstructs human values. It is safe to predict that neither in education, nor in the family and social relations shall we return to a pre-Freudian era.

SOCIETY

Social psychology, like the psychology of religion and the psychological principles of education, had formulated its position independently of the Freudian renaissance; which means that psychologists with that interest had applied their findings to social problems. Sociology, despite the indefiniteness of its contours, has a coherent purpose. It has taken over phases of human nature in the economic setting that constitute social problems. Among these crime is a form of behavior of pressing concern. The understanding and control of crime, more directly, of the criminal personality, welcomes illumination from every source; psychoanalysis traces crime and delinquency to conflict-situations. The contributions of Healy and Bronner support this position. Dealing with thousands of case-histories, they make plain that the psychoanalytic approach enforces the claim which the psychiatrist had already established. The neurotic factors in the etiology of crime extend far beyond the rather small percentage of pronounced psychopaths among the criminal population. Criminologists agree that the environment and the stress and strain of living, the economic stress notably, is statistically the dominant factor in crime production. In closer analysis, the liability to a criminal lapse parallels that to a neurotic surrender, especially among the youthful population; and crime is emphatically a problem of youth. The social failure—which is crime—and the neurotic failure have in common powerful urges and weak resistance. Some psychoanalysts, such as Alexander, would apply the psychoanalytic technique in all its details to the criminal offender, forgetting to what an extremely small minority this would apply. Others recognize in psychoanalysis an additional clue to the understanding of the behavior anomalies that arise from social and personal complications. Crime had already been recognized as a chapter in abnormal psychology. The many streams of connection between neurotic failings and crime, reappear through psychoanalysis; they bring personal conflict and social conflict into a mutually illuminating relation. Society's problem is the control of urges; their psychoanalysis is the first step. The social applications of psychoanalytical thought would alone make it a momentous contribution.

Crime is still a chapter in individual psychoanalysis. The other "social" application is of a different order. It transfers the findings obtained from the study of the individual to the group. E. D. Martin psychoanalyzes the crowd mind; Kolnai applies psychoanalytic concepts to sociological products; Rivers traces the play of psychoanalytic motives in the field of politics; Laswell portrays the psychopathic traits of political agitators and legislators and relates them to the neurotic traits and the family situation; Burrow proposes in abstruse terms a complete restatement of psychoanalysis in social concepts. The house of understanding that Freud built for the individual occupant has become a model for the communal relations. The concepts of psychoanalysis have been directly influential in establishing social psychiatry.

This development is foreshadowed in the inherent socializing of the urges, which psychologists had recognized and the psychoanalysts confirmed. Since self-display is set toward social recognition, whether recognized in a Freudian exhibitionism, a Jungian expansion of the ego, or an Adlerian ambition to prove superior, it requires a gallery. Moreover, all the urges develop in a social setting. The individual is ever in relation to and may be in conflict with social sanctions; the herd control appears as the Freudian censor, a concept made more truly sociological by Rivers. The social structure of collective groups, caste and class, party and sect, tribe and nation, inevitably repeats the motivations of the individuals who compose it.

The conflicts thus precipitated form a momentous issue. While adaptation to social structure is essential, the manner of accepting that obligation becomes a decisive psychic factor in normality; it may lead to the attitude of the radical and radicalism, which has been made the subject of psychoanalysis—the urge to protest or defy in one phase, the urge to be different in another. It may set in clearer relief the conforming tendency; that, indeed, goes back to the reaction to authority, for which the family—itself a social institution—is the training ground. Despite all the extravagant and remote delineations of the place of the father in fact and fantasy, he remains a figure of importance. The father as patriarch sets the patriarchal form of government; but assignments of power follow other patterns as well. Paternalism is a political issue. Governing others is a critical social relation. Forms of social control are liable to their own types of neuroses and maladaptations. So is every other institution, church or state, tyranny or democracy, assemblies or academies, and forces similarly operative with no definite institutional supports. Ideas and systems suffer similarly; there is a madness of crowds and collective manias. Out of the psychoanalytical view arises the ideal that society must provide wisely for the satisfactions of the fundamental urges; otherwise there will be rebellion, unrest, misery, and the sense of frustration and injustice. Governments exist for men; they must be judged in terms of human needs. Among the modern humanistic disciplines, sociology has responded sympathetically to the Freudianized versions of its concepts and purposes.

BIOGRAPHY

Psychoanalysis implies character analysis; * the transition to that application is inherent in the concept of the new exploration. Character-reading—what John Stuart Mill long ago projected as a science of Ethology, and the Germans, following Bahnsen, call Characterology—is among the persistent purposes of psychology since the days of Theophrastus and before. Freud was absorbed in the significance of neurotic traits and case-histories; the complex—a term furnished by Jung —is the first stage in a constellation of traits; character is a further integration which Freud recognizes in the constitutional trend but applies sparingly. Yet detecting the hidden motive in every-day behavior is congenial to a scheme of character reading. To Jung the type became the significant synthesis; in that connection, he made contact with characterology. Adler's psychology touches the character concept in the life-pattern, character shaped by goals set in an environment.

In addition to his many other honors, Freud may be credited with an influential part in establishing psychobiography, emphasizing, with the danger of over-emphasizing, the intimate psychic character of the great man whose genius the world acknowledges, often with a falsifying trend of hero-worship. That the hero is not such to his valet may be due to the valet's limita-

* The formation of character is an integral part of the psychoanalytic system. It is considered on pages 214 to 218 and critically on pages 220 to 225.

tions; that he may not be so to the psychoanalyst has another foundation.

It is less as replacing than as complementing the program of biography that the psychoanalytical post-mortem is conceived, holding a clinic with recorded data as the clue to an intimate personality study. The pioneer contribution is Freud's psychoanalytic study of *Leonardo da Vinci*. This lead has been followed closely or remotely by psychoanalysts such as L. Pierce Clark, who subjected a group of important historical personages to the psychoanalytic probe; and by professional biographers, such as Emil Ludwig, notably in his study of the German Kaiser. The purpose is to reveal the "real" Abraham Lincoln, Mark Twain, Napoleon, Byron, Nietzsche * in terms of motivations, normal and abnormal. Independently of Freud, the realistic school of Zola had reached the conviction that the biological man should be intimately, somewhat cinematically, recorded, alongside of the "career" personality.

The same procedure appears in literary creations in

---

* Dr. Lucile Dooley contributes this list of "analyzed" great men. Such "analyses" range from a psychoanalytical interpretation of the complete life down to incidents, critical or trivial in childhood, in dreams, in personal relations and in career, pointing to complexes or significant Freudian revelations. There have appeared psychoanalytical interpretations of the personalities of Jesus, Paul of Tarsus, Francis of Assisi, Luther, Swedenborg, Mary Baker Eddy among religionists; of Alexander the Great, Henry VIII, Queen Elizabeth, Napoleon, Louis Napoleon, Queen Victoria, Roosevelt, Woodrow Wilson, Lenin, among rulers; Leonardo da Vinci, Michael Angelo, Andrea del Sarto, Beethoven, Schubert, Van Gogh, among artists; of Socrates, Darwin, Schopenhauer, Fechner, Nietzsche, Rousseau, Tolstoi, among thinkers; of Homer, Anatole France, Charlotte Bronte, Emily Bronte, de Maupassant, Dostoiewski, Dumas, Flaubert, Francis Thompson, Goethe, Hebbel, Knut Hamsun, Mark Twain, Oscar Wilde, Poe, Schnitzler, Strindberg, among writers; and to literary creations, as Lady Macbeth, Shylock, Hamlet, Salome, Liliom, Peer Gynt, characters in the tragedies of Sophocles and in the dramas of Richard Wagner.

which the Freudian clue to personality finds varied expressions. Freud's own contribution is an analysis of the fantasies and the dreams in W. Jensen's novel: *Gradiva*. Though these dreams were never dreamt but composed by the poet and assigned to his character, they conform to the dream origins; which to Freud proves that the ways of poetic insight, as similarly the fantasies of children, may be interpreted psychoanalytically. From this the transition is easy, once the Freudian clues are accepted, to develop fictitious characters —in novels and the drama notably—upon the Freudian model of motivation. A conspicuous instance is O'Neill's play: *Mourning Becomes Electra*, in which the Oedipus situations are reproduced in modern setting, serving as the source of the personal and situational conflicts with which the play deals. By such complete acceptance the author becomes a Freudian dramatist; whether this "becomes" the drama is a different issue, turning as do so many of the personalized applications, upon the measure of normality or abnormality which inheres in the Oedipus situation.

The application of depth psychology to the understanding of the personalities and achievements of those who affected notably the current of human affairs is a legitmate enterprise. The personal intimate man dominates above and appears in the public man. Official biography needs the complement of the program of motivation, of character assets and deficits, which is the very core of psychoanalysis. As the carrying through of that illumination reflects the theories and assumptions of Freudian analysis, the project in its execution is subject to the same critique as the tenets of personality formation. That chapter in Freudianism is one of the most disputable and controversial in the entire field; it is shot through and through with the assumptions of psycho-sexual development, under which rubric these tenets will be reviewed. Even though rejected in detail, the fundamental thesis, that personality is the subject matter of the psychologist, and consequently that the biographical procedure may, and even, must follow this clue, remains unassailed. Personality, and by the same token career, which is however so largely a matter of circumstance, is a fusion of primary and secondary traits operative at the higher level of integration in which lives—civilized lives notably—are lived. The reflection of depth psychology in personality study is a permanent acquisition, deepened and enriched as well as popularized—and by such vogue distorted—by the Freudian approach and its venturesome applications. The same understanding that is applied—whether wisely and authentically is another issue—to our own lives, serves to elucidate the lives of others in support of the biographical interest. Writers sympathetic to psychoanalytical views portray their characters as thus animated and motivated; sex emancipation is a frequent theme; at times the human scene as it appears in literature approaches a clinic. As literature both reflects and affects life, making models for life and taking its models from it, the Freudianizing of what men live for and by has invaded every intimate relation. We live and think differently since Freud, whether or not in all respects we approve the change.

THE ARTS

What is true of literature applies equally to the arts, though the connection becomes less definite. The creative impulse is itself a problem in psychology, subject to psychoanalytic interpretation. Through the ages the subconscious has expressed itself pictorially; symbolism in painting is as ancient as in literature; in religious symbolism the canvas popularized the doctrine. With increasing development of technique and the modern freedom in subject, the art of the painter acquired a larger subjective expressionism. Painting may be psychoanalyzed, and music is subject to the same interpretation. The modernistic note has a complicated source, but it is an authentic expression of the psyche. Indeed art has been interpreted as compensatory activity, a recourse to fantasy in an escape from the too rigid demands of the reality principle.

This thesis, if elaborated, would enforce the principle of living or completing in fantasy what is denied or imperfect in reality. It projects a psychology of the artist who lives in many if not in every man. Since art is essentially creative, the temptation to ally it with the intimate creation of the racial succession, for the poet to speak of his poetry as the child of his brain, is an additional lure to identify parallel but not comparable urges. The artist labors to realize dreams; art scores in media favorable to subconscious assimilation. The relation of art to psychoanalysis is two-fold: to explain the artist psychoanalytically, and interpret the artist's, particularly the dramatist's, employment of Freudian themes.

One professionally interested in the vicissitudes of human behavior, from whatever approach, may equally have an interest in the arts. It may be a doctor who "looks at literature" as similarly he looks at love and life which likewise and with an allied interest literature portrays. There is a psychoanalyst in every psychologist and in many an artist, which will find expression alike in creation and criticism. I must leave it to the qualified literateur of the present or the future to survey the penetration of the Freudian theme in literary productions. Accepted as a clue, it may determine a plot, and a section of interlocking lives at any age, in any setting. The present development of the arts demonstrates the appeal of themes which the psychoanalytic clinic has revealed. Freudian ideas in literature as in life have re-interpreted the human relations by the intrusion of the clinical consciousness. Whether this addition aids or hinders the literateur's craft, is an open question. No other phase of psychology could have exerted so wide an influence. The reach of application of Freud's ideas is stupendous.

CIVILIZATION

The most momentous of all applications of psychoanalysis is to civilization itself; in Freud's hands it becomes a drastic critique of our civilization. It proposes an unprecedented form of revolution by way of a reconstructed insight of our inner life. Our civilization is brought into the clinic for psychoanalysis with the patient's hope of emerging with a better understanding of himself. The conflict is between the life of impulse and the life of reason. The question arises in the words of Zweig,* who has written an effectively dramatic account of Freud, mind and man, whether "the socialization of the Ego which passes by the name of progress has not really cheated man of his innermost self." Here is a modernistic version of the theme suggested years ago by Edward Carpenter: *Civilization, Its Cause and Cure*. Civilization is not precisely a neurosis but presents a dilemma, for which every philosophy is a solution by escape, or the abandonment of solution in pessimistic despair. Freud is troubled, deeply troubled, recognizing the supremacy of the impulsive life, yet with reason the only hope of its control.

* Zweig: Masters of Healing. 1932.

The proper close of this chapter is a tribute to Freud as philosopher. His essays written in war time, including reflections upon death, show an enviable temper of contemplation, when quite too many intellectuals failed in the privileges of their position. *The Future of an Illusion* (1928) is a masterpiece of exposition of the sceptical religionist. Like its successor *Civilization and its Discontent* (1930), its tone is pessimistic, despondent. It offers neither hope nor consolation. His position is consistent with the fundamental points of view arising from the conflicts whose neurotic aspects engaged his professional attention. In view of Freud's own confession that his tendency toward medicine was not of the strongest, and that he was a clinician by the route of analysis, one is tempted to regard the application of psychoanalysis to the philosophy of life as the most congenial of Freud's occupations. Equipped with principles he is free to carry them to their ultimate conclusions. He becomes a clinical philosopher.

I have carried this survey of the applications and implications of psychoanalysis far enough to make clear that Freudianism attempts far more than a scientific theory of the neuroses and related mental substructures, consists of more than a therapy and a pedagogy, and becomes a comprehensive philosophy of living. The applications of psychoanalysis, so many of them by thinkers not directly concerned with psychology or psychiatry, illustrate the wide influence of Freudian ideas. In that lies its appeal and its challenge. It proposes a reconstruction of the *Geisteswissenschaften* an attempt to bring the psychic procedures and values within the control of the scientific method.

What as science, as a scheme of understanding, would affect but the thoughtful minority—the intelligentsia who shape their course by critical reflection—

as a plan and policy of living, as a scheme of aims and values, affects a far larger group, if still a minority, eager for precepts of guidance in the personal conduct of their affairs. Therein lies the capital significance of the house that Freud built; it proposes a new, modernistic style of psychic architecture. If accepted, it makes a different home of the human habitation. On the apparently incidental issue as to whether and how far Freud is right or wrong, depend momentous consequences in the entire range of humanistic concerns. That importance, authentic or alleged, forms a major incentive for the present critical undertaking.

PART TWO

INTRODUCTORY NOTE

A critique of a monumental system of interpreting the human psyche, its nature and all its works, was introduced by a survey of the composite parts of the structure and design and composition of the house as Freud built it. Among the great interpreters—including those whose ambition or conviction of illumination however derived, outran their performance—Freud has an assured place, it may be a place of honor and pitying censure combined, as often befalls the heroic in any career. If his group in the hall of fame is that of the philosophers, he is the first representative who entered it by the route of a pioneering psychology.

I have attempted to present the system objectively, when possible neutrally—but have departed from this policy by introducing the critical note where it best served the reader's convenience to consider text and comment in one vista. From the outset my purpose is critical, writing under the assurance that the crisis in the fate of Freudianism is at hand. With that task behind me, I proceed to the critique. Since psychoanalysis is set forth as a science, the primary obligation is to examine how far it meets the scientific criteria. In so complex a structure, the execution is as essential as the design; a cause gains favor or fails by the manner of its support as well as by its platform. Psychoanalysis is an art, and the analyst a practitioner. The critique proceeds from principle to argument to practice. Whither psychoanalysis? is the concluding considera-

141

tion. The critic in confronting Freud and all his works, faces a peculiar situation: a partial and reserved approval of principle, a profound distrust of execution. He cannot commend the greatness of a great delusion, nor yet condemn the delusion utterly, when he considers the merit of the venture that runs through its intention and formulation. Both positions require candor, but require as well discriminating standards and emphatic verdicts. The decisive verdict lies with the critical public; for the moment it is in the reader's hands.

CHAPTER VI

PSYCHOANALYSIS VS. SCIENCE

Logic as Censor

I am inviting the reader upon a logical inspection of the house that Freud built with life-long zeal, with rare creative powers, with a distinctive flair for applications —admirable qualities, contributing to the wide interest in his striking contributions, but with slight bearing upon the final judgment: which is whether the monumental structure can pass the engineering test. The excursion is not one to fill the idle moments of an empty day; it is an exacting task, but indispensable for an appraisal of the comprehensive body of ideas by means of which Freud has profoundly affected the world of mind we live in.

Were it not for such insistent realities as laws of gravity, stresses and loads, fixed properties of wood, brick, stone and steel, wear of wind and weather, architecture might be a casual, arm-chair diversion. Intellectual construction meets similar inexorable conditions in the written and unwritten laws of logic, likewise determined by the building material of thought. Logic governs the constructions that minds built in first aid and further support of the thinking enterprise. Logic inspects the result, closely examining the criteria of evidence and the warrant of conclusions. Logic is blind to dramatic appeal, deaf to aesthetic satisfactions.

143

Logic, too, is a censor, though of a different order than the Freudian; both guard the "reality principle," the truth of seeing things as they are. Released from the one set of limitations, we build castles in the air or in an imaginary Spain, instantaneously perfect and complete; interpreting logical loyalties laxly, we indulge in speculations beyond the sanction of evidence and reason. We require no permits for thought constructions; they are judged after erection. Can psychoanalysis pass the censorship of logic? That is the question.

Responsible thinking does not yield crudely to wish; but in building theories on foundations of fact, there is opportunity at every turn for the subtle intrusion of favored interpretations, of finding what one is looking for, of construing data to conform to theory. This temptation applies particularly to constructions, such as those of psychoanalysis, in which the interplay of predilections and findings is inevitable. Bacon's immortal reminder may be particularly recommended to psychologists: that nature is more subtle than argument.

A strictly logical censorship would forthwith exclude Freudianism from the province of the sciences. Dunlap takes this position in *Mysticism, Freudianism and Scientific Psychology*. His judgment is unreserved. In appeal and method and conclusion, Freudianism is declared a form of mysticism; it derives its vogue and its appropriate place on the shelves of bookshops, where it consorts with phrenology, "new thought," spiritism and fallacious systems of character-reading, from the persistent longing for complete revelations and dramatic solutions of human problems. Its claims to recognition as a science are considered negligible. Believing it fairer to temper logic to the imperfections of psychology—if not a shorn lamb, at least an immature one—I cannot accept this sweeping condemnation.

The logic of a Daniel come to judgment, when judging so complex an issue, may well render a more tolerant verdict.

The fallacies of Freudianism are indeed manifold, and its violations of good sense and sound reasoning diverse and flagrant; but the scientific intention inheres in the Freudian quest. Freud's search is a legitimate extension of the psychologist's pursuit in understanding human nature; his clinical therapy is conceived as an effective diagnosis of neuroses and their relief. If he goes amiss in construction and becomes one of the *Builders of Delusions*, as Ward suggests; if he is to be classified, as Gillis places him, among the *False Messiahs*, it is not by taint of a paranoid streak nor of a messianic confidence. If he carries on his project so loosely that he misleads others and deludes himself, the cardinal error is a logical misjudgment of another order. How far the house that Freud built is scientifically designed is one question, how far it is scientifically constructed is another; both considerations are fundamental. When Watson, behaviorist, predicts that in the near future, anyone using the psychoanalytic procedure or terminology will be classed with the phrenologists, I dissent as positively, for the error in the program of phrenology arose from a complete misreading of body-mind relations. Upon flimsy, preposterous evidence, Gall announced the pretentious discovery of a complete cranial-cerebral-psychic code. Through the lure of a mistaken idea, a good anatomist became an absurd psychologist. The decipherments were as wrong as the psychology of the day was crude and the anatomy forced. Freud in action may be as extravagant, as creed-bound in supporting his thesis as was Gall in his; but the principles of the two solutions of the whys and hows of human behavior were quite otherwise arrived at. Though separated by only a hundred years, they are logical centuries apart.

If, seeking other disparaging analogies, we turn to Gall's contemporary, Mesmer, and his theory of an "animal magnetism" and the cures by its means, we come upon a mystical, an unsubstantiated system, in defense and employment of which theorist and physician and charlatan are uncertainly combined. Yet this unscientific intrusion did not deprive the "magnetic" phenomena of their reality. In some respects Mesmer's clinical observations were nearer the truth than the academic denials, and aroused an interest which led to the discovery of hypnosis; this in turn led to the recognition of suggestion and the subconscious workings of mind. Precisely in these now accredited mechanisms of the psyche, Freud, continuing the scientific quest, found the ground-clues of his interpretation. The case of Freudianism cannot be thrown out of court; to do so would be as unjust to Freud as unwise for psychology. In asking what is wrong in his presentation, we must grant Freud the same scientific intention as inspires adherents of other psychological schools with whose renderings we may for different reasons disagree. If psychoanalysis were not a worthy claimant for scientific recognition, this book would not be written.

The physical and the mental sciences, with equal loyalty to logic, meet their obligations differently. The claims of psychoanalysis must be tolerantly considered. The truth of psychoanalytic principles will never be confirmed with a Q. E. D. finality. They will become more or less acceptable to critical psychologists and psychiatrists by reason of their coherence with a large though irregular body of experience, of the support they find in biological foundations, of their applicability to clinical histories and to character analyses within the ranges of normal behavior; and they will be rejected by reason of defection in these respects. Freud's feeble grasp of logical principles is a cardinal misfortune for psychoanalysis; it should not discredit the entire structure.

THE FREUDIAN HOMO

How Freud discovered or constructed *homo psychoanalyticus* has been presented. We are now to examine the nature of the creature, not as he emerges concretely in the flesh from the clinical sanctum, but as the insight there obtained leads to the reconstruction of *homo* in general. As such a *homo,* I may ask in personal, practical vein, how much better do I understand what manner of creature I am or my fellow-beings are, as the result of spending a goodly number of hours and much mental perspiration in reading Freud and the Freudians, or even by being psychoanalyzed myself. As a peculiar variety of *homo* called a psychologist, I am interested in placing the Freudian in relation to other psychologies, in formulating the basic positions from which results the Freudian view of *homo* with all his contradictions. Yet in asking these questions, I have ever in mind the underlying query: How far is the Freudian *homo* authentic, how far an artefact, how far a neurotic, how far a libel?

But first, what goes into the making of this *homo,* real or alleged?

In curtest summary I find three guiding concepts. The first is the *subconscious homo*. Psychology has come to recognize that no amount of study of the comprehensive illuminated mental life which appears in conscious reflection, however aided and abetted by exploratory devices, will ever reveal the inward and complete man; that revelation requires the inclusion of the subconscious, indeed the emphasis upon it. Subscribing to that doctrine, I in so far enroll in the Freudian guild. Freud did not discover the subconscious life and its mechanisms; much had been contributed by others before and far more since, concerning submerged psychic behavior. So universally was the existence of the psychic Atlantis recognized that when, years ago, Stanley Hall proposed the analogy of the iceberg, with a segment above the water-line representing the conscious and the far greater and invisible mass below representing the subconscious, the simile was eagerly accepted. Furthermore, Freud's general plan of exploring certain phases of the submerged life and his clues to their sources, appeal to me as in principle sound; he has added much of primary importance to our total view of human motives and mechanisms. But whether the *specific manner* in which Freud conceives the subconscious and elaborates its participation in the psychic life is warranted or correct, is a *totally different question*. On that issue I must register a far larger measure of rejection than of acceptance, with the rejections pertaining to matters fundamental. The Freudian "unconscious" seems to me in the main a concept scientifically weak and in its applications variously misleading. My many and emphatic protests against Freudian conclusions would doubtless exclude me from the guild, if not being with them, I am declared against them.

The second leading concept, shaping the nature of *homo Freudiens,* is libido, the *libidinal homo*. The nub of it all is so simple as this: that it is useful to have a word—a most generic word—to summarize the basic *x* that keeps life going. Call it energy; call it the *élan vital;* call it the composite of the vital urges; call it the zest and the interest in living; recognize that it is biological in core, but acquires a rich psychic overgrowth in which it lives and moves and has its complicated being; and you have libido. That something keeps us going is so obvious that it seems strange that we got along so long and so well without this handy coinage. But a welcome addition to a technical vocabulary does not of itself make new knowledge; and what insight it confers may readily turn to confusion if the forces constituting libido are predilectively conceived. If all libido is sexualized, the psychological game becomes a totally different one. The critical problem recurs: What is the nature of this complex drive to live and to live abundantly? Has Freud interpreted it rightly? On this issue, my reaction is a mixed one. I recognize the utility of the term and its place in psychology, but cannot accept the Freudian development of it. Libidinal psychology is legitimate, indeed fundamental. To Freud belongs the credit of turning psychology in this direction, and with the proper inclusion of subconscious motivation, of primary function, even in the exalted reaches of secondary development. Libido has a fundamental subconscious component, however readily *homo sapiens* comes to recognize and consciously direct his libido, wisely or unwisely.

The third fundamental concept in the Freudian scheme is *sublimation*. This term I would extend beyond the limited meaning which Freud usually gives it. Sublimation is the directing of a specific urge, which may have an undesirable or a limited outlet, to a more desirable and higher-grade expression; sublimation is involved in all redirections of the urges by which the upper-level, refined, socially elaborate and acceptable products of the psyche have emerged. An important phase of sublimation is socialization, the completer adjustment of behavior to others, in all sorts and conditions of relations, and with consideration for others. Men would not go far in sublimation without the social influence. In sublimation the original impulse is preserved and its higher expression attained. Sublimation epitomizes progressive development. It is closely associated with the richer and derivative satisfactions of the surplus life of leisure and luxury, when the fundamentals have been provided for. Sublimation accompanies the process of development; we sublimate as we grow in psychic stature.

Without successive stages of sublimation we should still be close to the primitive status of the cave-man. The civilized life is the sublimated life. Since libido is the comprehensive name for the urges, it is in a sense profoundly true that libido is what is sublimated. In all these respects Freudian psychology is a *depth* psychology, including the submerged or suppressed subconscious; it is a *libidinal* psychology, referring behavior to basic urges; it is a *sublimation* psychology, tracing the course of the psyche from the primal trend to the final form. If a subscription to this program as a vital one entitles one to be ranked as a Freudian, I claim that appellation. Such depth psychology is peculiarly the proper study of mankind.

FREUD AND CONTEMPORARY PSYCHOLOGY

The conclusion upon which the motif of the Freudian symphony converges is not necessarily that of his composition in any of its movements. As I conceive or interpret it, there is nothing in the Freudian theme, nothing in Freud's approach to psychology—including its clue in the abnormal—that compels the program of the actual performance, the amazing elaborate score of Freudiana with all its discordant, inconsistent, extravagant, distorting variations. I can project imaginatively a depth psychology with the leading parts assigned, as in the actual presentation, to the subconscious with its submergences, fusions and suppressions, to the basic urges whether designated as libido or otherwise, to sublimation in all its repertory of transformation, which would advance our insight into human behavior, strengthen our control—that of neurotic impediments specifically—and yet read altogether differently and be conducted in a wholly scientific temper. This possible Freudianism would have been a far less dramatic reconstruction than the actual system, but a far more wholesome as well as more authentic one.

Yet the fact remains that the architectural signature on the house of psychoanalysis is that of Freud; plan and execution are as he presents them. We can no more choose in intellectual history than in the sequence of human events, political and economic, how the shifts of change shall come about. The fact remains that through the compelling intimacy and broad scope of its appeal, psychoanalysis has proved an effective challenge to the reconstruction of psychology and psychiatry; it has affected ways of living and thinking comprehensively. That fact places Freud in the history of ideas, and incidentally justifies the present venture.

Other trends in contemporary psychology were already moving toward the same desirable direction and emphasis. Child Psychology and Social Psychology and the increasing consideration of personality in General Psychology express the same interest in the deeper, affective, primitive, every-day reactions of every-day life. This vitalized study of human behavior in its setting of urges and motives has supplemented and in large measure replaced the too limited and academic investigation of the intellectual processes and the machinery of mind—all with great benefit to human understanding and the conduct of life. But it remained for Freud to give a direction to psychology which it will retain to the end of human reflection. "Know thy hidden self": thus spake Freud.

The major occupations of modern psychology, as they took form in Wundt's laboratory at Leipsic, concerned the outer machinery of intellectual operations. The impetus of that school has spent its initial force; its important contributions leave untouched the vital problems of the deeper and more intimate psychic life. The animus and purpose motivating the Freudian conspectus expressed the spirit of the times, which its vogue has come to represent. It was not the *proposal of a depth psychology but Freud's version of it* that aroused protest, because it presented a repulsive, distorted semblance of the admittedly idealized human psyche of the moralistic and intellectualistic psychologists. Psychoanalysis as first encountered seemed to be the embodiment of the improper study of mankind. The disinclination to envisage man as he really is, added to the academic absorption in specialized phases of mental expression, goes far to account for the initial and intense opposition to the Freudian doctrines. On this issue, the logic of the argument is wholly on the side of Freud. Truth is independent of acceptability on moral or aesthetic grounds; yet morality and beauty are themselves vital expressions of sublimation.

The proper offset of the "denatured" academic *homo* way to be found in the biological reconstruction, deriving its impetus from Darwin. The human psyche, however exalted by culture, must come to terms with the biological, evolutionary *homo*. What Wundt had in mind in naming his pioneering text *Physiological Psychology* was little more than its close affiliation with and dependence upon physiology in accounting for the mechanisms of the sensory and motor apparatus, and in supplying the cerebral substratum for the psychic coordinations: more simply, in recognizing a soma for the psyche. The vital recognition that all our sensory and motor patterns are scripts of an evolutionary language, into whose idiom psychology, no less than physiology, must be translated if its meaning is to emerge, was far from adequately present in the Wundtian movement; it has come triumphantly to the fore since. I have called this conspectus Naturalistic Psychology, in the spirit of the older use of the term, natural history. The psychologist is a naturalist in the field of mind. He may be studying a child in the nursery, or an animal in its native haunts, or a bit of reflex mechanism, or an elaborate reaction-pattern of an adult, or the social customs of primitive or civilized man; he is ever a naturalist, even if an academic one. If he shares the Teutonic fondness for large-calibre words, he may dwell upon the fusion of the *natur historisch* with the *cultur historisch;* for the most significant fact about man is his capacity for culture. History is but the upper-level humanized sequence of events that wander far but are not detached from their biological roots. In the same movement for deeper understanding arose the engrossing study of the abnormal, which so variously reflects the entire range of the human endowment, as in a spectrum with the color-scheme disarranged. That, too, falls within the naturalistic picture; it portrays how the psychic nature goes wrong. These collateral interests were moving in parallel orbits to what came to expression in the Freudian movement.

Beginning with a clinical insight, Freudian psychology grew to a general interpretation of the psyche. As such, it must pass the naturalistic test; it must be nat-

uralized within the greater empire of mind in nature.
The realities underlying such concepts as subconscious,
libido, and sublimation must somehow be provided for
in the biological inheritance, and integrated with it. I
cannot recall that Freud has inquired how the psychoanalytic complexities, which form the central concern
of his system and complicate human existence to the
breaking-point, came to possess *homo* and harass *libido,*
nor why so much of original nature must be sublimated;
which is an equally pertinent inquiry. It is precisely
these questions that I regard as the most fundamental
of all; they must be raised even if they cannot be answered. Otherwise, the foundations of any psychoanalytical system remain detached and questionable, a
speculation without roots. This survey of the relations
of Freudian to other contributions to psychology may
serve the fairer appraisal of its validity and value,
whatever may be the final view of the solutions which
Freud proposes.

THE "UNCONSCIOUS"

The Naturalistic Approach

A regard for the logic of science raises reservations
in the mind of a naturalistic psychologist as he con-
fronts the important innovations of Freud. Equally to
be considered is the status of psychology in which
Freudianism appears as an applicant for recognition.
The conflict of the psychologies is an additional reason
why it is not a simple matter to set forth how Freudianism should be weighed, and just where and why it is
found wanting. The project, the scheme, the system,
the doctrine, the total interpretation which is summarized as psychoanalysis, is not just either true or
false. It is not to be accepted as replacing accredited

psychology nor yet to be denied a place in that structure. Nor is the status of psychology so well defined, nor its basic principles so precisely formulated, nor its contours of content so definitely outlined that its program of progress is established. The flexibility of psychology is as much the result of uncertainty or of floundering, as of tolerance. Were this not so, the rivalry of solutions would not present such sharp contrasts, nor the babel of tongues among the psychologists be so confusing. The builders are suffering from more than a division of idiom; they are laboring upon different designs, with yet a faith or a hope that the façades will compose, or, it may be, with complacent neglect of the others' projects. That situation is unfortunate; it would be made far more so if Freudianism were to set itself up as a rival to them all, which in its present temper it presumptuously claims to be.

Convinced that the naturalistic approach offers the best hope for an inclusive reconciliation, I shall consider psychoanalysis from that approach. First to be examined is the most fundamental and distinctive of the Freudian concepts, without which there would have been no psychoanalysis—the subconscious. The entire movement arose upon a solution, an ingenious answer to a pertinent question. The query, parallel in moment to Newton's curiosity concerning the falling apple, was why hysterical symptoms should assume their special forms of peculiar, suspiciously unbiological disabilities. Physiologically they were "unnatural"; could they be made to appear psychologically "natural"? They could, if the psychic nature included an "unconscious"; for the patient seemed the victim, not the agent, of the symptoms. He felt their compulsion strongly but seemed ignorant of their *provenance*. The symptoms conformed to no physiological pattern and to no pattern of conscious construction. The paralysed arm, the blurred vision correspond to no course of impairment in nerve or muscle; nor yet are the disabilities imagined or imaginary. How do they arise?

Yet it will hardly do to assume an "unconscious" because one needs it for explanation. Much earlier in the stages of understanding, hysterical and allied symptoms were explained as demon possession. If you are willing to assume that there are demons and that it is their "nature" to inflict these plaguing symptoms upon their victims, the explanation of the symptoms is completely adequate. On this assumption, witches were accused, tried and executed. Our minds balk at any such "unnatural," crassly unscientific explanation. The logic of witch trials is as offensive to our logical standards as the execution of suspects is inhumane to our moral standards. The Freudian "unconscious" that devises and imposes hysterical symptoms, is plainly conceived as a natural and not a supernatural agency; it arises somehow within the psyche.

There were recent as well as ancient unscientific conceptions of the subconscious, arising as did Freud's, from the study of the obscure borderland of the psychic—not quite the same area of it but still "hysterical"—including, along with hypnotism, the alleged and abundantly testified accounts of clairvoyance and telepathy. The theory of Hudson in his *The Law of Psychic Phenomena* attained wide currency (though not among critical readers) forty years ago. He boldly announced that we have two minds, the "subjective" and the "objective." The "objective" is the conscious performer in our accredited mental daylit life; the "subjective" is the subconscious and is responsible for all the apparent mysteries and the peculiar phenomena of the rare, the transcendent, the abnormal. Hudson extended the hypothesis to spirit communications; but his assumption was comprehensive enough without that application. If we have two minds, and if such are their functions, psychology is supplied with a comprehensive solution, rather more acceptable than demon possession but equally unsubstantiated. The idea was suggested by Carpenter's earlier and wholly scientific study of this same field in his *Mental Physiology,* in which he set up tentatively the hypothesis of "unconscious cerebration."

Hudson's views fell outside the range of legitimate science, though he, too, advocated a therapy based upon them. Today this episode in the history of the subconscious is interesting only as a chapter in the story of error; the moral of which is plain. Freud's "unconscious" must find a possible naturalistic basis, or it, too, will be relegated to another, though far more important, chapter in the same book. As Dunlap considers that Freud's "unconscious" has no scientific basis in fact, he rejects it as completely as he would the theologist's "demon possession," or Hudson's "subjective mind." Others, indeed the majority of psychologists and psychiatrists, concede its naturalistic intent, but regard the evidence for it as so weak that they cannot accept Freud's account of the unconscious as valid. In my opinion, the Freudian "unconscious" (Freud does not, of course, posit an "unconscious mind," only a variety of "unconscious" procedure), is in the main an illegitimate, somewhat distorted extension of an actual relation, for which a naturalistic explanation can be found. I regard it as most important to look for it, though Freud does not recognize the need of such foundation, nor is he disturbed by its absence. Accepting the reality of his "unconscious," and convinced that he has unearthed its habits and habitat, he develops and explores its nature and applies it confidently to the further explanation of the many realms and borderlands of the psyche. In this extension upon so hypothetical a basis and with such far-reaching applications, lie the grounds for rejection of the concept.

Biological Foundations

It was Rivers who recognized the importance of seeking a physiological basis for the subconscious. If the world of mind is in fact organized about conscious and subconscious functions, the foundations for this distinction must penetrate deep down in the organic structure. Head and Rivers found a clue in the distinction between *protopathic* (primitive) and *epicritic* (discriminating) sensibility. By experimenting upon themselves, they observed that when a nerve in the arm had been cut, the restoration of sensibility as the two severed ends healed, followed a definite order. Vague, crude, gross, pain sensation reappeared before the definite, localized and specific tactile sensations by which we use our limbs, joints, skin discerningly. Generalizing this distinction, he reached the suggestive conclusion that there is a *protopathic* life, which may set the limits of psyche in lowly organisms, crudely reacting to changes pleasant or unpleasant; this by far antedates and underlies the higher type of sensibility that fills the conscious horizon. Such is the *epicritic life* of distinction, skill, correlation, purpose. The sensory-motor mechanism offers a clue-pattern of neural organization. The two types of sensibility persist and combine and compose the dermal psyche; in the fusion the epicritic sensations dominate and the protopathic recede, leaving some irregular vestiges, like tickling and goose-skin, as biological curiosities. The dermal senses may be accepted as biological clues to the primary sensory life; the eye and ear are far more exclusively epicritic in evolutionary status.

Extending this distinction, the conscious life is clearly epicritic; the subconscious life harbors a phase of the protopathic, not the ultra-primitive palaeozoic protopathic thus discovered, but something biologically analogous. As the "conditioned reflex" experiment of Pavlov furnishes a physiological prototype for simpler forms of habit, the Head-Rivers experiment supplies one for an ultimate distinction of far-reaching consequence. Both refer to components and patterns entering into behavior. By extending the bearing of the salivary gland experiment, "conditioning" has grown to a momentous chapter in psychology and by that route in education. The nerve-section experiment may prove even more significant, prefacing the great chapters of the subconscious and the conscious life. Prototype, or bed-rock psychology is not conclusive; but it is objective and suggestive.

The details offer further suggestions. During the recovery stage, the normally epicritic skin reverts to a protopathic condition, in which there is no exact localization; the sensation radiates and may be felt at a distance from the point of stimulation. As the nerve heals, epicritic sensation is restored; but for a time it could be banished again by applying cold to the skin. Normally the epicritic crowds out what protopathic sensibility persists. Rivers' dramatic interpretation reads that while the divided and then re-united nerve in his arm was recovering its epicritic sensibility, he was actually experiencing a sensation which has dropped out of human experience aeons ago, being biologically "suppressed" in the fusion of protopathic with epicritic elements. "Utilization by means of the process of fusion is the fate of the greater part of the complex processes which make up protopathic sensibility. It is only the smaller part which undergoes the other fate of suppression." If we accept what happens in the nerve-tracts supplying the skin as a prototype of more elaborate structures higher up, substituting "mental activity and mental experience" for dermal sensibility, we may conclude that the key-relation of subconscious to conscious is "utilization by the process of fusion"; yet physiology provides for a factor which "required the more drastic measure of suppression."

The object in citing this experiment is to indicate that a scientific concept of the subconscious or unconscious must seek a biological foundation, or at least be compatible with it. When found, it is not a proof, but a clue; its evidence may tell as much or more against the Freudian "unconscious" as for it. The discovery of a physiological form of "suppression" strengthens the case for psychological suppression; it does not identify or even assimilate the two. Salivary psychology or dermal psychology is not a model for cerebral psychology. Human behavior at the ordinary complex level which the Behaviorist or the Freudian have in mind is the issue of a highly integrated nervous system. The contention of Watson that upper-grade human behavior can be explained by "conditioning" comparable to the Pavlov type, is a wrong rendering of a biological analogy which Watson constantly has in mind. A Freudian would commit a similar error if he held that intricate varieties of human behavior are to be explained by "suppression" comparable to the Rivers type. Yet both offer a biological analogy which Freud never has in mind.

Without the nerve-section experiment, a strictly naturalistic psychologist might well question whether there could be any radically suppressed experience as

Freud postulates; without the salivary gland experiment, he might equally question whether habit formation of that type is basic. With both established, it still remains true and important that the complex life of our trained habits is not a complicated "salivation" experience, nor is a complex a complicated "dermal" experience. The primal form is not the final form but has bearing upon it. Later and higher forms of "conditioning" or "suppression" are not of the same order; for other factors arise independently and also fuse with it. The panorama of behavior is illuminated from the "conditioned" footlight; a parallel illumination emerges from the protopathic-epicritic base and the consequent integration by fusion.

Having in mind this rudimentary paradigm, we do better to accept the more inclusive terms of "primary" and "secondary" function. This biological category is indispensable to depth psychology, whether developed upon a Freudian basis or otherwise. Primary function fuses with and is replaced by secondary function; the secondary is distinctly conscious, elaborately epicritic; the subconscious (typically more "conscious" than "sub") contributes the primary function that ever supports conscious behavior. The submergence may be to any measure of depth, the emergence with any degree of clarity. But the principle of it all is *fusion*, fusion at all levels, in all varieties of integration. Fusion dominates above suppression; it is a fusional psychology that I have presented in my volume: *The Subconscious*. The term "subconscious" is far more acceptable; for "suppression" is often a minor factor, if indeed it be suppression and not merely submergence, an underground variety of both fusion with and detachment from the conscious stream. For the many varieties of this relation, the concept of *dissociation* seems to me, as to many other psychologists, essentially correct, but subject to further extension, including the important Freudian factors with their quality of censored suppression, at times strangely, at times simply motivated.

Dissociation and Suppression

How dissociation occurs, the dropping out of a phase of psychic traffic from the major current—somewhat as in a river a by-stream is formed by an obstructing sand bank—is a problem of moment. It sets up association and dissociation as collateral functions. It is to Freud's everlasting credit that he recognized the comprehensive spread of this range of psychic movement and indicated a vital factor regarding its source. That key other psychologists who had studied subconscious phenomena—myself among them—had largely, yet not quite completely, but rather stupidly neglected. It is the dynamic factor of motive. Before Freud we were studying "the subconscious" too much on a descriptive level. (I use this objectified but not personified term as a label of convenience, not as indicating an independent reality. There is no "the subconscious"; there are subconscious phases and components in the total psychic stream.) We were analyzing relations of what was retained and what lost in the main stream and by-currents and motivations. We neglected what forces caused the divergent channels.

This neglect was intelligible, because the standard phenomena recognized as subconscious were of the type of automatic writings and similar automatisms in which intellectual purposiveness amid detachment was the striking feature. The problem was how knowledge and intelligent control could be exercised apparently without contact with the standard directing self. Super-capacity, rather than incapacity, was manifested; only the trance state, light or deep, suggested a deprivation of function, along with the exercise of other functions not ordinarily at command. Expressed quite simply, hypnosis dipped deeper down into the primary stream. Yet motivations appeared in somnambulisms (I had called them "quests"), in fugues, as indicating escape from home ties, in dual or conflicting personalities to express frustrated or denied phases of desire. In all these amnesias there was the type of complete dissociation suggesting suppression, if once thought of as such. By the single stroke of an illuminating idea, Freud wrote the word "suppression" on the psychological map; and it has come to stay. Ideas, systems of sensibilities or of memories, of coördinations of movement, could be forgotten in the ordinary sense; but amnesia might also under circumstances be a dynamic product, as though the river threw up its own detaching sandbank. The principle of subconscious determinism was "discovered"; psychology was enriched. The mechanism appears in the hysterical and allied impairments which occupied Freud. Here was unearthed a novel phase of the subconscious, not an automatism, but a strangely motivated disability. Forgetting, which ordinarily is a dropping out, may be thought of as a being pushed out; the mechanism that worked the trap-door of oblivion merited careful examination. Again the critical question: Has Freud developed this vein of underground psychology profitably, correctly?

Continuing the development of a naturalistic (physiological) basis for the subconscious, Rivers points out that in *inhibition* we have a mechanism, common to low and high levels of behavior, essential to every phase of activity, subject to abnormal expression, and underlying the limitations of anaesthesia, hypnosis and much else. To begin with, there are nerve tracts of excitation which discharge muscle-fibres singly and in correlated groupings, or induce secretions of glands; and there are inhibitory fibres which hold back and check. Nature, it has been well said, drives by two reins, and one is a check-rein. The far more complex inhibitions of shyness, the difficulties in the release of impulse through the presence of counter-impulses, the paralyses of fright, the hypnotic rigidities, the hesitations of embarrassment or doubt, are as familiar to every observer of human behavior as in simpler form they appear in the physiologist's experiments. They represent conflicts between letting go and holding back. "Suppression by which experience becomes unconscious is only a special variety of the process of inhibition." This important formulation of Rivers goes far to naturalize suppression; it strengthens the Freudian concept, not necessarily Freud's application of it. Rivers goes farther and sets forth how the cruder "all or none" type of reaction—as in the violent responses of children— give way to the graded and shaded responses characteristic of mature, controlled, discriminatingly inhibited behavior. The child completely lets go or completely holds back; the adult adjusts one tendency to the other. The association of the thalamus as the seat of emotional response (by Cannon and others) as opposed to the cortical control, again suggests a physiological basis in the brain structure for that far-reaching distinction between primary and secondary function, that is the very Hamlet of depth psychology.

Because of their fundamental importance and my belief that the substitution of the terms primary and secondary, both as vocabulary and in our thinking, for the Freudian terminology, will do much to clarify the relations and avoid obscuranting identification, I add a word as to these valuable terms. As to their origin, Jung, who uses them freely, explains in a letter to Dr. Roback that he borrowed them from Otto Gross: *Die Cerebrale Secundärfunctionen* (1902). They are there used physiologically, but are most significant in their psychological implications. Primitive and derivative psychology, the psychology of low and of high estate, carry the suggestive distinction. The whole forms a comprehensive concept indispensable to much that underlies the modern, including the Freudian approach. I shall use the terms freely and interchangeably, and with their combined implications, harking back to physiological and psychological beginnings and endings.

I summarize them thus: Reflexes and glandular stresses and organic sensations and fixed coördinations, innate aptitudes and instinctive urges and the dispositions, inhibitions, the level of infant life and simpler animal structures and early cultural stages, are all representative of the primary function, either wholly or dominantly. Distinction, habit, direction, reflection, matured emotions, sentiments, tastes, skills, proficiencies, controls, withdrawals, anxieties, opinions, beliefs, ideals, standards, scruples, principles, reflections generally, are secondary function, wholly or predominantly; and in the interplay psychology finds its problems, and life its perplexities. There is much opportunity in so complex a dynamism for relations to become mixed and functions to go wrong. This method of consideration is of permanent value to the psychologist, whether theoretically or practically minded. Like much else, though it is by no means a Freudian contribution, it has been enriched (as well as decidedly confused) by the psychoanalytic use of it, which makes of it something very different from what it naturalistically is.

It is well to explain again that the use of the same term for processes wide apart in the physiological, and especially in the psychological scale, does not identify or even assimilate them. The contrast in status may be far more significant than the analogy, which, however, for comparative purposes may justify their inclusion in one evolutionary series. In that sense inhibition extends from the infant's withdrawal from a strange pair of arms to a religionist's conscientious scruple; but the one is in no sense the other; neither is the shyness a scruple, nor the scruple a shyness. The fact that a mechanism is provided for both varieties of checkings, supplies the concept with a naturalistic sanction. Taboos and inhibitory reflexes must be wholly differently considered; yet, given the appropriate psychic mechanism, we arrive at the latter from a foundation in the former. Such is evolution within the psyche conditioned by evolution within the soma. Similarly, the biologist may start in one organism with an eye-spot, and end in man with a pair of binocular foveal retinae; or Darwin may call the roots of a plant its "brain"—all analogies, but not realities. For these and allied reasons, the trend of Freud's project and intention, whatever our opinion of its execution, is in line with the fundamental progress of psychology. It is useful to consider the primal origins of final forms of behavior, and see the exalted in the lowly.

To a naturalistic psychologist this is important. It gives him a sense of security in following as far as he can the ramifications of subconscious behavior, even when its trail becomes obscure. It disposes him favorably to the principles of the Freudian project, while yet it insists that the development of the subconscious shall remain true to a naturalistic conception logically carried out. To recognize resemblances and relations within an evolutionary scheme is the very key-note of naturalistic science; to identify them and ignore their wide separation in status and meaning is a misleading fallacy, of which Freud and the Freudians have been flagrantly guilty.

Critique of "Ucs"

My general conclusion in the light of all the phenomena referable to subconscious participation is that the Freudian "unconscious," which is curtly written "Ucs.," plays a minor but real part within the orbit of normal human behavior, and that the part it plays is far more correctly interpreted as a factor in the total subconscious phases of psychic organization. In that process and product the *major rôle is fusion, a fusion of primary and secondary function,* and of successive integrations within the vast primary range. Fusional psychology dominates; when it recedes or the integration fails, some form or measure of recessive dissociation may be involved along with the dominant association. It may proceed in those constitutionally disposed to a fairly deep, temporary or prolonged dissociated state, which in turn may be partly physiologically, more commonly, psychologically conditioned. In this comprehensive scheme of *dissociational states* (or processes) the Freudian "unconscious" can and should be fitted.

Freud, of course, acknowledges the fusional aspect; he calls it the "fore-conscious"; I refer to it as the supporting subconscious, supporting the conscious; the primary supporting the secondary function; in remote analogy, the protopathic supporting and giving way to the epicritic sensibilities and activities. For this concept of subconscious functioning in all ranges, there is sound biological support in the integration-patterns of the nervous structure. When dissociation occurs—in moments of "absence," in lapses of the attention, in trance-states, in automatisms, in dreaming, in somnambulism—there is a rearrangement of rôles, which affords an additional insight into the normal relations of subconscious to conscious components.

One important phase of that relation it remained for Freud to point out. Because it appears markedly in the analysis of neurotic conditions, one might tentatively call it the "neurotic subconscious," as one might call the dissociated phase, the "trance or automatism subconscious." Each of us may be temperamentally more or less disposed to one or other of these tendencies. In both there is a wide range from slight to marked, from normal to abnormal. That all such relations, sharpened and exaggerated as they are in the abnormal, appear also in milder degree in the normal, is a general principle of abnormal psychology, well established independently of the Freudian evidence, but strengthened and enriched by it.

The statement just made that the characteristic "neurotic subconscious" occurs throughout the normal series makes it unfair so to designate it; it is more precisely a phase of motivation at times (but not universally, as Freud claims) present and in certain neurotic conditions playing the decisive rôle, also there assuming a neurotic quality, which it does not display ordinarily. By this I mean that all of us harbor and entertain, build up and come to terms with a Freudianized (along with a supporting) subconscious, but which does not at all attain the neurotic proportions or physiognomy; that we all have our conflicts in which conscious and subconscious factors interplay. Because such conflicts are dominantly emotional, one may equally designate this phase as the "emotional subconscious." If it be understood that the term implies only a trend in the direction of the alibi, escape, transformation mechanisms of Freud, the "Freudianized subconscious" is at once distinctive and acceptable.

My criticism in a nutshell is this: that Freud drags in this "emotional subconscious" when the "dissociated subconscious" (a failure in fusion) is adequate, far more natural and convincing. An illustration may be helpful. Let it be a minor point with no important bearing on Freud's major thesis, only upon his logic. The mild dissociative factor of a distracted state of mind may, usually does, account completely for a lapse. When a rector, delivering a sermon on the occasion of Queen Victoria's Jubilee, pronounced the words: "Yes! We have a very queer Dean," the parishioners knew that he meant: "We have a very dear Queen"; for they knew that he was given to these inverting, and in this instance, diverting, lapses; and they knew that he was likewise not on cordial terms with the Dean of the Cathedral church in which he was preaching. Accepting mildly the subconscious motivation, one may infer that the sentiment expressed a deeper thought diplomatically suppressed. Since he had been guilty of similar lapses with no such motivation, it seems far more consistent to regard this also as an accident of distraction, and refrain from making mountains of molehills, and elaborate and fantastically labored books on the *Psychopathology of Everyday Life* out of a topic suited for a casual after-dinner address at a psychologists' convention. The most serious of all lapses is a lapse in the sense of proportion.

Similarly, a drill sergeant in a moment of confusion gave the order: "Squaward Fod!", which the amused recruits readily translated into: "Forward Squad!" Had there been an ingenious Freudian among them, the slip might have been analyzed. Why should just this order be reversed? There must be a reason. "Squaw" is the Indian for wife. The drill sergeant must be at odds with his wife, fears her, takes orders from her. The subconscious clue is found. But is this science, or a game that anyone can play who finds it amusing or worth while?

It was as familiar before as after the Freudian emendation that there are collateral conscious and subconscious streams of thought, the subconscious supplying the conscious, with occasional interferences and breaks in their fusion or integration, and with now and then a fragment of motive precipitating the issue. That is all clearly within the play of the subconscious, subject occasionally to the stresses of suppression; it does not demand a distinctive "unconscious" suppressed so deeply—*spurlos versenkt,* to revive the submarine phrase, sunk without leaving a trace or clue—as to be assigned a separate category. One may readily admit from what we know of abnormal dissociation that in the neurotically disposed, here and there, now and then, the sinking may be profound, unrecoverable except by an appropriate diving technique, be it by hypnosis, by release through dissociation, by a free flowing talk aided by free association, by dream interpretation or what not.

This more plastic and elastic view of the subconscious range, as equally of the motivation factor, which may have any value in the game from pawn to king, is far more consistent with the total knowledge of psychic integration of primary and secondary function, is more consistently naturalistic. It protects from extreme application of either motivation or deeply sunk suppression; it compels a constant reference to the hierarchy of function in which the relations develop. It would have saved Freud from the unpardonable sin of universalizing the complexes, making it the fate of man born of woman to be doomed to everlasting sex damnation.

In addition Freud confuses the two sources of the subconscious content. The one subconscious content is derived from the individual experience; it represents the sum total of all that I personally want to forget in my own past and present psychic assaults or guilts or difficulties, my personal concealments, of which incidentally I may and must also be partially aware. The other is the far more rudimentary, primitive source, so archaic as to be racial, evolutionary, reaching its tide in infantile stages, all operative in an undeveloped form of psychic life. Yet it is precisely this vague, early, inchoate "unconscious" which is endowed by Freud with a magical potency to make its reverberations felt long years afterward, with all the detailed clarity and effective reinstatement of an eidetic impression. The "unconscious" may be one or the other; it can hardly be both, certainly not on equal terms. The adult can hardly be subject to revival of foetal impressions leading to desires to return to intrauterine shelter, and to having a claustrophobia at twenty because shut in and frightened at seven—all by the same mechanism.

This early, primitive, archaic subconscious, if it continues at all (which is more than doubtful, since its natural course is completely vanishing fusion with later stages of related interest-development) would be in the nature of vague, nebulous, sensory feelings and motor tensions, which would be of no value for psychoanalytic purposes, certainly not in the form of thoughts, ideas, recollections and the finished products that figure as complexes in clinical analyses. Jung, facing the same problem, boldly assumes in addition to the personal a "collective unconscious"—an un-naturalistic hypothesis, which introduces further irreconcilable complications. Freud turns from the primitive to the personal reservoir arbitrarily and confusedly, as suits his purpose. Like Jung, he is consistent at the cost of a far fetched, "unnatural" inference. He finds it necessary to assume a genetic unfoldment in which the earlier archaic-infantile episodes are given specific, articulate and potent values in the formation of mature traits generally, and of neurotic symptoms specifically. Hence the truly astounding assumptions of infantile sexuality, interpreted on the adult pattern; hence the family romance; hence the nuclear complexes and fixations; hence birth traumas; hence oral, anal, and urethral character-traits; hence much else that has been characterized as Freudian "mythology," all of it a crass violation of the fundamentals of naturalistic psychology. The Freudian interpretation is additionally unnatural, in that the completeness of suppression, so far as the conscious psyche is concerned, must be reconciled with the amazing resurrective power of the suppressed. The Freudian "unconscious" is buried, but buried alive. The decease and funeral rites appear as suppression; the disturbing *revenant* in conflicts, fixations, complexes, perversions and what not—lively ghosts indeed, making a long continued Walpurgis of our supposedly dead selves on which we fail to rise to higher things, indeed rather descend to neurotic depths of misery and perversion. In such various ways has a false conception of the subconscious disastrous consequences for the understanding of the human make-up and set-up; and by that route it contributes to dubious, pernicious methods and false solutions for the direction of the intimate life.

What may seem a slight slip, and in the main a

theoretical one, leads to the sharp divergence of psychoanalysis from science. A slight deviation in the foundations throws the whole structure out of plumb. In the detailed execution of the plan, which determines the special features of the house that Freud built, lie the sources of its errors and confusions. Freud's "unconscious," I must conclude, is a magnificent myth, growing out of violations of logical principles.

The effect of this objection and rejection is a negative reaction to the great bulk of psychoanalytic contributions, while yet recognizing in the approach and framework a distinctive and illuminating contribution to modern psychology. I might say that I accept the table of contents as chapter headings, but not the contents; or that I agree to the *dramatis personae* but not to the drama as staged; or, more colloquially, that I believe that psychoanalysis is in the right church but the wrong pew. A fusional psychology built upon the relations and integrations of primary and secondary functions, would, in my opinion, adequately incorporate the essential truths of the Freudian dispensation and avoid its exaggerations, distortions, and pernicious fallacies.

LIBIDO AND SUBLIMATION

In critique of the concept of libido, I take a similar position. For a proper appreciation of the libidinal aspects of the psychic life, our generation and all future ones will be indebted to the genius of Freud. It is the *course* of libido that becomes the issue, its *argument* not its *principle*. I shall accordingly resume that discussion in consideration of Freudian argument, where, indeed, it forms the very crux of the controversy, dividing Freudian from non-Freudian and anti-Freudian camps and camp followers.

Sublimation, by the very dimension of its scope, falls beyond the limitations of this essay; the story of sublimation is the story of civilization. Sublimation as a process in development, and sublimation as an instrument of mental hygiene, I accept completely. But this is not precisely the psychoanalytic point of view. Freudian sublimation is "the exchange of infantile sexual aims for interests or modes of pleasure-finding, which are no longer directly sexual, although psychically related, and which are on a higher social level." Sublimated activities are thus presented as "desexualized" or "aim-inhibited." Sublimation also includes substitutional trends in functions associated with sexual processes, including narcissism. That term itself epitomizes the limited Freudian concept: that all later forms of ego worship derive from the autoerotic satisfactions of one's own person considered as a love object. Similarly an inherent libidinal sadism sublimates into general cruelty or into choice of profession—from butcher to surgeon—affording parallel outlets.

Since the legitimacy of both these concepts is intimately bound up with the story of psycho-sexual development, which penetrates every phase of the Freudian argument, it will be more profitable to consider it critically in that connection, for the present only anticipating the conclusion that the Freudian version of libido and sublimation is distorted through over-emphasis of the sexual factor, as the account of the "unconscious" functions goes wrong (along with other reasons) by over-emphasis of the suppression factor. The two orders of distortion converge; though the critique of Freud's sexology and of his psychopathology offer distinctive as well as common points of attack.

Freudianism when weighed in the scales of science is found seriously wanting. The cardinal defect is the false rendering of the "unconscious" phases of the psychic economy; its great merit is the direction of attention to that phase and its motivating value. I have dwelt upon these logical premises in detail by reason of their many consequences, and because of my preoccupation with the Freudian psychology. The second great defect is the gross sexualization of libido. That affects the practice of psychoanalysis and shapes its popular appeal as well as determines the content of Freudian argument. These pragmatic issues are considered in the following chapters. If psychoanalysis is ever to become a science or its practice a scientific art, its principles must be recast and its temper and procedure reformed. In its present form it is an amazing conglomerate of unsupported conclusions and unnatural assumptions carried out with a speculative abandon close to irresponsibility—all of which make it an outlaw in science.

In this chapter I have had to present for the psychologically minded, the reasons why the Freudian "Ucs" is completely unacceptable. For the lay reader, I can state the conclusions more simply. There is no evidence that any such region or process exists; the functions attributed by Freud to the "Ucs" are unnatural. That subconscious processes appear in the neuroses, in dreams and in lapses is abundantly clear. Their legitimate explanation forms a large problem in psychology.

CHAPTER VII

FREUDIAN ARGUMENT

A thoroughgoing analysis of psychoanalysis is an urgent need; that is the justification of this book. Following the evidence in the case of Freudianism versus other psychologies is an argument. *Freudian argument* refers to the methods by which Freudians derive their "facts" which in turn they interpret, formulate as conclusions, and confidently apply. Such "facts" are not just come upon; they arise from an intensive search for them and commonly in the interests of establishing a thesis. That procedure is perfectly legitimate, indeed often indispensable; one cannot look just in general. Important facts in all fields of research have come by the same route which the Freudians follow. Such facts are often tinged with theory—again not an objection, if so recognized; but the value of fact and theory is one, capital and dividend in the same investment. The "stock" may have a high standing in the market of science; it may be of slight and dubious value, or even worthless and worse. This statement summarizes the nature of the evidence in the case.

In my opinion, Freudian argument in all its objectives—and in each partly for the same, partly for different reasons—is so riddled with fallacies, that my final rating of it is low indeed, though not indiscriminately so. It is because I have confidence in the possibility of a rational psychoanalysis, that I deplore the actual course which this promising movement has taken. My brief maintains that psychoanalysis is guilty of reasoning unbecoming a candidate for scientific status, together with disorderly "logical" conduct injurious to the public mental welfare. The theories of Freud are based upon a web of assumptions fantastically speculative; the conclusions conflict sharply with established relations well supported by psychological evidence from many sources. Freudian argument ignores, distorts and runs the gamut of speculation from the superficially plausible to the completely ridiculous. Freudian argument is so involved, fatuous, specious, ambitious, cryptic, inconsistent, has been spread so wide and so irresponsibly, that I can do little more than sample its grosser errors and major transgressions. These appear in the explanation of lapses; in the interpretation of dreams; in tracing the course of sexual development; in accounting for character-traits.

This is a sweeping condemnation and a comprehensive charge. I am well aware of its implications. It carries the counter-charge of presumption in maintaining that hundreds of able minds have been led into serious error and have in so far wasted their talents and contributed to confusion and retrogression. Such episodes in the tortuous history of ideas are not uncommon; this chapter in that history is in many respects unique. I must give the reader an opportunity to judge the grounds of my conclusions. This involves a long excursion; for the Freudian theory covers a vast domain. In each of these provinces I ask the reader to have in mind the Freudians' positions as I have presented them, at times with critical comments. If the way seems long, let it be remembered that the literature is of staggering proportions. I must at the least supply an eclectic documentation to present the quality of the conclusions which I oppose.

Symptomatic Argument

Freud maintains that certain familiar orders of mental misadventures,—slips of tongue or pen, mishandlings, forgettings, lapses generally—are motivated ruses or escapes of the "unconscious." The first difficulty with this argument is that in terms of the order of behavior in which the principle is supposed to be exemplified, it for the most part just *does not apply;* how important, if and when true, is another matter. The argument regards these common failings as bits of motive, which escape by breaking through the barrier of "unconscious" resistance; they manage to seize the muscles of organized habits and pull the strings, once they are let out of the bag of repression. Such are *positive* (action) lapses. For forgettings or losings (except as the latter are also mislayings), the unwelcome items are said to be pushed out; they are *passive* lapses. By explaining *all* lapses by this formula, Freudian symptomatology ignores the obvious and adequate explanation that the human mental mechanism is imperfect, that the mind is constantly dropping stitches. It is human to err; it seems to be Freudian to divine cryptic causes for the self-evident.

Everybody knows, as every elementary text in psychology explains, the readiness with which delicate coordinations are upset. The evident "cause" of lapses of both orders, positive and negative, is that they arise as inevitable, "natural" consequences of distraction, confusion, inattention, inadvertence. As these occasions occur constantly though irregularly, and often concern trivial matters, most of the pertinent incidents have the quality of "human" accidents. Liability to lapses happens to be a painfully common, highly inconvenient and costly failing. All sorts of articles of convenience and value are lost, mislaid, exchanged, forgotten at every point of the human traffic. Every railway-system, every department-store maintains a "Lost and Found" bureau. If each of the articles that reach these storage-places involved a Freudian tale—lost because of unpleasant associations—it hardly seems probable that they would promptly be reclaimed, or be advertised and rewards offered for their return. Perhaps only a meticulously or fanatically orderly person escapes spending many irritating *quart-heures* in following consciously the clue of his subconscious lapses. Subconscious they are in the sense of handlings in the half-attentions of distraction and the inevitable dropping of some of our memory parcels when our minds are too full, or respond to too many calls. One might as well explain the "wrong numbers" on the telephone exchange by Freudian conflicts in the private affairs of the operators—surely a "lame and impotent conclusion, of which many more, equally lame, equally impotent, are to follow.

A fundamental misgiving arises. If Freud, the master mind of psychoanalysis, in pushing an argument to the extreme, is prepared to ignore such glaringly obvious experience, how can one have confidence in *any* of his conclusions? Dr. Tannenbaum, who at one time practiced psychoanalysis, but abandoned it when convinced of the error of his and its ways, points out the manifold errors of the "psychology of errors" *à la* Freud. He cites a domestic incident. Mrs. T. was peeling potatoes, when three insistent and attention-demanding summons occurred simultaneously: the door bell rang, so did the telephone, also the soup on the stove boiled over. Undecided which summons to attend to first, in her haste she cut her thumb with the paring knife. Setting into action conflicting groups of muscle-habits involves the risk of incoördination; hence the slip and the cut. One could invent a Freudian explanation of self-punishment or other guilt; one could symbolize the thumb and the knife and the onion, or whatever the offending vegetable, delicately or obscenely—*chacun à son goût*. But how unnecessary! and why should the inner compulsion coincide with the outer disturbance?

The retort discourteous would be that the ardent Freudian forgets the obvious because it is inconvenient for his theory; but the reply scientific is that the presence of a minor motive, granted that it is of the censored Freudian order, does not displace the many other factors that enter into the psychology of errors. The fundamental flaw in the entire symptomatic argument is the plain ignoring of familiar workings of the mind. No one questions that the Freudian formula now and then and in part—at times quite shrewdly—applies; the credit for the explicit recognition of what was not quite overlooked before the days of the new analysis, belongs to Freud. He brought these actions into the motivation orbit; he included certain mannerisms which, as character traits of minor import, are similarly revelatory. Symptomatic slips will take their place among the mental automatisms, which by their occasional failure suggest or reveal the subconscious switch that, when mis-set, throws the train of thought or behavior off the track of intention. But the actual chapter as Freud has written it, instead of being slight and simple, cautious and suggestive, proceeds by a series of cumbersome mental acrobatics that make a fictitious mountain out of a factual molehill. The gist of the argument holds. The remoteness of the motives and contortedness of the mechanisms that are resorted to in explanation, make propagandist sophistry of what, soberly carried out, might be a modest scientific contribution.

Immediately as we read, and more strongly as we re-read the motley samples of Freud's symptomatology, are we tempted to ask whether he or we have lost our senses. If the first reading was casual, will the reader re-read critically the exhibits and explanations of Freud, the analyzer, of Freud's the analyzee's, lapses, in item one: walking up, in *abstraction,* a superfluous flight of stairs (page 75); in item two: picking up *in haste* a tuning-fork for a hammer (page 76); in item three: sweeping, *by an awkward movement,* an article off a crowded desk (page 77); in item four: kicking off a dressing-slipper *in a moment of exuberance,* and bringing down a statuette (page 77), and ask himself in all seriousness whether this labored exegesis is science or a scientifically worded jest.

Who has not walked beyond his destination, when his mind *wanders* from the errand to some reflective business of its own? Who has not *in haste* picked up one article for another? Who has not upset things through *inadvertence?* Who has not in an *impulse* of the moment failed to be circumspect? Abstraction, haste, inattention, impulse account for these lapses adequately, and quite as far as they require or permit of explanation. Imagine what life would be if we psychoanalyzed all our lapses continually. It seems almost preferable to go back to the age of superstition when every little action was looked upon as an omen, every event a foreboding of good or ill, and even bits of physiological behavior, from sneezing to ears burning or limbs falling asleep, were "explained" on the fanciful principle of a magical determinism. It is not the inconvenience but the absurdity of the procedure that offends. By such logic one can prove anything, and by the same warrant nothing. If such is the method of Freudian proof, I blame no profitably occupied and clear-witted mind for wanting none of it, for responding when a Freudian rings his telephone: "Line busy," or by hanging up the receiver.

There is also current in the Freudian employment of the symptomatic argument an overlooking of the familiar, which appears like a bit of presumption, making an original discovery of what everybody knows. This tendency to make much ado about very little is so constant and characteristic that it compels attention; it lays bare the mental habit, the making of the psychoanalytic complex,—a complex responsible for a larger share of Freudian literature than any other complex invited by nature or induced or invented by man.

Thus Freud speaks of a bit of stage craft by Elenore Duse which shows "from what depths she draws her art." Jones follows suit and adds: "The action illustrates the profundity of the great actress's character studies." And what is this profound "symptomatic act"? Nothing more than that in a reflective moment, after a quarrel with her husband and the entry of her lover, she plays with her wedding ring, taking it off, putting it back, and finally removing it—a perfectly obvious and familiar bit of stage "business" and quite conscious; for if it were not so, the audience would not follow it understandingly, and the effect would be lost.

The "much ado" distortion spreads over so much of the Freudian doctrine that it makes every critical reader suspicious; it gives him the feeling that under the guise of learning and with the imprint of science, an advocate is trying to "put something over" on him.

Science, it has been frequently observed, makes the unknown known, and the known more intelligible; pseudo-science, in one of its erring moods, attempts to impart to the familiar a specious air of the recondite. Symptomatology, like much else in the rich repertory of Freudian discoveries, proceeds by a disregard of a certain sane perspective for which we have no better and no more complimentary name than common sense.

The Limitations of Determinism

Unquestionably now and then, more or less, plausibly or probably, the argument in one or another of its phase applies. We are constantly playing a game jestwise and seriously between our expressions and our repressions. Certainly, little strands of minor motives mingle with the major motivations and in their failures betray their unsuspected source. All of which is moderately significant if kept within the limits of the reasonable. Escaping that restraint by whatever route, a belief, a theory, an explanation begins to assume the quality of a delusion. The argument is not a reduction but an *elaboration to an absurdity,* a form of fallacy so characteristic that it may in the future become known as the "Freudian fallacy." Above all other mortals the psychoanalyst needs the qualification which he claims, of seeing more truly, more deeply, and more objectively than the untrained mind. If by acquiring depth vision, he overlooks the obvious panorama on the surface, his last estate is sorrier than the first. If to be Freudian, one must become fanatic in one's devotion, that "lapse" will hardly inspire confidence in the psychoanalyst's fitness to restore direction to a disoriented mind. This comprehensive charge against Freudian argument holds aloof many a student otherwise sympathetic with the essential Freudian insights. Reason carried to excess becomes unreason.

The *elaboratio ad absurdum* may be relatively mild in the four cited lapses of Herr Doctor Freud; it becomes flagrant when applied to negative lapses, such as the omission of the word *aliquis* in the elaboration of the Freudian tale "of liquefaction" which will be found by the reader (if it escapes the censor) on page 82 or the positive lapse of the confusion of eye-drops, on page 84, which, if it is typical of an analyst's habit of mind, will not dispose one to entrust one's spiritual welfare to a follower of that profession.

I have stopped to analyze the errors of Freudian ways as applied to the "psychopathology of daily life" for a group of reasons: it is not intensely vital to the central theory which focuses upon the neuroses; it is versatile, touching upon varieties of familiar behavior; the underlying principle is sound, its theory quite correct, and in part familiar; it illustrates the unfortunate quality of Freudian argument in ignoring, in assuming, and in carrying the plausible to the extreme. As actually carried out, its net issue is confusion, distortion, falsity.

I have dwelt upon it for another reason of considerable importance: to make clear at the outset that there are limits to the rational applications of the principle of determinism, which is the thread on which the Freudian beads are strung. Determinism we all admit, for it upholds the principle of cause and effect in the mental world. But to suppose that we can trace the course of determinism in minute detail, and to insist upon doing so by hook and by crook, is to abuse a truth mightily. That way lies the error of charlatanism in character-reading, and the error of superstition as well. Many forms of pseudo-science arise from an originally wrong assignment of antecedent and consequençe, which is another type of error; but straining a right principle beyond the load it can carry, is a mental habit often found in followers of false leads. Ignoring the obvious, disregarding alternative and familiar explanations makes one error; overlooking the limitations of determinism makes the other. In symptomatic actions, in dreams, in our behavior generally, much inevitably remains unaccounted for. A rational view of the principle of determinism is resigned to have it so. Beyond a rather readily recognizable limit, the asking of questions and insistence upon minute answers is a mark not of exceptional curiosity, but of a not well ordered interest. Carried still farther in the temper of Freudian analysis, it vitiates its own merit.

DREAM ARGUMENT

Dreams and Oneirology

Back of the Freudian *dream argument* stands a set of assumptions, some verifiable, others plausible, but for the most part a tissue of near-truths as misleading as unsupported prepossessions. These predetermine the interpretations. The general thesis seems well established that dreams represent an order of psychic procedure closer to the primary fantasy, a compromise between expression and repression, an escape of subconscious trends, a symbolic dramatization in which the surface episodes arise from more deeply motivated meanings. For these enlightenments dream psychology is indebted to the psychoanalytic approach. But when the argument proceeds upon such assumptions as the specific sexual stages of development—presently to be examined—ignores all other factors than the motives or wishes in dreams, injects into the thesis dubious propositions without evidence; when the scheme of interpretation is carried out arbitrarily and even absurdly, the entire structure is jeopardized. In theory and in practice Freud's theory of dreams, when weighed, is found seriously wanting; its measure of insight cannot save it. The result is far more a novel pseudo-scientific brand of oneirology than a scientific study of dreams. My rejection of the larger portion of the general and specific contributions in Freud's *Interpretation of Dreams*—and decidedly so in that of the oneirologists among his followers who, at first leashed to the master's guidance, later run recklessly at large— represents a protest against any brand of diagnostic psychology founded upon a logic so loose and subjective that its conclusions do not, almost cannot acquire, scientific sanction. I do not question that there are some completely Freudian dreams, and many more composite or multi-motivated dreams with a Freudian component. I agree that the explanation of the dream-incident as a veiled symbolic expression of a suppressed erotic desire or of an attitude derived from it, may in many cases be a permissible and even plausible explanation, or the best available. The decipherment can never be assured. An oneirology based upon such conjectures, though far removed from the arbitrary absurdity of the news-stand dream-books, is not a project to be commended. The logical psychologist must decline to be an oneirologist even in the psychoanalytic sense, if he wishes to remain a serious student of dreams.

A scientific study of dreams would proceed by collecting *all dreams without selection* and leave their *interpretation to non-partisan* judges; it would recognize the limitations of "reading" dreams. Nothing less than such a survey could establish such assumptions (stated by Freud as facts) as that dreams protect sleep, that dreams never concern the trivial but only the important, that dreams *always* express desires. These and other propositions are asserted by psychoanalysis without adequate proof, indeed without the ordinary control of checks and balances exercised by any responsible experimentalist. That cautious mode of inquiry is not at all congenial to the spirit of the Freudian logic; had it been so, the formidable and pretentious body of psychoanalytic conclusions would never have been developed. It is safe to predict that any such inquiry, though certain to reveal instances favorable to each such thesis, would not result in the clear-cut, universal generalizations which the Freudian hypothesis requires, and requiring, maintains. As the baffled pupil in arithmetic, "gets" the answer indicated as correct in the back of the book by ingenious but mathematically unaccredited processes, so the Freudian disciple has the answer in the front of his mind and proceeds similarly. Whatever the measure of truth in the Freudian dream theory, the verdict upon the total structure—principles and argument—is decidedly negative. It is so on both counts: the propositions concerning dreams set down as established are not proven, with a large presumption against their validity; the dream interpretation is carried out as an indefensible oneirology. So partial, extravagantly elaborated and fancifully applied a theory hardly merits the equally elaborate investigation requisite to refute it. There is slight purpose in discussing minutely the improbability of statements so irresponsibly set forth.

Not to leave the argument without illustration, consider the psychoanalytic theory of nightmare. It is difficult to understand how these most terrifying of all dream experiences protect sleep. Ernest Jones, interpreting Freud, makes this the exception that proves the rule. "When the distortion of the wish-fulfillment is insufficient to conceal from consciousness the nature of the suppressed desire, in other words when the conflict is so great that no compromise can be arrived at, then the sleep is broken and the subject wakes to his danger." Another Freudian suggests that the slumbering Ego sets off the censorial alarm-clock, arouses his bed-fellow, the Super-ego, to help him squelch the Id; the emergency call is a nightmare! But Jones continues, true to psychoanalytic form, that the only deep enough concern requiring such drastic methods, is sexual—specifically incest. So the completed formula reads: *"An attack of the nightmare is an expression of a mental conflict over an incestuous desire."*

Since it must be so, it remains only to develop devices of interpretation, though as illogical and unpsychological as the young arithmetician's devices are unmathematical, to bring the premises in accord with the answer. Dr. Jones discusses other causes of nightmare, cautiously. He recognizes the influence of posture, of digestion, of faulty respiration, and most of all the individual susceptibility: some persons are by their nervous constitution peculiarly mune or vulnerable to nightmare and others wholly immune. But the italicized statement—italics his—shows the unreserve that vitiates so much of Freudian argument. He is not content to enumerate the psychoanalytic, including the sexual, factor which undoubtedly operates in (some) nightmares, but insists that it is *the* factor, and in detail is an expression of the nuclear sexual complex which is the universal Freudian answer to all psychic disturbance.

The Cult of Dream-Symbols

The addiction to a form of argument which turns dream-psychology toward oneirology is likewise responsible for the Freudian psychoanalytic dictionary of *dream-symbols,* hardly more respectable for all its learned assurance than the arbitrary and fanciful assignments of popular "dream-books." His adherence to a minute determinism is his ruin. His dictum is absolute: *"It is always a strict law of dream-interpretation that an explanation must be found for every detail."* (Italics mine, but the dogmatism his.) It is precisely the use of "always," "strict," "law," "must," "detail," that exceeds the logical warrant of the thesis. The second lure is the cult of symbols; for without that dream interpretation—legitimate and otherwise—is limited in its operations.

Obviously symbol-making abounds; metaphor, simile, analogy, words themselves are variously symbolic. Minds sharing experiences and emotions, traditions and environment, will "naturally" develop similar symbols; though, as Freud fully recognizes, most symbols are individual; each dreamer uses a dictionary of his own. "Free association" is required to determine the clue to the symbol as it arises in the individual's mind. There is, indeed, a legitimate study of symbolism, to which study psychoanalysis has furnished an additional incentive. Jung is the psychologist of symbolism *

* I take this occasion to repeat that the readiness with which we dream and in such dreams use symbols and similarly imaginative procedures, has its basis in the naturalness of fantasying, in the primacy of this mental movement in the child's mind, to all of which Freud has given renewed and enlightening attention. Through the Freudian psychology fantasying and day-dreaming has come to its own. As Freud employs the fantasying tendency in the development of neuroses through fixations of the libido, the argument will recur

par excellence; he values it for its embodiment of the mind's predilections, of the method and mood of the freer mental movement, as well as for its psychoanalytical employment, and follows it into the deeper obscurities and higher mysteries of mysticism. At its best, symbolism is acceptable and often obvious; at its worst it is oneirology pure and simple, only not notably pure and not conspicuously simple.

The motivation factor in dreams and the disguising symbolism of its expression is peculiarly complicated by the sex motif. The result is a *sexualized oneirology;* and that at its worst is a crude as well as a lewd form of "cross-word" puzzle. Kings, queens, children, snakes, horses, fishes, figs, apples, seeds, bananas, canes, umbrellas, caskets, closets, ovens, wagons, barrels, revolvers, drain-pipes, sprinkling pots, targets, balconies, windows, doors, entrances, exits, airplanes, Zeppelins, water, landscapes, hills, mounting, descending, entering, withdrawing, flying, falling, swimming, boating, losing trains, wandering in the dark: all these have been genitalized—male or female, only not fine or superfine, by psychoanalytic imagery, and placed on the uncensored side of the dream dictionary. On the censored side, appear all the organs and operations, incident to sexual acts and their antecedents and consequences. Thus is established the psychoanalytic thesaurus of synonyms.* The distortions necessary to construe the dream situations into the sexual conflicts adds personal

in that connection. On the value of fantasy, its relation to the pleasure principle, and its employment of symbols, there is a fair agreement.

* The extravagance of the method invites ridicule, most appropriately in terms of the science which is the exemplar of rigid demonstration. Birdwood's *Sex Elements in the First Five Books of Euclid* is wittier and intrinsically no more far-fetched than the sexualization of canes and ovens. A straight line bisecting a circle becomes hardly a fit proposition to present to adolescent minds versed in Freudian symbolism.

insult to logical injury. Obviously anyone so disposed can take any dream and subject it to this process, and it will come out genitalized and revelatory.

The Freudian dream technique has other resources. By tapping in turn the associations of each item in the dream, one can go on and on through indifferent or non-sexual associations, until something is reached capable of the desired interpretation; if enough hands are dealt, some will be vulnerable. If it has the wrong meaning, the dream symbol may be reversed; if the patient recognizes, admits, or even volunteers the sexual and guilty meaning, the point is proved; a denial shows that the association obtains in the "unconscious," or that his resistance impedes its recognition. Yet this wilful execution does not exclude the soundness of the approach; for dreams must in the nature of things point at times vaguely, at times definitely to intimate conflicts and desires, including sexual ones. Freudians are not content to stop there; creed-bound, they show the same courage of their convictions as animates the fanatics, paranoiacs and monomaniacs whom they analyze.

The composite fallacy of Freudian oneirology arises from its false sexology, its strained symbolism, its exaggerated determinism. With one's allegiance to logic compromisable, and the employment satisfying to one's temperament, anyone could take the parts of the house in which Dr. Freud lives, the objects on his desk, the furnishings of his study, bedroom, bath-room and kitchen, the articles of his wardrobe, the contents of the show-window of the nearest hardware shop, or sports shop, or china shop (with or without a bull in it), and genitalize them all with no more distortion of their primary intention nor violence to the logic of sobriety than obtains in constructing the Freudian dictionary of dream-symbols. One's disinclination to engage in this enterprise is not a latent Puritanic resistance, but an enlightened prejudice in favor of logic and sanity.

The fallacy of oneirology reaches the height of absurdity when significance is attached to a single detail arbitrarily. That appears in Jung's numerology.

He cites the fragment of a dream of a married man engaged in an extra-marital affair. The detail appears as a "subscription" and a "manager" who comments upon the high number of the subscription, 2477. It is suspected that this number has a financial signifiance. As the dreamer has a frugal mind the number may represent the expense of his illicit venture, which a more exact reckoning makes *2387* francs "which could only be arbitrarily translated into *2477.*" By "free association" it was determined that by adding the numbers of the birthdays of himself, his mistress, his wife, his mother, his two children, his present age, and the present age of his mistress (together with two other numbers not wholly intelligible), the total is *2477,* the numbers being derived by writing his own birthday (Feb. 26th) as *262* or the *26*th day of the *2*nd month. The sum is *2477;* and it is assumed that the calculation was made by the "unconscious" who also devised the code.

When the number *152* appears in a dream as a stake in a game, the house-numbers of the residences of this complaisant but migratory lady afford the clue. For she lived successively at number *17* on one street, number *129* on another, then at number *48:* which added make *194; 194 — 48 = 146.* At present she was living at number *6.* Hence the dream equation: *146 + 6 = 152.* The dream is now solved!

The problems of the patient "are mirrored in the unconscious of his wife." Her whole dream was: *Luke 137*, which interpreted as *Luke i, 37* refers to the annunciation; and as *Luke xiii, 7*, refers to a fig-tree, "from antiquity a symbol of the male genital," which symbol is again brought into relation with her husband's impotency regarding herself. As she, the dreamer, is not conversant with the Bible, the dream-number must be conceived as "cryptomnesia," or a form of second sight!

The absurdity of the conclusion is exceeded only by the paranoiac illogicality by which it is reached. Yet this example occurs in a learned treatise by an eminent scholar. I bring this critique of dream argument to a climax with this specimen not as typically Freudian—for Jung is the numerologist, though Freud is quite as *outré*—but to illustrate what indulgence in such logical contortions can do to an otherwise able and creative mind. Oneirology may be regarded as an illicit venture in argument for which the defense of absurdity is the price. For Jung defends this "Significance of Number Dreams" by such specious explanations as that

the study of free creative fantasy "requires a broad empiricism" and "a high measure of discretion as to the accuracy of individual results"; "but this in no wise obliges us to pass over in silence what is active and living, for fear of being execrated as unscientific. There must be no parleying with the superstition-phobia of the modern mind; for this itself is a measure by which the secrets of the unconscious are kept veiled."

Whom the gods would destroy they first make mad! One is tempted to suspect that a similar preliminary operation is performed upon novitiates into the psychoanalytic brotherhood of oneirologists.

It may seem unfair to conclude the dream argument upon this fantastic note. Freudian principles of dream interpretation do not inevitably converge to this height of the ridiculous or depth of the absurd; the diagnostic insight may be maintained on the level of reason and plausibility. But there seems to be something in the intellectual atmosphere in which the Freudian culture thrives, that inclines to carrying faulty premises to extravagant conclusions. The followers of Freud, deriving their license from the example of the master, enter upon the enterprise with loose standards of evidence and a conviction of the irrelevance of accredited areas of established psychology. Travelling with such light logical luggage and sighting their goal ahead, they go fast and far, though often circling tortuously before making the desired landing. Of all psychic products, dreams have the most varied composite of determining factors, most of them vague, shadowy, sinuous, chaotic, shifting, enigmatic. To select one of these factors— the private or neurotic conflict—as *the* supreme one-and-only, universal determinant, and then impose upon it a highly conjectural formula with a fore-ordained set of sexual values, is a bizarre parody of the methods of science in the interests of a crudely disguised prepossession. A dream psychology, not without valid support, is thus blighted from root to blossom. The logical sins of an erring though creative theorist are visited upon the disciples to the third and fourth generation. Even Freud cannot make oneirology creditable.

PSYCHO-SEXUAL DEVELOPMENT

Sex in Psychology

Freudian argument rarely moves far from sex. Freud finds the sources of neurotic symptoms in the formative influence of childhood impressions, and increasingly in the part played by early and intense sexual attachments within the family, as well as in traumas or emotional shocks and in the course of sexual enlightenment. This addition to the theory of the neuroses was destined to become the corner-stone of the completed structure, as that assumed its sexual dominance. Adding one "discovery" to another, through revelations obtained in the psychoanalytic sanctum, Freud reconstructed or resurrected the lost, suppressed biography of libido, as it may have existed not in the primitive cave-man, but as he finds it persisting in the aboriginal infant. Such was the "discovery" upon which he staked his professional fortune. Thus man in the Freudian version became *homo libidinalis*.

The freer and franker recognition of the sex life in the human make-up is all to the good; it is well to see sex steadily and to see it whole. The trend in that direction was well set in advance of Freud. Havelock Ellis is the most influential of the pioneers of this enlightenment. The twentieth-century spirit of emancipation served as a powerful social factor in the same direction, meeting with the usual revolutionary hazard that liberty may turn to license. Within the domain of psychology, the reaction had set in against what Wheeler—an entomologist who looks at the *Foibles of Insects and Men*—calls the "rose-water psychologies of the academic type," . . . "born and bred in a belfry." The protest was expressed long ago by Stanley Hall, who recognized the momentous play of sex-derived, and sex-tinged traits in the near and far evolution of human character as projected in careers and institutions. Hall's genetic psychology emphasized the sex component in personalities, in religious expressions particularly, such as the renunciations of the cloister in reactions to frustrations of the hearth. He found the major defect of James's *Varieties of Religious Experience* in its neglect of this vital factor. Wheeler turned to psychoanalysis for illumination and in a measure found it there, albeit in a "veritable cesspool of learning." His comment concerning psychologists, that the habit of "sitting down together or with the philosophers and seeing who can hallucinate fastest or most subtly and clothe the results in the best English, is not helping us very much in solving the terribly insistent problems of life," may be accepted as a deserved reproach; and yet the psychoanalysts, definitely bent upon human service, have introduced a form of "hallucinating" far more ambitious and far less defensible than the armchair indulgence. They specifically accept the obligations of a science and present their conclusions under that aegis. The best of insights applied with feeble logic parallels the failure of good intentions.

To bring sex into the focus of psychic motivation was an essential step in depth psychology, though the transition from sex secretive to sex incandescent came with unhygienic suddenness. The credit for its establishment may in part be assigned to Freud; the discredit of the untenable execution of the project is responsibly his, and flagrantly that of his followers. Freud's over-emphasis of the sexual libido and the manner of its dominance was a major point of issue that led to Jung's secession. The detailed plot of the psycho-sexual development as asserted and applied, is of all the questionable Freudian doctrines the most so. Infant sexual-

ity is the one nub of contention; the Oedipus relation
the other; the determination of character-traits by fixation in the stages of sex development is a third member
of the strange sex-trilogy. If the extravagant and hypothetical pronouncements on these three aspects of sex
were eliminated from the psychoanalytic gospels, or
had never been incorporated into them, there would remain a fairer possibility of a serviceable psychoanalytic
sexology. In view of the actual position this suggestion
would be regarded by orthodox Freudians as even more
emasculating than the dreaded loss of potency which
plays such a lurid part in the dismal drama; which
drama may prove (as I believe) to be a Freudian nightmare.

Infantile Sexuality

The cardinal error of Freud's conjectural genetic
psychology is the assumption that the *primal form* in
psychic development is in essence the *final form,* that
its meaning must be read by anticipation, thus introducing a unique "inversion" psychology. He seems to have
forgotten that the stages of genesis are not reversible
and not prophetic; growth is a one-way traffic. There
is indeed, a unitary development, binding and bridging
earlier and maturer phases of expression. The child is
father to the man in a genetic, not in an anticipatory
sense; the child is not the master of the man, as Freud
insists. One might as properly interpret the infant's
chuckle as a precocious anticipation of a subtle witti-
cism, or Freudianize it as a secret infantile enjoyment
of a Rabelaisian jest; or endow the infant's tears at the
loss of its bottle with the grief of mature tragedy; or—
distinguishing neither urges nor situations—see in the
infant's addiction to said bottle the prognosis or infan-

tile stage of the drunkard's indulgence. To ignore every-thing that occurs between the nursery caress and the seal of betrothal, and read the mature "cathexis" of the latter in the soothing effect of the former, is about as completely unpsychological a procedure as a perverse psychologist could devise. Such "genetic psychology" is crassly ungenetic.

What similarity of general pleasure-stimulation there is between the infantile overture and the dénouement which ensues many acts and scenes later as the issue of the gradual development of the psyche, including prominently its sexual components, offers no basis for composing an elaborate, detailed love-sick drama upon a minor infantile incident. Since life is growth, the *primal* form of an urge is not the *final* form; the *germinal* is not the *terminal* situation. A tyro in psychology would avoid such a gross confusion; only a boldly original but prepossessed mind would be tempted into its acceptance.

Once this fallacy is committed and all logical con-science abandoned, one is indeed free to elaborate the consequences of such unwarranted identification *ad libitum,* which in this reference becomes *ad libidinem.* Freud's proclivity to accept the abnormal as the stand-ard for the normal—not as its end-term or as deviation from it, which is the legitimate employment *—lured him into naming the infantile manifestations in terms of what, if persistent in maturity, would constitute a per-

---

* Let me repeat, since Freudians are as adept in misunderstanding what psychologists accept as what they reject, that the principle of abnormal psychology which recognizes the abnormal as the end-term of the normal with analogies and similarities of processes in the graded series between, has no relation to making the abnormal the standard of the normal. Freudians cannot take credit for the assimi-lation and affiliation of normal and abnormal behavior, for that was established independently of their specific interpretation of the relation.

version. Consequently the infant is classified as a creature "polymorphous perverse"—truly a horrible example, not of original sin, but of logical violation in conception. Having at that inexperienced stage no other pleasure-field—falsely called love-object—than its own body, it is pronounced auto-erotic (a term suggested by Havelock Ellis for sexual self-love); or Narcissistic, a far maturer sin with a wider connotation. By the same untenable identification, any marked attachment at a later stage to playmates of the same sex becomes evidence of a latent homosexuality; and early and late, the bond of devotion between a male child and his mother is set forth as embryonic incest: "a general human characteristic decreed by fate" and Freud. Such perversions, since they occur sporadically among the adult abnormal, are inferred to be present universally by inherited taint *ab initio*, with no more warrant than a superficial resemblance in one phase of expression which, in the two settings, has totally different origins and values.

This crude *fallacy of identification* is invited by a set of *theoretical assumptions* underlying it. The "genetic fallacy" alone would never have developed the "family romance"; one false assumption led to another, and to the strangest of all: that we attain the normal by passing through the abnormal; as though we attained sanity by successively being inflicted by, and "dissolving" the several varieties of insanity, or saintliness by way of an exhaustive repertory of sin. The whole of this bizarre doctrine is impure assumption, and unpsychological besides; which means that there is adequate basis for a completely different version of the genetic story. With infantile sexuality once assumed, later perversions are explained as regressions to it—again a valid concept, invalidly applied. And so the orbit of Freudian fallacy, cycle upon cycle, cumulates and diverges farther from the truth in its gyrating complications.

The pleasure principle stands, and psychology is indebted to Freud for its richer formulation. There are certain pleasure-giving zones important in infantile life, which were unfortunately called erogenous. Had they been spoken of as *hedonic*, the "infantile" catastrophe might have been avoided, and Oedipus have remained a classic myth, known only to the elect. Pleasure is at first simple, diffuse, primary; the infant cuddles for warmth, security, nourishment, as do cubs of other mammals, whose incapacity for anthropoid cerebral development saves them from the charge of embryonic incest.* The fact that primary and earlier pleasure-sensations enter and combine with secondary and later-appearing effects, gives no shadow of a warrant for reading the mature connotations into the immature manifestations. F. Lyman Wells, a close student of hedonic psychology and wholly favorable to the better established Freudian principles, neatly labels this Freudian confusion as a "great anticipatory misnomer." "Polymorphous perverse" psychology probably contains more loose and false thinking than any fallacy of our enlightened and yet blundering attempts to explain ourselves.

The "great misnomer" is part of an inverted "genetic" psychology on a great scale. In consequence thereof, "sexual" in psychoanalytic usage, has been

---

* Apparently intelligent animals are not quite spared the tribulations of the genetic sexology that afflicts humans. "When a dog licks his injured paw tenderly for hours on end, it is an unjustified rationalization to assume that he intends this to be a medical treatment, the disinfection of his wound or some such thing. Much more plausible is the presumption that an increased amount of his libido has been directed to the injured limb, so that he regards it with a tenderness otherwise reserved only for his genitals." This medley of absurdity is the serious opinion of an eminent psychoanalyst. It is not a parody.

spread so thin that it covers everything in the line of bodily incited pleasure; is so attenuated that a trace of it is discoverable everywhere, even though in homeopathic doses. Yet this partial ingredient is regarded as determining the entire affect and as justifying the name appropriate to the consummation which becomes in due course specifically sexual. This playing fast and loose with words is an unworthy casuist defense. The composite fallacy is far more than verbal; it involves a complete inversion of the actual relations of general bodily pleasure and specifically erotic affects.

"What we have to start with are a number of possibilities for pleasurable reaction, between which a developmental selection takes place; and for the best of evolutionary reasons, those are the most likely to survive and flourish, which are involved with the reproductive instinct. But, of course, the underlying *Lusttrieb* of the organism may develop in various ways, without relation even to the genital areas, not to mention sexuality."

Such is Wells' lucid formulation of the actual psychology of hedonic development. Underlying the "infantile" fallacy is the allied fallacy of the *libido* concept, which vitiates in so many ways the entire Freudian sexology. Its critique will appear in later considerations. Through the vestibule of infantile sexuality, we approach the throne-room of "Oedipus," the king-complex and his court.

Oedipus, the Rex Complex

The "Oedipus complex" is indeed complex; it is a tangled tale of many tissues; its logical analysis requires a patient following. It is prolific, however regarded, in my opinion a prolific progeny of assumptions issuing from a false premise. Assuming it is the original logical error; the universalizing of it, the dissolving of it, the elaborating of its issues follow. The "family romance" would be an absurd comedy of errors, were it not so dismal a tragedy when accredited as a doom. Yet running through it all is an erratic vein of validity; this strand of truth is far from validating the plot in all its circumstance. The relations of the family circle are indeed formative; their strong hold upon the plastic stages of development, not the destiny of an inherent tendency to perversion, makes them so.

Yet in all the Freudian flood of communications, as copious as unsavory, recounting the adventures of the Freudian "Oedipus," I find no definite statement of how the incest theory arose. One may read and re-read that it was "discovered" in the analysis. This, stripped to its factual content, means that the theory was found acceptable by some neurotic sufferers submitting to analysis; that incidents and relations in their childhood, including fantasies, could be described in such terms by the usual procedures of the Freudian confession in which fact, fantasy, suggestion and prepossession are intricately interactive. And once started, it was accepted eagerly by the disciples as a shibboleth of their faith. The best established and most common finding could be quite adequately described as an overattachment to the mother, a case of imperfect psychic weaning. This genetic hazard has been known through all times, as the phrase: "tied to mother's apronstrings" testifies. The sexualizing of this relation is the truly novel interpretation. If I Freudianize and declare that the apron-strings symbolize and indicate the umbilical cord, the interpretation would be as novel and as warranted. To convert this idle suggestion into a "discovery" of an "Umbilical Complex" requires only that one ignore biologically the function of the umbilical cord and the developmental stages at which it functions, and to ignore psychologically and sociologically all the circumstances that lead to apron-strings, confident that all meanings are sexual; then, with this beautiful if not aesthetic thesis in mind, delve into the unconscious of a few complacent patients, tap a few free associations—free, but guided toward the complex—add disdainful remarks concerning Puritanic resistances, and a new dogma and not a few pages will have been added to the annals of psychoanalysis, which is the Rialto where assumptions congregate. Of the making of complexes on this pattern of construction, there is no end; for the welfare of psychology, there should have been no beginning.

As to the name, the classic Oedipus myth happens not to fit the Freudian circumstance at all. The storied Oedipus was reared by foster-parents, and knew not his mother until he was mature, indeed as a post-marital revelation; otherwise the oracle would have been unfulfilled. It is the intensive infantile attachment that is made responsible for the Freudian fate. No matter! *Oedipus* the king of old, could have had no "Oedipus" fixation. If the "Oedipus" had been called the *X complex*, the name would have served as well. The puzzling point is how anyone conceived the idea that such a relation inhered in infantile psycho-sexual development. It seems clear that the "incest" theory came first, the name later.

Dr. Ramus, though a follower of Freud, comments that to interpret an intensive son-to-mother attachment "as incestuous, either consciously or subconsciously, strikes me as being labored and unnatural. It suggests that Freud, or whoever first thought of it in this connection, had deliberately searched for a myth on which to hang his new incest theory, and having found the Oedipus myth, adopted it as being the nearest he could find to what he wanted.

"Infantile sexuality"—such is my analysis—was a needed premise for the assumption of the "Oedipus complex." Only a strongly sexualized being would develop an "Oedipus" at that tender age. As every man has an "Oedipus," ergo, we must all be infantilely sexualized. The circular reasoning would at least have the barren merit of consistency if the circle had a factual center; as a fact the entire construction is spun around an hypothesis and an unnatural one.

However, we must not linger in reflection at the threshold. Undismayed by the eccentric logical behavior of our guide, as intrepid voyagers we enter the kingdom of the Freudian Oedipus.

This "most characteristic and important finding in all psychoanalysis" includes infantile sexuality, which "is the most novel and important of the psychoanalytical contributions" (Jones). The Oedipus complex is "such an important thing that the manner in which one enters and leaves it cannot be without its effects" (Freud).

First, it is *assumed* that there *is* an Oedipus situation; second, that it *is important* for future development; third, being important, it follows that *it is important how one enters it or leaves it*. All of which *is* important, if true. Looking for facts subject to observation, one meets the over-attachments within the family.

The needs of maturing emphasize the desirability of growing out of them. The evidence is strong that in the neurotically disposed the failure to outgrow these bonds is far more than the usual liability, and that the over-mothering of the spoiled child has untoward consequences; yet this handicap may have any value from zero to the main factor in any given case.

That these childish attachments are reanimated at puberty, amongst them the emotionalities of the "Oedipus complex" is an anti-genetic assumption. What occurs at puberty is not a "reanimation" in any sense; as well expect creeping and crawling and sucking and tantrums to be "reanimated." And granting a liberal extension of the later effect of the too concerned and too closely guiding, and again of the doting and hot-house type of loving parent, it is certainly a remote though not impossible issue, that the fixation upon father or mother by daughter and son respectively, prevents or affects choice in mating because the daughter is looking for father in all her suitors, the son for mother in his courtship; or in turn, that the over-mothered son is looking for a mother more than for a mate in his wedded life. Such eventualities may be considered sensibly and not as issues of an "Oedipus" tie. For obviously it is the continuance of false parental and filial relations through many years, and the adolescent and later relations and frictions of family life that affect the issue. Jung's assumption that Freud's assumption of an incest desire is a symbolic expression to return to the arms or the womb of the mother, or Rank's further assumption that the so-called "Oedipus" is a "rebirth fantasy, reverberating the anxiety associated with the birth trauma," is equally wild, equally baseless; yet all cannot be true. One assumption is as valid as another, for all lack even the possibility

of proof. How such situationally explicit urges become
developed in a cortically immature brain is a mystery,
and how these traits got into the heredity passes understanding or escapes consideration. Such assumptions
serve as springboards for more ambitious somersaults
into the unverifiable, which may be followed with shocks
or thrills in what Henshaw Ward would call the circus
of the Freudian intellect. "Hallucinating," fabricating
and improvising with the aid of an appropriate vocabulary results in the Freudian sex extravaganza.

Freud's Oedipus complex develops a progeny of
secondary complexes, all parthenogenetically conceived
by the same fertility of assumption. The *incest* assumption, as love of mother, entails *envy of father*, and
that in turn generates *hostility* and the desire to *displace* him. But the father is also *feared*, for the father
is *authority*, and the father *threatens*. But *what* does
he threaten? To answer that question the same "hallucinating" facility is put to work. Since the answer
must be a sexual threat, there comes into being another
bizarre complex, the *Castration complex*, upon which
uncensored volumes have been written. Not a vestige
of proof outside of childish fantasy or a nurse's or
parent's unwisdom. But what a choice addition to a
sexual theory!

One might suppose that assumption had reached
its limits, and confusion could not be worse con-
founded. But there remains one slight difficulty:
Oedipus was a male, and psychoanalysis taking its
clue from sex, must be made applicable to either
sex. Nothing daunted, the psychoanalyst makes the
plot reversible, a garment suitable to both sexes and
all psychological climates. Electra in peculiar mourning comes to the rescue; for what she mourns is the

very loss which the father threatens. It is assumed by the childish fantasy that she is the castrated being, and there is "discovered" by the method of assumption raised to a higher power, that she so regards herself and is consumed with envy of the male's more complete anatomy.

Nor is *this* the limit of assumption. A psychoanalyst of the feminine persuasion has discovered a feminine phase in the male's development, a *"Femininity complex,"* when like the girl he accuses the mother; while the girl blaming the mother for her own defective anatomy turns for compensation to the father; and, not to be outdone, a male psychoanalyst describes a *"Masculinity complex"* in the female, engendered by the same fatal knowledge of conspicuous sex differences—which surely is not such a recondite secret that its discovery should be either a mystery or a shock. While the stern, paternal attitude which makes the young son cringe before the father, is sexualized as the "Castration (threat) complex," the corresponding attitude in the young daughter becomes a "Castration (accomplished) complex"; thus both "Oedipus" and castration are successfully universalized to fit all genders. "As we learn from our psychoanalytic work, all women feel that they have been injured in their infancy and that through no fault of their own they have been slighted and robbed of a part of their body; and the bitterness of many a daughter towards her mother has as its ultimate cause the reproach that the mother has brought her into the world as a woman instead of a man"—(Freud).

Whether question-marks or exclamation-marks would be the more appropriate unverbalized comment upon this choice morsel of Freudian logic, I leave to my feminine readers.

However, Freudian sex is versatile. The "Oedipus" is affected by "the complicating element introduced by bi-sexuality."

A *"complete Oedipus"* is both "positive" and "negative" or inverted, combining in various degrees of emotional intensity (cathexis) "a father identification and mother object-love with a mother identification and father object-love"; likewise, the "amount of cathexis (emotional intensity) distributed to either the positive or negative situation depends partly upon the relative strength of the innate masculine or feminine disposition in the boy and also upon experiential factors." The "Oedipus" has an "anaclitic" origin, which means no more than the familiar mammalian dependence. The attachment of boy to mother as nurse and protector "results naturally at the phallic stage in her becoming the love-object." The girl begins in the same way, but changes when she discovers her lack of the male organ. The "girl's libido must now slip into the new position and take the father as love-object," and her "Oedipus" culminates "in a desire which is long cherished to be given a child by her father as a present." This leads to hostility toward the mother; while in childish fantasy even the culmination of the boy's "unconscious Oedipus wish is to give birth to a baby in some vague manner."

I can find no slightest warrant in biology, physiology or psychology for the remote possibility of any item of these "hallucinated" relations. I find well established principles in all these sciences that point to their utter impossibility except as fantasies in which children indulge as non-logical beings, and Freudians as "illogical" adepts. It is all a medley of confused relations taken *ad lib.* from any and all stages of the genetic development and fused with all the contradictions of scrambled stages. The reply to this charge is always that these unnatural relations, urges, reflections, take place in the "unconscious," which is a dark cavern where nothing is visible but anything may be reported as happening, as free from verification as what goes on on the other side of the moon. Or it is dream or fantasy which *ex hypothesi* has equal validity with fact. Freudian argument thus becomes Freudian casuistry. Without the confirmation of quotation-marks, readers would suspect me of maliciously inventing this unique "genetic" psychology. It is actually developed as learned doctrine by trained men of science in technical treatises caviare to the general public, whose deprivation I have attempted to relieve.

Even this is not the climax in the series; for there is also an "anthropological" psychology, autochthonous on Freudian soil.

"In the soul-life of present-day children the same archaic moments still prevail which generally prevailed at the time of primitive civilization." Back of this pretentious formulation is the lame logic of the recapitulation theory, in that application long since exploded. Truly evolution leaves its recapitulatory trail and atavisms occur, but not in a fashion supporting such a remote application. The child's unconscious is here supposed to reënact adult urges for which social relations of aeons ago evolved complex regulations. The taboo against incest (on the origin and significance of which anthropologists are not agreed) is held as evidence of its "natural universal occurrence." That we are unaware of our fate is the result of our "Ucs," seething with suppressed incest-strivings, bequeathed from cave-man days and ways. And paralleling anthropology is geology.

"Educational and analytic work must both alike repeat the latency period (which I have made bold to regard as a residue of primeval deprivations dating perhaps from the Glacial Epoch) and bring it to a new and successful conclusion. In this work the physician must take over the rôle of father or primal father, whilst the patient must be in that state of susceptibility which involves regression to the group mind" (Ferenczi).

Geology leaves its psychoanalytic residue in "glacial" character-traits. Perhaps the next stage is to account for "frigidity" in the female of the species by a parallel argument. Truly fearful and wonderful are the ways of scientists, when they have official sanction to hallucinate, like Macbeth, "thick coming fancies."

The fantasies and fallacies of Freudian forensics continue trailing clouds of glory, as ordinary logic is left behind in the earthly dust of fact. A further bit of confusion, neither genetic nor archaic, but modern and sophistic enters: the amazing thesis that what is prohibited must be strongly desired. Like many another argument, it harbors a truth in its right setting, and becomes an absurdity in a false rendering. Do we infer from the severe penalties attached to murder that we are all constantly struggling against that impulse? That we began, as infants with homicidal urges in the cradle, and the actual murderers were either *fixated* at the stage of "social" development, or later *regressed* to it? Or, reversing the argument, do we infer from the

Honor thy father and thy mother precept an inherent, deeply unconscious urge to degrade them? What is astounding in all this flight of logic-free fancy is the deliberate ignoring of obvious areas of experience that go into the formation of human prescriptions and proscriptions, from the Ten Commandments down. We must also bear in mind the "socialized" factor in taboos. Many orders of prohibitions, noble and ignoble in intent, rational and irrational, flourished and continue by virtue of tradition and possibly of a legalized prejudice. These suggest an unexpected field for further psychoanalytic research. There is the controversial "deceased wife's sister" episode. Shall we assume a strong universal, infantile suppressed sister-in-law incest-striving at the basis of such prohibition . . . which curiously affected only Englishmen—likewise an interesting psychoanalytical inquiry! Or we may recall that among some less enlightened tribes, a brother is obliged to take into his family wife and offspring of a deceased brother. Surely and somehow this confirms the theory by the usual reversals of relations and identifications permissible in Freudian argument! Not to leave this temptation without a name, let us call it the "Leah-Rachel" complex and await its psychoanalytical confirmation. By such logic, we can easily construct a sinner's calendar of complexes, and like "Ruddigore" commit a crime a day in the unconscious to appease an ancient doom. Or it would be tempting to write a Freudo-Mosaic Decalogue, beginning: "Thou shalt not covet thy mother, nor murder thy father, except in the Ucs—where thy days are numbered," and ending, who knows where?

It would seem as though the inscription over the doorway of the Freudian house read: *All logic abandon, ye who enter here.* Yet "Oedipus" is the keystone of the arch: *"All other conclusions of psychoanalytical theory are grouped around this complex, and by the truth of this finding psychoanalysis stands or falls"*; the italics are mine, the pronouncement that of the most distinguished Freudian apostle in England, Ernest Jones. If so, the edifice crumbles into a pitiful heap of débris; it is built upon the sands. "Oedipus" reflects a morbid imagination, disordered by intoxicating draughts of fermented reasoning. In my opinion, the valid part of the psycho-sexual theory is more secure without the unwarranted assumption of the "Oedipus" as a universal genetic stage of development. For no one questions that development is psycho-sexual in a true and important sense. If psychoanalytical psychology is to make any authentic contribution, it must refrain from wild psycho-mythology. At present the "hallucinating" goes solemnly on, projecting as fact what seems to fit the initial theory, and in learned jargon developing as doctrine relayed in the psychoanalytic clinic, the scores of figments that emerge annually from the psycho-analytic mills, which though they do not grind slowly, grind exceeding fine.

Sexualized Personality

Our excursion into the realm where "Oedipus" is king may at times have suggested the travels of a psychological Gulliver to strange peoples of strange natures with strange ways. That impression will be strengthened by the further account of the sources of character-traits of the Houyhahnms that dwell in Freudland, in whom we are bidden to recognize the replicas of ourselves. The key to character analysis *à la* Freud is found in the inconsiderate anatomical dispensation of nature, reflected in the medical specialty known as "G.U." (genito-urinary). Freud "discovered" a "G-U" stage in childhood which extends to a general "excretory" occupation. The "discovery" comes out of the Pandora's box of analysis; it is supported by childish fantasy; it appears in childhood interests, readily confirmed. The taboo that extends from G to U by anatomical dispensation extends by physiological kinship to the excretory functions. It is assumed that pleasurable as well as interesting sensations attract the child to them. The interest is reënforced by the privacy that grows about their performance, and the emphasis placed upon their control. Toilet and bath-room form a legitimate group of nursery interests. They hardly constitute the inner sanctum of the psychic life of any normally occupied child. That they influence its future in such momentous ways as character-formation is a long-range conclusion indeed. Had the idea arisen in folk-ways or as a nurse's belief, it would have been recorded as a weird superstition; in the book of Freud it becomes scientific gospel.

The prelude to the tale is on safe ground. The first book—the genesis—of this development is wholly in accord with genetic psychology. The first center of active interest is the mouth. "Oral" psychic life is as authentic at the infant level as the thymus or the fontanel. By the primacy of the sensory field of the intake, the mouth becomes the apprehensive center, antedating the hand; pleasure is nature's sensory lure, like honey to the bee. To call the resulting range of interest and its accompanying sensations *oral-erotic*, instead of *oral-hedonic*, is the first step in the descent into Freudesque error. That initial break in logic portends fatal consequences.

Equally in accord with genetic principles is the

persistence as well as the outgrowth of this primary oral-hedonic zone. Normal adults when they fall in love do not revert to sucking their fingers. When the erotic urge is in flower, it utilizes the earlier hedonic field and brings the lips into the erotic technique, but with a maturer meaning. There's many a stage between the lip psychology of the infant and that of the adult. All of which is so commonplace that only a learned man with a thesis to establish would overlook it. The Freudians seem to forget that the lips are ever used for other than "sexual" purposes. Upon the assumption that all is sex and sex is all, there arises a comprehensive genetic psychology and a characterology, which to my regret I must impose upon the reader to set before him the ways of Freudianism.

The specialist in the "oral character" is Abraham. He has "discovered" two infantile sub-stages of the mouth zone: the first localized in the lips; the second in the gums and teeth. If the unweaned "you" in some measure is fixated or overindulged at the sucking stage of life, the influence of this "pleasure in taking" develops into a general "taking" type of satisfaction, and you will mature as an optimist. If the unweaned "you" is over-indulged, you develop "a carefree indifference and inactivity, perhaps even make no attempt to gain a livelihood. The whole general attitude in the case of such individuals is one of expectation that some kind person (a mother representative) will 'flow for them eternally.' Generosity is also frequently brought about by an identification with the bounteous mother" (Abraham, after Healy). If, however, the unweaned "you" fails to "achieve gratification in the sucking period," that infantile thwart "may result in a later asking

or demanding social attitude (either modest or aggressive), a tendency to cling to others, a dislike of
being alone. Impatience is a marked characteristic
of this type." Such is the foundation of a pessimist,
making the worst of everything, finding difficulty
everywhere. Or those who fail in proper infant "oral"
satisfaction, may "communicate themselves orally to
other people." This results in an obstinate urge to
talk, and to attach value to what they say. Loquacity
and conceit, no less than pessimism, result from inadequate sucking.

The second biting stage of oral eroticism "leaves
its definite mark on later personality," foreshadowing
a contrasted gum-and-teeth psychology for the adult.
This type of infantile concern betokens pronounced
attitudes of hostility and dislike and also abnormally
developed envy. The entire later behavior, choice
of profession, and hobbies may be 'rooted in oral
eroticism.' " Office-holders, it is suggested, are persistent "suckers," not, however, in the sense of the
"easy-marks" one of whom is born every minute; how
these are "erotically" accounted for in the nursery is
still uncertain.

These are, indeed, amazing derivations; and a century ago deluded Gall read quite similar traits in cranial
bumps! Truly the world moves and science with it.

When a learned M.D. in a fourteen-page paper discusses in scientific jargon such ridiculous suppositions,
infantile even as jests, one may throw discretion to the
winds. It is even more in order to call nonsense nonsense, than to call a spade a spade. Between such
pompously learned character-readings and the shrewd
guesses and "hunches" of a gypsy fortune-teller, or
the superstitious pronouncements of the befuddled as-

trologer, there is little choice; and what there is favors the ignorant craft, for they may not know what they do, or knowing, exploit those who do not. But there is more and worse to come. The second book in the Freudian characterology is Exodus. The genesis of character-traits is at the entrance, the next stage at the exit of the food-tract. In the psycho-sexual development the interest is transferred from oral to anal processes. The method of interpretation is the same, the elaboration more involved. It will be sufficiently convincing to indicate the conclusions:

> Freud's cardinal triad of anal characteristics comprises (a) orderliness (bodily cleanliness, reliability, conscientiousness in performance of petty duties)— in an over-accentuated form, pedantry; (b) parsimony, which may become avarice; (c) obstinacy, which may become defiance and perhaps also include irascibility and vindictiveness. These three personality qualities are found regularly together, the last two forming a constant element.
>
> The child in whom anal erotism is constitutionally strong derives great pleasure both autoerotic and narcissistic, from excretory processes and feels intensely the "deprivations" associated with sphincter training and the taboos placed upon expression of his anal-erotic interests. There are two varieties of anal character-formation derived respectively from pleasure in the act and pleasure in the product. "The form of the future personality-characteristic is largely determined by whichever aspect of the original interest predominated."

By what process of biological evolution cerebral qualities have been developed upon the sewage-disposal-plants of metabolism, is not indicated.

A general Ego attitude of possessiveness and proprietorship is an outstanding characteristic of object-relationships, as found with the anal character. This is to be traced back to the original psychic pleasure in retention. Anal love also expresses itself largely in the bestowing of gifts rather than tenderness upon the love-object. This may be carried over into social relations at large in acts of philanthropy, benefaction, and patronage. The possessiveness of anal love shows itself clearly in the collector; the objects collected are associated with excrement. "The pleasure in looking at one's own mental creations, letters, manuscripts, or completed work of all kinds" has its prototype in "looking at one's own faeces."

Parsimony as an anal-erotic trait can only be understood by taking into account the underlying process of symbolization. The unconscious identifying of faeces, gifts, and money influences many later social relations involving money. The interest in money plays a rôle in the anal character, and has attracted to itself "the psychical interest which was originally proper to . . . the product of the anal zone." Dislike for waste and efforts to make use of it; time-saving devices—carrying on two occupations at the same time, mark the "anal" man. Also a more practical caution: he is apt to forget small debts. The conservative is an "anal," the liberal an "oral."

Sublimation plays a large part in taking care of infantile coprophilic interests and impulses which are, of course, especially taboo with adults. Later interests in painting, sculpture, cooking, metal molding, and carpentry are believed to be traceable to coprophilic pleasure in smearing and molding. The choice of occupations and professions is thus largely dependent upon the process of sublimation of anal interests.

The bright sociable individual who has been gratified in the early oral stage is also to be contrasted with the hostile malicious individual whose characteristics in this respect are to be traced back to the biting stage, and with the morose, aloof, reticent individual whose trends are derived from the anal stage.

These citations are not from an unexpurgated edition of *Believe It or Not,* but from the sober scientific compilation of Freudian doctrine of Healy, Bronner and Bowers. The accidents of etymology must be blamed for an unsavory pun: yet such is psycho-*anal*-ysis.

Another pearl beyond price clamors for mention, an *"urethral* personality formation," represented as a by-product of the anal stage.

Very little seems to have been discovered as yet as to the specific characteristics deriving from urethral eroticism. Freud speaks of the "burning" ambition found to be closely associated with childish enuresis.

Hitschmann claims that both ambition and predilection for play and working with water—for example, excessive bathing and washing—have been empirically deduced from urethral erotisim.

Glover mentions ambition, envy, and impatience as all of urethral origin. Abraham derives ambition from oral eroticism and thinks it is reënforced by urethral impulses.

Frink cites the case of a baseball pitcher who felt that he was getting much the same pleasure in pitching ball as he had in early urinating exploits.

"A gentleman who well remembers his infantile bladder weakness became later a passionate volunteer fireman, which after what has been said above does not greatly surprise us" (Ferenczi). His later career is still infantilely "conditioned"; turning to medicine, he became an urologist.

This truly original, if not elevating, chapter in characterology suggests that if some alert and creative paranoiac, such as form the élite of insane asylums, had been driven by his psychopathic ruminations to formulate the theory that character-traits such as obstinacy, refractiousness, parsimony, pedantry and others just cited, are the issue of a marked reluctance in discharging excreta and an associated tendency toward constipation, the case might have given rise to a new rubric in the rich repertory of psychiatry as "anal paranoia." The Freudians variety is a deliberately cultivated paranoia, the rationalistic madness of the academic mind. It may be necessary in the future to recognize three orders of individuals: sane, insane, and Freudian.

We have now learned how character is formed partly in the nursery, but even more influentially in the lowlier services of the bath-room. The Freudian child-psychologist follows infantile love in its troubled course from oral to genital; and he reads adult traits, even such complex ones as pedantry and liberalism, as aftermaths of anatomical occupations usually conducted in privacy. This exotic chapter Ferenczi calls the "metapsychology of habit." Certainly such derivation has no place in any psychology hitherto known to the sensible sons of men.

Transition to the genital stage likewise develops its peculiar psychology and after-effects.

According to Jones, anal eroticism appears in "the tendency to be occupied with the reverse side of various things and situations. This may manifest itself in many different ways; in marked curiosity about the opposite or back side of objects and places e. g., in the desire to live on the other side of a hill because it has its back turned to a given place; in the proneness to make numerous mistakes as to right and left, east and west; to reverse words and letters in writing; and so on." Abraham adds: "There is no doubt that the displacement of libido from the genital to the anal zone is the prototype of all these 'reversals.' "

The genital stage is more or less safely reached at puberty, with, however, a "reanimation" of the primary infantile (phallic) genital stage. Libido then comes to its own, and the guiding principle, as Ferenczi proudly proclaims, becomes *genitalism*. "Genetic" psychology shifts to a genital center. There appears another "sexual" source of personality-traits: not "Oedipus" alone but other varieties of sex aberration threaten and characterize the maturing of the ever sexualized self. "Narcissus" and "Sade" and "Masoch" join the company of "Oedipus" in shaping the Freudian homo. *Narcissism* is a useful term; though as bandied about by Freudians, it suggests a subtle, scientific insult. Self-admiration has a large repertory; it includes the pleasure in display of personal charms, possessions, achievements, from childish showing off to the sophisticated "Peacock Alley" and play to the gallery. It extends from the intimate personal self to the acquired social and professional ego. An integral phase of social competition is sexual competition. The trait includes an emphasis upon that appeal, which may indeed dominate. So far, fair agreement. The questionable usage as well as diagnosis is the sexualization of the entire phase of any trait because it contains a sexual component, thus assimilating all phases to the sexual origin and pattern. That is false psychology. Narcissism is a more useful term when confined to its specific direction and emphasis. The same comment and correction applies even more sharply to *sadism*. It is a logical perversion to hold that every sexual perversion is inherent and is represented in the total sexual life. To derive all cruelty, from a boy's pulling of a beetle's wing, to teasing and bullying, to a brutal attendant's harshness toward prisoners or patients, from an inherent "sadīsm," is a "genetic" confusion. The same unwarranted tendency appears in the complementary *masochism*, which belongs to the general *Wonne des Leides*—the pleasure in pain, which may develop to a "martyr" complex. The universalizing of sexual extremes serves no useful purpose, and completely confuses the psychology of the emotions.

The fallacy here involved is disguised because the terms Sadism and Masochism are unfamiliar, and so carry the potency and conviction of an abstruse and profound discovery.

Their origin is this: Count or Marquis de Sade (1740–1814) had a checkered career. He was accused of poisoning as well as of unnatural offenses, was a victim of sexual perversion accompanied by pleasure in inflicting physical cruelty upon the objects of his passion. While in the Bastille he wrote obscene novels, sending a copy to Napoleon. He was committed to the insane asylum, released and recommitted as incurable, spending the last eleven years of his life at Charenton. His vice or insanity has attained the distinction of a scientific term. Sacher-Masoch (1835–1895) was a minor writer, an Austrian, who wrote of Galician life, including tales of women craving and taking pleasure in being treated with physical cruelty in connection with sexual embrace, a morbid trait doubtless described from life. He, too, is now immortalized in science.

The fallacy becomes clearer when applied to a more familiar perversion, *homosexuality*. That this is an abnormality is usually acknowledged; but it does not appear so in the Freudian sexual theory; for that supposes a "homosexual" trend common to all, which must be suppressed, outgrown, transmuted, or dissolved. There is assumed a homosexual component in libido— an assumption as ungenetic as gratuitous. Libido is parcelled out into trends and tendencies, as though the analyst were behind the scenes and arranged the plot of the human drama. It would follow equally that boys' gangs and men's clubs, and girls' gatherings and women's organizations, all more or less harbor disguised "homosexual" trends. For the restraint in making the application quite so broad, the censorship of common sense is responsible. By the same logic by which all son-to-mother attachment harbors incest, all affection is erotic, all cruelty sadistic, all joy in suffering masochistic, are all gatherings for men only, or clubs composed exclusively of women, homosexual. If consistently Freudian, we should similarly designate Princeton and Williams or Vassar and Wellesley as "homosexual" colleges, though not as yet so described in the catalogues, and substitute for "co-educational" the more appropriate Freudian term: "heterosexual" institutions, for State Universities.

The dire consequences of an initial false step appear

in the applications that follow: the reading of mature (and perverse) traits into infancy; the derivation of mature traits from "sexualized" infantile episodes; making the sexual component dominant in all emotions and relations in which it enters. We are accordingly assured that the choice of occupations is determined on the one side by the suppositious overattachment or fixation of oral, anal, urethral and early genital trends; and equally by sadistic, masochistic and narcissistic urges. Soldiers, barbers, butchers, surgeons and even tailors find outlets for sadistic trends as they cut and handle sharp weapons; while with equal gravity is it concluded that the sons of these "cutters" are apt to develop a neurosis which is a "monstrous exaggeration of castration fear." The initial error vitiates the entire outlook and makes these phases of psychoanalytic psychology an absurd caricature.

Sexualized personality becomes genitalized personality by the same error that plays fast and loose with the concept of libido. By such route Ferenczi discovers a *"Cornelia complex,"* setting forth that when the mother of the Gracchi referred to her sons as her jewels, she was in her "unconscious" displaying her sex appeal. The adept Freudian sexualizes every act and object, finding strictly dishonorable motives for every apparent item of the day's occupation. He reads sexual incidents and attitudes in the golf player's stance and handling of his club, discusses learnedly whether smoking is oral because the cigar is held in the mouth, or anal because it leaves an ash, or genital by reason of its form. He reduces all manners of special interests to offshoots and derivatives of sexual occupations. The desire for knowledge is but a converted offshoot of a craving for sex enlightenment; interests in movement active and passive, rhythmical and restless, derive from the sexual sphere; sports, art, choice of profession, hobbies, types of belief, from politics to religion, to superstition, fears, shames, hates, attachments, are all by-products of a primary sexual activity.

All this illustrates what I have discussed previously as the reduction process (and error) of the "nothing but" psychology. All these derivative trends and activities, trivial and serious, are analyzed as "nothing but" disguised and modified sexual occupations. If that is the Freudians' notion of sublimation, they have deliberately prostituted the term and robbed it of all its virtue. True sublimation is the enrichment of the psychic life by surrounding the urges with the issues of a cultivated life. That is another chapter in the tale that Freud should have told.

To illustrate the reduction process and how seriously it is taken, I mention a 65-page disquisition by Dr. Karl Abraham, the late leader of the psychoanalytic movement in Germany, on "Restrictions and Transformations of Scoptophilia in Psycho-Neurotics, with Remarks on Analogous Phenomena in Folk-Psychology." Scoptophilia is medico-classic jargon for the intense desire and pleasure in seeing, in psychoanalytic reference to sexual pleasure in gazing upon the erogenous zones; it is in Gallic phrase *voyeurism* and in Anglo-Saxon vernacular *Peeping Tom*. When this inquisitive curiosity is directed to any other pursuits however remote, then the initial sexual scoptophilia is said to be transformed or displaced. The motive of the higher form of investigation is reduced to the primary. Chemist and geologist and philosopher are thus reduced or accounted for as transformed scoptophilists.

To enable the reader to follow the course of these "scientific" derivations, I cite them in detail, in terms of the analysis:

"What interested him most in chemistry was the *status nascendi*. On going more closely into this, it appeared that the moment in which a substance was formed or in which two substances united to form a new one had a positive fascination for him. His interest in procreation (combination of two substances in the formation of a new one) and in birth (*status nascendi*) had been displaced on to scientific problems in a successful way. He unconsciously discovered in each science the problem that was best suited to afford a veiled representation of the interests of his childhood. The field of palaeontology supplied another very instructive example of this sublimatory tendency. The geological period termed pliocene—the period in which man first appeared— particularly engrossed his interest. The child's typical question concerning its own origin had been here sublimated to a general interest in the origin of the human race."

"We owe to von Winterstein some very excellent remarks on the unconscious motives of philosophic thinking. According to him the philosopher desires us to see his own thoughts. His libido is no longer directed to the forbidden (incestuous) aim, no longer to that which one *must not* see, but to that which one *cannot* see. At the same time it has turned back upon the ego in a way which we can only comprehend as a regression to the position of infantile narcissism."

Such are the ramifications of psycho-sexual development in the Freudianized homo. That there is a psycho-sexual development in the human species; that it is of supreme consequence in shaping our composite psychology as equally in the total business of living, remains as true as important; for the completer recognition of that truth and its importance, the world will ever remain indebted to the genius of Sigmund Freud. It will do so, in my opinion, despite its almost complete rejection of his scheme of sexual development. The true psycho-sexual development, as psychology traces it, reads quite otherwise. It centers about the concept of *sublimation,* which Freud duly recognized, and then so largely forgot. The sexual was magnified, the psychic neglected; or if not quite that, the psychic was assimilated to the sexual, sexualizing the psyche; the actual course is the infusion of the sex life with psychic values. That consummation forms the nucleus of the true story of libido, which will be written by a psychologist emancipated from the Freudian complex that sex is all.

CHAPTER VIII

PSYCHOANALYTIC TECHNIQUE

"Psychoanalysis" has come to be used as a general term for the entire Freudian structure: theory, principles, argument, applications. It refers particularly to the probing, confessional, exploration of the personal intimate life. The patient who goes through the process or ordeal is said to be psychoanalyzed—in popular parlance—"psyched." The sources of his neurosis are thus brought to light, and the measures for its relief determined. This is a *clinical* procedure. The technique of this art and practice next comes before our reviewing stand.

ATTRIBUTISM

There is also a logical technique employed in reaching the principles which direct the practice. The present brief challenges that technique as variously fallacious. One such fallacy permeates pages and volumes of psychoanalysis: the fallacy of attributism. It consists in accepting as a reality an abstract concept devised by the thinker for the convenience of his thinking. When a scientific Pygmalion "animates" his Galatea, an engaging fantasy becomes a subtle delusion. A concept is little more than a mannikin in the intellectualist's workshop. But *Id, Ego,* and *Super-ego* stalk about in the Freudian clinic as living realities, deriving their vitality from clinical evidence. Clearly the *Id* exists in the human make-up only as a convenient label for what I prefer to think of and speak of as the assemblage and integration of primary function; these are realities. By thus thinking and speaking of them, I am constantly referred back to their substructure in the nervous system, and am under no temptation to think of them as superstructures, or entities of any kind. The fantastic powers ascribed to the *Id* and to the galaxy of associated concepts, violate the naturalistic oath, which—paralleling the Hippocratic oath—should be administered to all psychologists.

If the reader, with attributism in mind, will re-read what the *Id* and *Ego* and *Super-ego* are supposed to be and do (pages 92, 94, 95), he will realize what an attributistic fantasy the entire tale is; or, if not, let him read the tale at length, at great length, in the original version, unabridged. Attributism culminates in the superstructure, but it makes its appearance early and often; it pervades the "unconscious" in many a mood and phase of that pervasive and evasive concept, cast in several rôles in the Freudian drama. "Oedipus" is attributistic through and through; the "infantile" is attributistic; the endo-psychic censor is attributistic; and libido also in its upper registers. Attributism in concept formation is the bane of Freudian argument, a series of Galateas come to life. Though the term "attributism" is mine, the recognition of its danger to right thinking is well recognized by critical minds, ancient and modern. The Greeks had a name for it; they called it *hypostasis*. A great Teutonic mind, Goethe, thus phrased the temptation.

"One studiously works one's way into a terminology, and then using it to suit one's purpose, acquires the assurance of understanding, or at least of saying something. . . . Anything may be maintained, if one takes the liberty of using words now in a broader and again in a narrower sense, in a liberal and a remote application."

This reads as though Goethe had the Freudian sexual theory prophetically in mind. And by fortunate chance, one may cite Breuer, the Columbus of psychoanalysis, in the same cautionary vein.

"All too easily one gets into the habit of thought of assuming behind a substantive a substance, of gradually understanding by consciousness an entity. If, then, one has got used to employing local relations metaphorically, as e. g., 'subconscious,' as time goes on an idea will actually develop in which the metaphor has been forgotten, and which is as easily manipulated as a material thing. Then mythology is complete."

Attributism invades the cerebral mechanism and becomes a fallacious mental habit. When imbedded in argument it vitiates the entire structure, which William James would have described as nothing but a scheme. Consequently, one cannot readily dissect the argument and indicate that this, that and the other item is wrong. The objection is more fundamental: it reads that a logical mind, accustomed to logical expression, does not think in such terms, does not indulge in such elaboration. Until Freudians think more rationally and cautiously, their cause is hopeless. The fallacy of attributism subtly, insidiously, comprehensively invades every phase and phrase of the psychoanalyst's technique. He has forgotten the realities and put in their place a mythology of forces—Ucs., Id, Ego, Super-ego, Oedi-

pus, libido in many guises, and other animated concepts—which he then uses to account for the clinical
data which suggested them. As a consequence the sense
of hypothesis is lost, and the assurance of reality sub-
stituted; that is the essence of delusion.

There is a special temptation to this transgression in
the cultural setting in which Freudianism arose and
eventually flourished, despite academic discourage-
ments which were motivated by a suspicion of the conclusions rather than of the method. While any language
can be so manipulated as to conceal thought or its
absence, academic German seems especially devised for
the purpose. It gives the semblance of important meaning to cultivated obscurity, and by use of impersonal
and passive and reflexive voices transfers the responsibility for the statement to something seemingly as
objective and uncontrollable as the weather, while in
reality it is all the completely subjective and irresponsible fantasy of a logic-emancipated speculation.

It is not speculation alone, but a tendency toward
involved, didactic, pedantic formulation—even Teutonic advertising reads like excerpts from a dissertation
—which congenially combines with the academic tradition. Unbridled speculation is in some circles regarded as a perquisite of the Teutonic scholar; it seems
little affected by the realistic contacts of the clinician.
Mental spinarets are easily operated; each spinner
takes pride in the originality of his web. Consequently,
in a remarkably short period, a literature of a thousand
numbers arose. My protest is directed against the entire technique of the theoretical side of Freudianism;
the psychoanalytical psychology is false, in addition
to its many other transgressions, by the falsity of at-
tribution.

NEUROSIS

The technique that commands the central interest is that embodied in the *clinical* procedure. The pragmatic promise that set the current of hospitality toward the Freudian dispensation was the hope of understanding and relieving the psycho-neuroses. This problem in all its magnitude is the unfortunate heritage of the complicated age in which we live—an age superficially a machine age, in deeper analysis a psycho-neurotic age or, in the pristine meaning of the word, a psychoanalytic age. The twentieth-century homo has become acutely and disturbingly conscious of his internal difficulties; there is a troubled intro-direction of his psyche. In older days religious contemplation and consolation absorbed and drained off—*abreacted* in Freudian phrase—the troubled emotions. The management of our cerebral "souls" to attain our present peace of mind, makes mental hygiene a world-wide interest. The Freudian project made a direct appeal to that compelling need; once its promise was recognized, it found a following among troubled souls and those engaged in ministration to mankind's psychic failings. The neurotic problem, which by the turn of fortune's wheel, has for a span become associated with the name of Freud, must be projected upon a large canvass, that its momentous proportions may be fully realized. The psycho-neuroses reflect a goodly share of the world's distress.

We are told that there are more "mental" cases in our hospitals and similar institutions than of all other diseases combined; we are informed that if the mental disorders continue to increase at the present rate, in about thirty years there will be just about enough mentally fit persons to take care of the mentally unfit;

and there will be no other occupation. Facing this dismal forecast, it may be well to realize the scale of the incapacity, the loss of useful days' work, the interference with orderly schedules of behavior, the personal misery and intense unhappiness, the frictions and fractures of social relations issuing from the psychoneuroses. Presumably it exceeds that of the "mental" cases which compose the available statistics. The problem of neuroticism should be approached with the same sense of magnitude as well as of tolerance and insight as surrounds world disarmament; it is in a measure a psychic disarmament, the conquest of a great destroyer of internal peace. If Freud has really solved this problem or moved it appreciably nearer to solution, his place is secure among the immortal benefactors of mankind. These reflections should impart a sobering sense of their responsibilities to the contributors to psychoanalysis. And that responsibility should be further strengthened by the weighty consideration that a goodly share of humanity's most delicately organized and creatively useful citizens are peculiarly subject to the liabilities, the deviations in psychic pattern, that in one phase express themselves in the psycho-neuroses. This we may credit, whether or not we endorse Bergson's opinion that much of the most important work of the world has been done by those of this disposition, indeed by victims of neurasthenic ills.

Our initial step in the survey of Freudianism was to follow Freud's first case of hysterical impairment. Presently and increasingly Freud found the clue to the neurotic problem in the course of libido. There resulted two theses: that the psycho-neuroses are caused by conflict of urges, operating subconsciously; that such conflicts are libidinal. Freud developed this into an equa-

tion, and called it *symptom-formation*. This intensive
dwelling upon symptoms was in itself a false step and
detracted from a fair view of the larger problem of
the factors that go into the making of the neuroses. One
would not get far in the knowledge of stuttering or
blushing or insomnia or sleep-walking, if one confined
attention too much to the minute speech haltings, the
facial suffusion, the restless tossing, the somnambulist's
behavior—all of which are psycho-neurotic. The total
make-up of those in whom these symptoms occur, the
psychic occasions, are vital to the "causes" even if the
deeper causes elude us. And incidentally these more
physiological symptoms are just as legitimate items for
psychoanalytical accounting as the special symptoms
selected by Freudians for the very reason that they
seem to fit in with the formula; yet these have not been
included in the analyst's range. The Freudian approach
is not conducive to a broad view and an adequate solution of the basic problem of the neuroses. It illuminates
one important phase of the significant symptoms. To
substitute the part for the whole of so important a
problem is a false start. I can, indeed, cite Freud's ad-
mission—which, however, is contradicted by his practice and by a score of other citations—that "after decades of analytic investigation" he is still baffled as to
the "*leit motif* of the neuroses"; and so is the rest of
the profession. There is, so we assume, a *leit motif*,
perhaps the fusion of several with intricate variations.
How nature composes them is as yet the secret of the
neurotic sphinx.

The statement of a psychoanalyst, Jones, may serve
as a preamble.

"Formerly these states were explained by the co-
operation of two factors—inherited weakness of the

nervous constitution, and some current difficulty, of which disappointment in love and overwork were the most typical. Between these two, Freud inserted a third—namely, the effect of certain experiences during the early sexual development. He in no way denied the significance of the other two; on the contrary, he has done much to define more nearly the essential nature of them and the exact continuity subsisting among all three."

But has he? The constitutional factor is regarded by "orthodox" psychiatrists as the chief determinant. They entertain the hope that some neurological genius of the future may discover a bio-chemical basis for the neurotic vulnerability. The source of the liability is one problem, its manifestations another; both must be considered. The psycho-neuroses are classified as "functional nervous disorders" (in medical short-hand f.n.d.), with no assignable organic basis. The nervous system of the neurotic does not work properly; since we do not know why or how, there is slight possibility of attack from that side. A dominant characteristic is that the disturbing symptoms fluctuate decidedly through psychic (emotional) influences. There is convincing evidence that the f.n.d.'s represent distinct types of vulnerability; most distinctively the generally hysterical and the generally neurasthenic varieties, which are by no means one, despite overlapping symptoms; the term hysteria * may itself include distinct orders of impairment of function, concerning which there

* The general thesis that psycho-neuroses are resultants of conflicts of a sexual order leads to the discovery of the mechanisms or dynamisms by which the symptoms arise. These have been considered in terms of the situations; everyday lapses, dreams, neuroses. That part of the argument must be held in mind in judging the pertinence of Freud's "neurotic" formula.

is as yet no agreement. What holds for the anxiety neurosis may not apply to the compulsion neurosis, both of which disorders figure in Freud's clinical cases. Note again, that the two inducing factors above noted —work and love frustration—are likewise distinct. Work points to fatigue; the assault of fatigue upon the nervous resources is a definite physiological factor, though worry is far more upsetting than expenditure of energy. Both are strains; work under worry is many times more straining. But work is not a conflict unless there is distaste or the strong desire for other occupation; and love frustration is not fatigue, though it may equally impede the course of useful occupation. The neurotic equation is complex; the factors and their values are largely unknown and variable. Assurance is out of place.

Despite protestations here and there to the contrary, the actual Freudian diagnosis of the neuroses is confined almost exclusively to the "infantile sexuality" etiology, with a cavalierly reference to constitutional factors. Even the character-traits which enter into the neurotic picture are set forth as sequelae of polymorphous perversity and anatomical fixations along the G.-U. genealogy. No reader of Freud would derive any impression of the vital and decisive rôle that constitutional temperamental factors play in the tendency toward "symptom formation." Hamlet is assigned a lesser part even than the grave-digger.

Next, the *libidinal* emphasis detracts from the proper place of the *conflict* factor, which forms the intrinsically Freudian contribution, for which he will be remembered when the one-sidedness of his diagnosis is forgotten.* This limitation stands in the way of a cor-

* The reader, and especially the reader versed in the current views concerning neuroses, is asked to accept neurasthenia and hysteria

rect diagnosis even in Freudian terms. Jung parted company with Freud on this issue; for conflicts are of many orders, and the present dominates, despite the "dead hand" of one's genetic past. Jung insisted that the neurosis be interpreted in mature terms. And Rivers, a neo-Freudian, in psychoanalyzing a case of claustrophobia—morbid fear of shut-in places—which had previously been analyzed by a Freudian looking for sexual clues without avail, found the source in infantile experiences, but not sexual ones. So the "exclusive interest in sex may actually obstruct the discovery of an infantile experience which furnishes as good example as could be desired of unconscious experience and of the possibility of recalling it to manifest memory."

Rivers records that in his psychiatric service in the War, the Freudian principles were constantly useful, yet cites this experience to show the inadequacy of Freud's theory of the neuroses. The War brought forward a considerable contingent of hysterical impairments comparable to those emphasized by Freud. There was indeed a psychic conflict, an assault upon a deep fundamental instinct charged with intensive emotion; but it was not sexual. The stresses of war and of peace bring different conflicts into prominence. Indeed Rivers notes that sexual factors in neuroses among soldiers

as referring generally to disturbances of that type, without implying the specific and developed forms of the maladies thus designated. The need of such terms is recognized, as for instance Kretschmer's terms: "schizoid" and "cycloid," which refer to types of personalities and grouping of character-traits which you and I possess, without implying that we shall ever manifest the symptoms of dementia praecox or manic-depressive psychosis. Overstreet, popularizing the concept, speaks of "micromanic" and "micro-depressive" persons or trends. I find it simpler to leave the terms and broaden the meanings to include minor and related orders of personality-trends.

were uncommon.* The *danger* instinct, the menace to life itself, precipitated the neurotic catastrophe; and, true to one of the Freudian precepts, induced a symptom of incapacity which disqualified from service, and in so far represented a subconscious escape into illness. Obviously a smouldering "Oedipus" complex could not suddenly erupt under the stimulus of shot and shell and privation and exposure; the vulnerability that took the "shell-shocked" out of the ranks was not a mother fixation. The conflict formula holds and also the mechanism of conversion, which leads Rivers to speak of hysteria as "substitution" neurosis. The war neuroses confirmed certain essential principles of psychoanalysis, but as definitely opposed the specific diagnosis which more and more has become the basis of technique among orthodox disciples of Freud.

As Rivers and others observe, there is nothing novel in the concept of conflict as a potent factor alike in the play of normal relations and in the formation of neu-

---

* I cannot include so large a question as to whether and how far irregularities in the sex-life—frustrations of sex expression particularly—are a cause of the neuroses. The dictum which Freud makes universal that they are, that a neurosis where there is a normal sex life is impossible, he is said to have heard pronounced by Charcot, who apparently gave it the positive formulation (not quite the same thing) that there is always sex abnormality when there is a neurosis. The more plausible theory is that the neurotic tendency is apt to extend its disturbances to the sex activities, and quite naturally as these are highly charged with affective tensions; yet this does not exclude the other relation in the etiology. Peck, a psychoanalyst, comments that "Freud's axiom that 'with a normal sex life there can be no neurosis' might be changed to 'a normal sex-life is an index which marks the absence of a neurosis.'" There is abundant evidence of the occurrence of neuroses in persons leading a normal sex-life, and of persons with free sex-relations developing a neurosis. The subject is well worth extensive investigation by a neurological research institute. Only then will any trustworthy formulation be possible. Freud's absolute statement is premature.

rotic handicaps; and this applies to both the orders of conflict that disturb internal peace: those between one order of urge and another in the personal heirarchy of control—between Id and Ego, and between the individual urges and the social code—Id, Ego and Super-ego. "The feature which makes Freud's theory noteworthy" (and makes it equally so decidedly questionable) "is his scheme of the *nature of the opponents* in the conflict, and of the mechanism by which the conflict is conducted" (Rivers). The sexualizing of the "opponents" in terms of infantile fixations so completely dominates the Freudian theory of neuroses as to overshadow all else, and by such obscuration nullifies its illumination. In fact there is little evidence that Freudians have responsibly considered the problem of the neuroses in its larger perspective.

With a strange indifference for a clinical profession, Freudians ignore the physiological symptoms common in neurotic affections. A few of these happen to be so common as to be conspicuous. The typical neurasthenic—perhaps nine out of ten—develops a sharp headache at the base of the brain. Has the Freudian neurologist considered what there is in the "Oedipus" tragedy that induces a pain in the neck among all sorts and conditions of men and women, of all ages, sexes, and previous condition? And why is it that so many whose infantile experiences were closely similar to those who succumb, never develop that peculiar pain which is almost the neurasthenic's tell-tale? Another clue-symptom is the neurasthenic early morning disability, the aggravation of the symptoms upon awakening. What mystic factor of repressed infantile desire or family romance is reanimated in the morning? An ingenious Freudian may proceed to solve the puzzle; but it will be by the weird and baseless psychic alchemy that makes of his diagnosis a cultist parody of science.

In the hysterical cluster of typical symptoms, there is globus or "air-swallowing," a choking sensation and gulping spasm.* By what conspiracy among the "Oedipus" victims of the gentler sex, have they agreed to substitute for a phase of their emotional conflict this tracheal irregularity? Most of the "conversions" are so individual that it requires an analysis to find their source. Yet here is one which follows a common pattern with no common experience to account for it. What such symptoms actually point to is a common liability in the nervous mechanism. Unquestionably some of the hysteric's seemingly physiological symptoms are induced by the psychic mechanisms to which Freud gave a significant interpretation; and still more importantly, others are not.

The Freudian formula not only fails notably in the accounting for the neuroses; it fails equally to account for the total range of symptoms. It selects the symptoms to which it applies, as equally it selects the cases to which the theory is applicable. Small wonder that more conservative neurologists and psychiatrists look upon this ambitious project with its conspicuous limitations, as a false step, a disastrous episode in the progress of their profession.

---

*A symptom for which the Freudian explanation may be the best, is the hysterical distention of the stomach, which yields to suggestion or hypnosis; it has been interpreted as a pregnancy fantasy. If so, the Freudian mechanism applies. Yet it may be of the same order as globus. The diagnosis is replete with uncertainties.

TRANSFERENCE

Within the frame of the clinical procedure appear two "facts" which Freud regards as the pillars * of psychoanalysis: *Transference and resistance*. There is indeed a "fact" behind both concepts, and a good measure of theory also. Resistance refers to the natural tendency to screen the private self. We may not be saturated with sin or burdened with a past, and still prefer, even to our confidents, to clothe the intimate self with a presentable make-up. The tailoring of the self required by the social code may for the moment be ignored or taken for granted, as one prefers. The confessional demand of complete frankness is as honored in the breach as in the observance. Admittedly resistance is real, and the technique that insists upon overcoming it justified. It is an art well worth developing; the spotting of the concealed and repressed foci of psychic infection, often subconsciously withheld. But much so-called resistance is ordinary forgetfulness, and not the repression which blocks the work of analysis. With these reservations, one may concede the Freudian resistance, but not the common alibi that where no complexes are found, it is only because the resistance to their discovery was too great; for by that argument the Freudian croupier is bound to win every time from the critical player, whether he stakes on the red or the black. One may concede also and welcome the illumination, that much that we now forget or repudiate was once active and accredited, particularly the rich fantasy life which most of us have left behind,

---

* I may say incidentally that in the course of many thousand pages, Freud refers to so many doctrines as "pillars" of his system, that his house becomes a colonnade. Creative fertility and a shifting perspective invite this phase of the Freudian temper.

yet which many never had. There are variable layers of resistance swathing the inner sanctum of our being, past and present. That recognition is useful; no psycho-diagnosis can proceed without it. It was always recognized, never so clearly as in the Freudian technique; which addition is gratefully acknowledged.

Transference is quite another matter. The "fact" of it is the relation of confidence between patient and analyst. Transference either has a specific meaning, which must be justified; or it refers to what is so well recognized that it needs no special name or emphasis. The doctrine of transference to the orthodox Freudian involves the decidedly questionable theory of "regression" and "reanimation," and applies it in a peculiarly arbitrary form.* Transference is part of the technique, along with free association, dream analysis, and the general interpretation of his complexes to the patient. It is definitely an erotic relation. In plain English the patient must fall in love with the physician as a stage in the treatment, and fall out or dissolve the relation to complete the cure. I am well aware that the relation is often described as warm affection and regard. But I see little evidence anywhere of platonic nuances in the Freudian considerations of sex. The complications introduced by the man-to-man, or man-to-woman relation are either naïvely disregarded, or are supposed to be neutralized by a cautious professional objectivity; though "counter-transference" is recognized, in which the analyst responds to the advances or attrac-

---

* The word "transference" is also used in Freudian doctrine to designate the shifting of erotic feelings from one object or person to another; for that process Freud prefers the word "displacement." He confines "transference" to the physician-patient relation.

tions of the patient. Emotional alchemy seems a flex-
ible art. Earlier we were told that (nearly) all affection
is sexual in origin or implication; now we learn that
an emotional relation of decided intensity may and
must be developed without such implications.

Again the interesting question as to how this factor in the technique arose. It is not a datum dug out
of the patient's hidden past, but created and encouraged for his present difficulties. How readily the
relation might occur or be invited by the intimate
nature of the conference, is obvious. It seems that
this was a reason for Breuer's withdrawal from the
original psychoanalytical "case"; and Wittels, in re-
telling the story fifty years later, offers as his explanation of the patient's speaking only English the
clue that Breuer was the only one in her immediate
circle who understood English; so that this was a
subconscious device to be alone with her beloved
physician to whom the transference had been made.
The same symptoms whose "formation" had been
found in childhood experience is under this additional
illumination quite otherwise accounted for. Thus does
clinical technique reflect back upon diagnosis. Freud
quite frankly explains that at first embarrassed by
these feministic attentions, he soon recognized that
it was not his own Don Juanitic person that was involved, but that he stood only as the surrogate (or
emotional draper's model) upon whom or which the
patient hung her therapeutic affections. These ramifications are intriguing.

However, *revenons à nos moutons;* for there is a
bone of contention to pick. The entire notion, including
the affective acrobatics, rests upon the wholly prob-

lematical—to put it mildly—theory of reanimation of affect. Doubtless hysterics do, as Freud says, suffer from affective memories. That source of phobia and compulsion is real. It may be variously accounted for. Hollingworth has developed the "redintegration" theory. Psychic scars must somehow be explained. The reanimation or resurrection idea is defensible, but not the use of it in support of the transference technique.

The rationale of the transference rests on the "re-animation" doctrine. Transference requires the patient to go back not in memory only but in feeling, and relive the erotic relation of his infancy or early period; only that the analyst now replaces the original love-object. Such commanding of the emotions is as credible as a love philter. Freud's confidence in the process and in the fantastic assumption behind it, so utterly unpsychological and so combinedly naïve and dangerous, is one of the strangest exhibits in the entire fantasia.

"The decisive part of the cure is accomplished by means of the transference through which new editions of the old conflict are created. Under this situation the patient would like to behave as he had behaved originally, but by summoning all of his available psychic power, we compel him to reach a different decision. Transference then becomes the battlefield on which all the contending forces are to meet. The full strength of the libido, as well as the entire resistance against it, is concentrated in this relationship to the physician; so it is inevitable that the symptoms of the libido should be laid bare."

"In place of his original disturbance the patient manifests the artifically contructed disturbance of transference; in place of heterogeneous unreal objects for the libido, you now have only the person of the physician, a single object, which, however, is also fantastic. The new struggle over this object is, however, raised to the highest psychic level, with the aid of the physician's suggestions, and proceeds as a normal psychic conflict. By avoiding a new suppression the estrangement between the Ego and the libido comes to an end, the psychic unity of the personality is restored. When the libido again becomes detached from the temporary object of the physician, it cannot return to its former objects but is now at the disposal of the Ego."

Thus is assumption twice compounded: assumption one, that the neurotic difficulty is completely determined by early shock; two, that a sensible mature person can by any process reinstate an emotional situation experienced at a tender age, and at will or by effort recast the rôles of the drama. The notion is as preposterous psychologically as it is futile clinically. The farce or tragedy of "transference" represents about the lowest level of logical degradation to which inveterate Freudians have descended. What an "Alice in Wonderland" a "Freud in Blunderland" would make!

The hallucinating proceeds thick and fast; and each analyst adds to the recipe or invents his own transmutation of the baser emotions into acceptable gold. They learnedly discuss whether the analyst is or should be the love object in person; or hold himself quite objective, the analyst becoming "a blank screen on which are projected pictures of the patient's infantile life"; or "a concealed figure" on whom the patient drapes his fantasies; whether at the beginning the analyst is or takes the rôle of the father, then becomes the mother; whether the patient is literally reborn, for re-birth fantasies at this stage "may be taken for more than a metaphor."

Jung will have none of this folderol and looks upon the analyst-patient relation as a psychological rapport: "an object of human relationship in which each individuality is guaranteed his proper place." The patient is to feel that he is "accepted" as he is, and will be guided to a better adjustment to regain his normal self and adjust to the trying circumstances in his situation. But this welcome oasis of common sense amid a welter of mirage speculation is promptly dispelled by the introduction of the "collective-unconscious" and similar Jungian fantasies. There still inheres in his technique a fictitious sense of something technically original in a relation which is one of tact and the usual requirements of high-minded integrity and professional responsibility. In fact, the very recognition of transference as a part of the technique, instead of accepting the confidential relation for what it inevitably must be, casts a lurid light upon the occupations of the analytic clinic.

And it is precisely here that the menace enters. I cannot close my eyes nor those of the reader to the disquieting tales of the abuse of the relation of analyst-patient which come from abroad and nearer home, in which the transference eases the way of abuse. Add to the fixation upon sexual causes for neurosis the legitimized technique of at least a shaped "erotic" relation, and remember that not all analysts or even all who hold a medical degree are saints, nor all patients circumspect, and the rest may be safely left to the reader's charitable though uncensored imagination.

At the moment I prefer not to distract attention from the baselessness of the clinical technique, by dwelling upon its dangers, important as that consideration is in the total menace of erroneous doctrine and injudicious application which surrounds psychoanalysis "as is." The fallacies and the perniciousness in the technique and temper of psychoanalysis are parts of one malignity. It does not fall within my self-assigned task to bring charges against practitioners nor to concur in or refute those that have been made, though I shall not sidestep the issue. I prefer to emphasize that this practice, like many another, not too well grounded in science or reality, becomes benign or malign according to whatever in post-Victorian days, we may still call the moral standards of the practitioner and the ethics of the profession. The Freudian analyst has deliberately placed himself in a precarious position, and has done so, in my belief, by the route of false assumptions and "sexual" predilections, to which we may now add the bizarre culmination in the invention of "transference" as an ordained technique.

Since not every patient can love every analyst, provision is made for a "negative transfer" in which she hates him or he her (for there are woman analysts), or he him or she her, in a fair promiscuity of genders and relations. (And how a busy analyst keeps track of all his "transferences" and knows how far in the straight or crooked emotional path he has proceeded with each, would seem to require even more diplomatic discretion than is imposed upon a chronic philanderer with marauding

proclivities). The negative transfer absorbs or re-
stages the hate episodes in the family romance. The
"transference" itself develops a neurosis which is
exchanged for the actual as one more readily dissolved, apparently by the same principle by which
the veterinarian who was strong on "bots" converted
the disorders of his animal patients into his specialty, for which he had an infallible remedy; or,
more respectfully, like Mesmer's performances at
the baquet (suspiciously like transference), which
consisted in inducing crises and then drawing them
out by passes and strokings. His *salle des crises*
seems to find a successor in the psychoanalytic clinic.

"The analyst's effort from the beginning to keep
the situation charged with affect tends to make it
take on an increasingly infantile coloring. Pre-
genital thwartings and sadisms are stirred up, and
the patient essays to bind all this affect in the analyst"; thus the transference neurosis arises.

Or, again:

"The history of the patient's development is re-
enacted in the analytic room." . . . There is a revival
and reëxperience of "incest wishes and incest bar-
riers" . . . and "the conscious conviction through
mental experience of the reality of the infantile
Oedipus in all its strength and horror." "This can
occur nowhere else in human experience."

Doubtless and *Gott sei Dank!* not.
But I cannot close the theme of transference upon
this tolerant note of amusement over its Quixotic flavor.
For the tang of it is not savory in any sense; and as it
falls within the compass of my critique, its banality as

an approved technique derived from an absurd principle, places the practice of psychoanalysis in quite too close proximity to the charlatanries of the pretenders calling themselves "applied psychologists," who talk glibly of Prama and akasic force and vibrations and sympathies between the psychologist and his patient or disciple. They, too, have taken psychoanalysis under their wing and have added that technique to their quack repertory. Wild psychology is not confined to the ranks of coin-raking pretenders.

ANALYSIS

It is a relief to reach a Freudian doctrine which in principle one may unreservedly approve. The analytic approach by way of the intimate exploration of the personal history, of distresses and conflicts particularly, remains a permanent contribution of value—not the only one by any means—of the psychoanalytic insight of Sigmund Freud. Analysis is an invaluable technique for the understanding of neurotic impairments and character deficits, as they operate and as they generate, and as they disclose their counterparts in the normal psyche. Just because our knowledge of the psychological bases of mental disorders generally, of the psycho-neuroses particularly, is so imperfect, is the approach from the analytical side indispensable. Long recognized as an aid to diagnosis, as a chapter in the patient's intimate story, it remained for Freud to give it its proper place in the total technique. Eventually the conflicts and their settings may prove to be aggravations rather than causes, forms of outlet and expression rather than the ultimate sources of deviating behavior, which (to make a concrete assumption), in some instances may be irregularities of glandular function;

they are none the less highly important. Their detection and removal forms an integral part of the psychiatrist's task. In many forms of mental disturbance, light and grave, this personal analysis is almost the only technique available; as supplementary, it is equally indispensable.

To avoid the implications which the story of Freud and Freudism give to the term "psychoanalysis," I propose a neutral and generic word for this analytic process: *psycho-diagnosis*. That indicates its intent, aligns it with other diagnostic procedures, and leaves its technique free to develop as knowledge progresses. The Freudian psychoanalyst is committed to one type of psycho-diagnosis, which for reasons recited is wholly unacceptable to large numbers of psychologists and psychiatrists. Psycho-diagnosis accepts the analytic principle enthusiastically. Its future development will be free to incorporate all that is well established in the analytic systems of Freud, Jung, Adler, the Neo-Freudians *et al*.

Within the psycho-diagnostic program we come upon the "free association" technique of Freud. That likewise is a valuable procedure, widely adopted by practitioners who are reservedly Freudian. It is more versatile than Jung's association technique which, however, has its distinct diagnostic uses. But the question turns, as so commonly, upon the skill and the objectivity—I emphasize both counts—with which it is used. Since we are told again and again with reiterated assurance that the "facts" come out of the analysis, and the major source of analysis is "free association," the evidential value of the entire technique converges upon the validity of this procedure.

As employed, I question it radically, fundamentally, comprehensively. The so-called "free association" is not free, not completely, not convincingly so. It is altogether too prone to be guided by the analyst's attitude, questions, known views, personal relations to the analysee. The opportunities for suggestion are abundant; they intrude subtly, however much one is on one's guard. I do not refer to the cruder forms of suggestion in the same physician-patient relation which deceived so astute a psychiatrist as Charcot into the "discovery" of three distinct hypnotic states, or the far cruder suggestion that led credulous Dr. Luys to "discover" that drugs in sealed tubes held against the nape of the neck or displayed in the presence of hysterical patients, produced all the characteristic symptoms that result from their injection. I do imply that the probing may readily have a suggestive effect, if there is, as in the instances cited, an anticipatory theory behind it and a knowledge on the part of the patients of what is expected of them. It takes a far more cautious, a more reserved, a better controlled form of psycho-diagnosis to keep the analysee's train of thought and emotion and fantasy free from the analyst's prepossessions.

The method is clearly the best we have; I have no substitute to propose. I believe it can be refined by suitable controls to yield as reliable evidence of internal conflicts and mechanisms as we are likely to obtain. I regret my lack of confidence in its employment by the majority of psychoanalysts, whose conclusions contribute cumulatively to the staggering psychoanalytic literature. The temper in which they proceed from principles to practice adds to the untenability of the conclusions. The operation is correctly planned; its execution faulty. Note carefully the vicious logical circle in which the argument runs: the evidence—let us say for the "Oedipus"—is derived from what the patient allegedly contributes to the analysis; the "Oedipus" thus found, the symptoms, fantasies, compulsions, entanglements, dreams, personal traits, are all interpreted Oedipus-wise. There is no control—let us say in similarly analyzing subjects free from neuroses—no objectivity, no standardization. The chain of conclusion is only as strong as its weakest link; and that is weak with the fatal weakness of a subjective intrusion.

The dream as rendered is indeed free from intrusion; yet free association as applied to it is subject to the same objections; likewise the explication of complexes in the form of character traits. Each one of these techniques—free association, dream interpretation, character diagnosis—is valuable, and its underlying principle sound. It is only the prejudicial employment that discounts the validity of the findings. A reformed psycho-diagnosis of the future will in my opinion repudiate largely the findings of Freud, yet regard Freud as the founder of an invaluable technique.

We reach or return at this stage to another factor in the analytic technique which raises an interesting question: Breuer's original *catharsis* and the question arising from it, why consciousness cures. This so fundamental query which gives the turn to the entire practice—namely to bring out the complexes into the light of day and dispel them like ghosts—has, so far as I know, not even been raised by psychoanalysts within the fold, but is admirably discussed by Schmalhausen,* a practicing psychologist distinctly hospitable to Freudian concepts rationally formulated. The matter is too complex for brief discussion. It involves relief of tension, realization, reëducation, inducing emotional control through intellectual objectification, for which proc-

* "Is Consciousness Curative?" in "Our Changing Human Nature."

esses different subjects have a variable and usually quite limited capacity; those who have it most may least need the services of an analyst. Not all consciousness cures; in fact consciousness—what we usually call self-consciousness—is precisely a malaise. Digging at the roots of sensitive growths is damaging. Imbedded in it all is a catharsis, the simple talking cure of Breuer which, however, has grown into months and years of daily scheduled and remunerative conferences, elaborating and magnifying the simplest incidents to a fictitious significance.

The protracted analysis, which has become the support in more than one sense of the analytic profession, is a cultist contribution. By what revelation has it been determined that the analysis must consume months and even years of confabulation and the payment of fees by the hour? Naturally this procedure raises a suspicion whether science is so generously favorable to revenue. But as I write, I am informed that in the Viennese citadel of psychoanalysis, curtailed periods of analysis have been sanctioned in deference to the prevalent depression. Science is not as inconsiderate in its demands as it is rated.

Meeting this objection, we are referred to resistance and the many layers of wrappings in the unconscious which must be gradually and carefully removed before the "true" psyche, infantilized and bare, is reached. One analyst sets forth that he does not venture to approach the intricacies of the dream life until the third month of analysis. Each has his own rules of technique, all arbitrary, all suggestive of the vagaries of a cult. Advocates of brief analysis are also found, but they are not popular with the profession; while Adler, who is confident that most difficulties—at least in children —can be diagnosed in one session and even better without seeing the patient, is considered a renegade; but that in all truth is another story. The central weakness in the analytic technique is its arbitrariness of procedure upon prejudiced assumptions. That makes of it a cult and not a science.

THE "CASE" OF FREUD

A protocol of a total analysis should somehow be brought into the clinical picture. The case of any one patient would involve tedious detail. The analysis of Freud himself would be of compelling interest. By his frankness in revealing his personal traits, he has placed himself upon the dissecting table; and a fellow analyst has evolved from this biographical material *The Tragic Complex of Freud.**

True in every detail to the psychoanalytic drama embodied in the Freudian "family romance," the tragedy begins in childhood, and the trauma there inflicted leaves permanent psychic scars; such is the *Tragic Complex.* When eleven or twelve years old, the boy Sigmund was told by his father of a ghetto-day incident, the point being to make plain to the son how much more favorable his own than his father's days. Said the elder Freud: "When I was a young man, I was taking a walk in my best clothes one Sabbath afternoon, when a Christian came along, tossed my new fur cap in the mud, with the words: 'Off the pavement, Jew!'" The knowledge that his "mighty" father submitted unprotestingly to this in-

* The author is Charles E. Maylan of Munich, who asks the revered master to accept this "hostile" book in paternal friendliness. This reception is not likely, for the study is invidiously selective and takes malicious pleasure in discrediting interpretations. Yet as an illustration of the possible result, it is as legitimate as many an analysis that a patient has received at the hands of a professional analyst.

dignity, started a conflict within the son who feared yet revered, even as he resented and hated his father.

The brooding upon the incident with the ambivalence which psychoanalysis makes characteristic, developed or combined with a "Hannibal" fantasy, in which Rome, the foe of Hannibal with whom Freud identifies himself, became the symbol of Christianity with its powerful organization, all in imposing contrast to meek Jewry. This antagonism persists and induces the mature Freud on a visit to Italy to resolve to pass through the hated Rome and proceed directly to Naples. When on another occasion Freud visits Rome, he is impressed by the stern mien of Michaelangelo's statue of Moses, which represents the threatening father, the threat being that of castration. Freud's *Moses of Michaelangelo* appeared anonymously—a significant instance of repression. Freud's own "analysis" of the pose of the statue reveals his guilty conscience at age fifty-eight, reflecting juvenile sexual offenses. The index finger of the *right* hand of Moses grasps the *left* half of the beard, turning it to one side and thus directing attention to the *left* tablet of the commandments—the left signifying the forbidden. This statuesque gesture in psychoanalytic cipher means that the beard represents the mother, the head the father, and that the emotional effect of the statue is motivated by the son's desire for the mother, and by the guilty fear in face of the reprimand by his father.

In another connection Freud is also identified with Hamlet; for Freud's father's ghost stalks through his life, bringing consternation and neurotic conflict. Freud's private life, his professional career, and his supposedly objective psychoanalytic system are all unmasked and made to reveal a tragic, composite

Oedipus-Hannibal-Hamlet, pro-Semitic, Martyr complex of embittered hate and revenge. One incident
in fact or dream, in reality or fantasy, is added
to another, and for the most part interpreted sexually or disparagingly.

Freud's *Ego and the Id* is interpreted as an emotional, a neurotic self-vindication. The *Ego* is Freud,
and the *Id* is his mother. But the important part in
the book is that of the *Super-ego,* which is the father.
The failure to insert the Super-ego is a suppression.
It indicates Freud's desire to be alone with his
mother even on a title-page. Indeed, the typographi-
cal arrangement is so cunningly devised that there is
no space for an additional insertion.

Serious analysis, invidious satire, parody, move so
nearly in the same manner that the distinction fades.
Complexes everywhere! Even the choice of profession is not a reflective consideration, but an issue of
deep affective, personal psycho-pathology—a dia-
bolical intrusion from the subconscious; Freud's
demonic urge toward a medical career requires explanation. "After 41 years of medical activity my
knowledge of myself informs me that I really was
not a true physician." And of the period of decision:
"I was not aware of a need to help suffering humanity: my sadistic inclinations were not pronounced,
so that traits thus derived demanded no development." The actual motive, according to this analyst,
was a desire to secure authoritative satisfaction of
his curiosity concerning what went on privately between his parents.

The Q. E. D. is this: Freud and all his works are
the product not of a scientific talent and intellectual
curiosity, but in essence a by-product of Freud's personal hate of all that is superior, joyous, free—a

hate of his father and all resembling him, a hate of Christianity, of Jehovah on the part of Ahasverus, the Wandering Jew. Speaking scripturally and psychoanalytically at once: "It is the unfulfillable yearning of the Jewish people for the 'promised land,' which is the familiar yet ever inaccessible stage of 'genitality' which Freud-Moses sees from afar and points out to his people, yet cannot himself enter, by reason of hereditary sin expressed as a sexual lust in envious dread of his father, directed toward his mother, and onanistically diverted."

The purpose of citing this wild example of psychoanalysis is to indicate how variously the game of reading subconscious motives in word and deed may be played. It leads to the reflection that few of us, if indiscreet enough to record our intimate motives or our behavior in moments of abandon, would fare any better—which reflection may serve as a consolation for obscurity. Truly we all live in glass houses and may rejoice that the Freudian rays penetrate only by our consent! Herr Maylan is clearly a more extreme, a less restrained Freudian than a more responsible representative of the movement. Yet, while his animus to belittle Freud appears throughout, his logic is hardly less strained than, in certain instances, Freud's himself in expounding his system or in applying it to the private foibles and tribulations of his patients. The distortion of Freud's personality in the hands of a prejudiced critic is intrinsically no more grotesque than Freud's general libel upon humanity, which I reject not on moralistic but on scientific psychological grounds.

The compass of this critique is set by the challenge of Freudian principles. If Freud's psychology is wrong, all is wrong; for the instigation of the enterprise was the conviction that psychology holds the clue to mental disorders. The fate of the technique is that of the underlying principles. I have focused upon what the analyst believes and why, as it affects his attitude toward his patient. The technique of psycho-diagnosis applies as freely to the normal man and his character-traits as to the neurotic. Treatment is a separate issue; it is the diagnostic technique that dominates in the total picture of the clinical procedure. It is by that that one would instantly recognize that one was listening in upon a psychoanalytic examination. We have thus reached the point of convergence of principle and practice, of the architecture and the occupations of the Freudian house.

The verdict upon the merit of both will, at my venture, take the form of prophecy. In forecasting the future of this momentous episode in intellectual history, I shall begin with its therapeutic phase and the temper pervading the practice. Principles, argument, technique, treatment are of a nature all compact. My brief ends here. I have deemed it important to present the mass perspective of the Freudian structure with its amazing originality, challenging contemporary psychology. Placed in the balance, I have found it wanting in naturalistic substance, and through that basic defect, aided and abetted by a disregard of the fundamental logic by which naturalistic science has come to be established, it has grown into a castle of delusion. Yet the paradox of the *dénouement*—not quite unique though possibly so on this scale of importance—is that within the maze of tortuous wandering lies a worthy prize, well worth an enduring quest.

CHAPTER IX

THE FUTURE OF FREUD

Temper

The motive force that has carried the psychoanalytic movement to a voluminous wave of popular attention and created for it a considerable following among those discontent with traditional methods and attitudes, is the frank direction of the psychological instruments of exploration to the insistent and intimate problems of human relations. However false or however true its conclusions, however weak or strong its arguments, however effective or defective or even pernicious its practice, its mission is broadly humanistic. Psychological enlightenment is presented as a program of salvation. By no other appeal could the service of psychology have become so glorified. The gospel of Freud seemed to say: Believe and prove it in your own person, and you shall be relieved and saved. As a motive, the hope of personal aid is far stronger, far more widely disseminated, than a zest for understanding. The strongly handicapped, the painfully inhibited, will listen to almost any voice, enlist in any enterprise that promises the release of their fetters; the maladjusted who sense their deviation will make the supreme sacrifice to be as others are; the miserable and perturbed and despondent yearn to be happy, with an intensity inspiring the last desperate ounce of effort. The therapeutic promise of psychoanalysis came as the most novel, most ambitious, most releasing of the long procession of curative systems that mark the history of mental healing.

To the contemporary trends in psychology psychoanalysis offered a rebuke, a challenge, a supplement, though its actual attitude assumed the undiplomatic form of ignoring them. With the practical purpose of applied psychology directed to human efficiency, it had no direct relation and thus no quarrel; these were but crumbs at the feast. The solutions of behaviorism, likewise bidding for popular approval by reducing adjustment to a program of conditioning, it inevitably found alien and irrelevant, as the behaviorist in reciprocity found psychoanalytic doctrine mystical, fantastic, assumptive, remote. Even to the cognate formulations of mental hygiene, as likewise in its contacts with related fields of psychology, psychoanalysis made no conciliatory advances. Toward psychiatry, clearly its nearest of kin, it took an unfriendly position, quite too plainly implying a disdain for an unprogressive relative. These estrangements affected its relations throughout the domain of mind and its ills; but they came to a head in the practice. It is psychoanalysis as an aggressively novel and revolutionary practice, free-lance in spirit, that determined the temper of a controversial campaign. A gauge of the future of this movement must be derived from its past and present reception. The encounter of Freudianism with established disciplines serves as the basis of prophecy, and places its therapy in the first line of attack and defense.

From the outset in its days of struggle, when it had but a sparse and scattered discipleship, to the present position of prominence, Freudianism went its own way, here and there making contact with problems and interests grudgingly considered, but for the most part neglected by academic psychology. Of dreams, lapses and neuroses, orthodox psychology had little to say. The second important reason for the impression made by psychoanalysis when once launched against the tide of academic resistance, was its recognition of *depth psychology,* so much closer to human motivation, so much more intimate and direct than the analysis of mental factors and the syntheses of mental elements. Psychoanalysis gave psychology a new center which it is likely to retain. For both its promises and its enlightenments the motif of psychoanalysis will endure, and the work inaugurated by Freud mark a turning point in the history of psychology and in the increasing knowledge of the springs of human behavior and their control. That phase of the future of Freud is secure and predictable.

In forecasting the future of the Freudian movement —the immediate prospect particularly—the temper with which it has been and is conducted is an important datum, even as in a legal trial the attitude of the defendant enters along with evidence and argument; and Freudianism remains on trial and re-trial, though it has outlived the prejudice against a fair hearing, and despite its extensive spread in recent decades. Contemporary opinion is formed by personal experience and the circulation of good and ill favor, from mouth to mouth. Along that route to verdicts, reputation turns upon cures rather than upon conclusions. Movements of this order wax and wane by the flow of popular attention, often with vaguely assignable causes. It is accordingly pertinent to consider the prospect first as affected by the success of the practice and as reflected in the total atmosphere surrounding it.

Most persons in trouble would be grateful for relief without too critical examination of the theory behind the practice that helped them. Anyone at all acquainted with the ebb and flow of "cures"—cures that cure and cures that fail—including the continuous procession of fakes and fads and follies stimulated in an advertising age, need not be told that the scientific basis of the system is often the least factor in its vogue. Many of these systems—forming rather a distinct group—arise empirically within a practice, which by trial seems to give results. This is conspicuously *not* the case *in re* psychoanalysis. Psychoanalysis belongs to the equally typical group of therapies in which practice is entirely a derivative of theory, however true that the suggestions for theory initially and in the course of elaboration grow out of clinical observation. Here the pertinent psychological principle reads: Create a belief in the theory, and the facts will create themselves. It holds, however differently, for psychoanalysis as for spiritualism. Unquestionably the more permanent and influential appraisal of psychoanalysis will be in terms of its principles; its fate for a decade or more will hang more intimately upon its practice. I can but repeat that I see nothing in that record to strengthen its hold, and I see much to weaken it. The crisis of psychoanalysis is at hand; the critical stage in its appraisal will presently be in full tide. That conviction has inspired this critique.

Psychoanalytic therapy comes into the frame of my project primarily as it reflects phases of doctrine. *Abreaction* is one such measure, as old as the confessional and permanently useful; "infected minds" discharging their secrets to "deaf pillows" can far more effectively discharge them to an understanding counsellor. As in the course of Freudian exploration, the emphasis was transferred to the unearthing of complexes, and in turn to the explorations of the infantile fixations, therapy shifted toward the breaking down or circumventing of resistances, and once again was transformed by the introduction of the entangling relations of transference. With each of these shifts, the therapy became more and more deeply involved in hypothetical premises, and, in my opinion, thereby moved farther and farther away from a verifiable basis and a promising art.

The procedure thus became controversial; innovations entered. There was much discussion—the issue is critical—as to how far the process of re-formation of character and readjustment to situation, which all agree to be the goal of therapy, is amenable to an intellectual factor of recall, or requires the emotional factor of reliving the experience, discharging it, substituting other gratifications, resigning ourself to its sway. Ferenczi introduces an "active" therapy in which there are assigned activities to release blocked motivations. This is in accord with established principles of mental hygiene, but in the form advocated is beset by fanciful suppositions which takes it out of that rationalized orbit. Rank introduces confusion by staking all treatment on "the reproduction of the intra-uterine state" hypothesis. Clearly there seems slight hope of a rational and consistent therapy in the contentious state of psychoanalytical Denmark.

Jung's positions shape the practice quite otherwise; and Adler takes it out of the psychoanalytic field, though readily included in general psychotherapy. His change of emphasis is of primary importance. He brings psychotherapy into closer contact with the moral-educational program, merging it quite too much so, as it thereby loses distinction and assumes an evangelical appeal. The procedure is spread thin and be-

comes commonplace and cultist in form. It does so
through insistence upon a single-tracked solution of
neurotic difficulties, by making superiority, which always masks inferiority or is a compensation wise or
unwise for it, the basis of a universal, weak and watery,
often meaningless solution, as miscast as all panaceas.
The error in his position is serious in that it so falsely
simplifies an actually most complex problem, as to lose
all grip and substance; it leaves little sufficiently tangible and practicable to serve as a basis of therapy. You
cannot convert a bootlegger into a missionary by calling
his attention to a false "pattern of life" associated with
his bringing up as the eldest in the family. Again the
cultist trend dominates. But one notable emphasis remains. Through the circuitous route of first "organ inferiority," then "psychic inferiority," then "compensation," then the dominant "pattern of life," Adler was
led to emphasize the "goal" as the guide to treatment
and stake his therapy on that. In contrast to an *urge*
psychology and its emphasis on *sources,* there results a
goal psychology with an emphasis on *ends*. The complementation is indispensable. In the entire range of the
"new" psychology there is no single idea of more fundamental consequence. No therapy can proceed effectively without concentration upon goals. The psychotherapy of the future will be equally a goal psychology
and an urge psychology. I present this picture of the
status of therapy to justify my minor consideration of
that aspect. Future therapy will depend upon a rationalized fusion of doctrines at present utterly confusing
and contradictory.

When the issue turns, as by the tide of popular interest it does and legitimately so, to the actual measure
of success which psychoanalytic therapy has achieved,

there must be borne in mind, the clinical experience
with the course of the psycho-neuroses. With due al-
lowance for exceptions, they have a self-limited term.
There is a period of incubation, of increasing difficulty
and concern, a culmination of despair, exhaustion, still
with fluctuations, and a period of subsidence, convalescence, gradual resumption of the normal tempo and
mood. The pattern is one of waves and ripples. The
pattern varies with temperament; now and then there
is a more or less sudden turn, and the patient snaps out
of it. Consider the evident sources of relief through the
very assurance that the patient's troubles are taken seriously, and that the patient, if of that kidney, obtains
encouraging satisfaction from finding himself an object
of interest; consider the long periods over which the
analysis spreads; consider the susceptibility, indeed the
suggestibility characteristic of certain forms (hysterical) of the psycho-neuroses; consider, by no means the
least, that there is no system which contains a modicum
of therapeutically effective moments, however fused and
confused with irrational ones; indeed, that there is no
system, however completely unscientific and even preposterous unless positively injurious, that does not
show a testimonialized census of cures and convales-
cences; considering all this, the success that has actually attended the practice of psychoanalysis is, in a
generous estimate, no greater and no better than was
to be expected. Certainly there are cases, many of
them, suitable for some varieties of psychoanalysis in
judicious form. But as applicable to the neuroses in
general or to any of its groups specifically, the procedure is just one of many, the others based upon different theories or frankly empirical gropings. As Hollingworth pointedly says: "Freud fails to show why
other methods of therapy than his own also succeed. If

his own theories are demonstrated by his own therapy, what shall we say of the reported success of the therapy of Babinski, Hurst and Rosanoff?"—which are distinctly not Freudian. There is nothing in the therapeutic experience that validates the method, nothing to offset its contradictions and violations of sound theory and established data; for it must be repeated that there is a great deal known about the varieties of the psycho-neuroses and their manifold factors that compose their versatile pictures—much of it of recent knowledge—which Freud completely ignores. In these rival approaches lie suggestive hints for the explanation of precisely the phenomena that attracted Freud's attention, and far more satisfactory ones.

There will be no available gauge of the actual efficiency until psychoanalysts of all persuasions publish impartially the statistics of their failures and successes, a consummation not at all likely in the present cultist temper of the Freudian movement. I much prefer to leave this phase of the verdict to professional practitioners in the field of neurology and psychiatry. Yet one criticism I must anticipate and rebut. It is the usual objection that no one who has not worked long and patiently with the system, lived it and practised it as an intimate part of his occupation, is in a position to judge its merits. That defense is lame and question-begging. It is used by proponents of cults and quackeries as invariably as occultists cite that there is more under heaven and earth than is dreamt of in our philosophies, not understanding what the "philosophies" quite rationally account for. There are too many more profitable occupations to justify such sacrifice; and from his detached conning tower, the critic, if penetrating, can see to advantage. Even if I had the proverbial nine lives to live, I should not feel the obligation to devote one apiece to the practice of physiognomy, phrenology, astrology, numerology, Christian Science, "New Thought," homeopathy, chiropractice, and Freudian psychoanalysis, in order to feel justified in reaching an appraisal of the intrinsic worth in principle or practice, or to indicate the gross and flagrant violations of logic and sanity which they present. I could not believe otherwise and write this book; nor can I consent in any measure to relieving all these proponents of the obligation to prove their theories to the satisfaction of scientifically minded judges. The survey of evidence and argument justifies a verdict.

Before passing on it is well to consider another factor in the turn toward psychoanalysis as a therapy directed toward relief by recognizing the reality of psychic ills. It is the cavalierly treatment of the psycho-neuroses by the medical profession, of the milder forms particularly as they occur among the most intelligent, deserving and high-minded men and women. The general practitioner, the internist, the diagnostician, have all too commonly taken an unintelligent and intolerant attitude toward patients in whom no organic disturbance can be found, whose "organ recital" is listened to with mingled and not well concealed expressions of pity, contempt and amused superiority. Physicians occupied with more tangible and to them more important and interesting "cases," fail to distinguish between the very distinct orders of intelligence, conscience, and courage among the patients who spend wearisome and agonizing hours in cheerless waiting-rooms.

A distinguished diagnostician, after examining an even more distinguished patient with negative findings, dismissed the latter with the patronizing remark that a man of his intelligence should certainly know better than to succumb to psycho-neurotic symptoms. The same undiscriminating and offensive reaction is repeated countless times daily in regard to worthy citizens generally. The medical profession has a large responsibility for the desperate recourse to less scientific practitioners, including charlatans, on the part of patients who have struggled long and heroically and could be brought to convalescence and cure by more sympathetic and understanding professional attitudes. Modesty would suggest a more appropriate deliverance, an acknowledgment that the difficulty was one in which the diagnostician is not versed and must be referred to those more competent in that type of disorder. Among the psychiatrists likewise, those peculiarly fit to deal with the functional neuroses form an elect minority.

The possible menace of psychoanalytic exploration cannot, should not, be overlooked. That it has been taken up by the "idle rich" lured to the novel by the attraction of a fashion, or espoused by prurient and unstable personalities as a thrill in sex or narcissism is but one side of the picture. Tales from Vienna * recount cases of distracted American husbands resorting to extreme measures to save their wives from psychoanalytic "transferences"; and of patients, bullied into admissions irritating rather than healing to emotional wounds, and of others driven to despair by emotional upset. These tales can be duplicated *ad lib.* in New York or wherever psychoanalysts have appealed to the same type of clientele. It is quite too easy for a practitioner to spend a few months in Vienna and on his return announce himself as a psychoanalyst ready to

* George Seldes: *Can These Things Be?* 1931

tamper with the holy of holies in the lives of bewildered patients. From unwisdom to indiscretion to scandal, and again from wrecked lives to suicide, the unsavory rumors accumulate. More than any form of practice that has sought scientific sanction, is psychoanalysis open to the abuse of confidence,* to the sex-degradation that is mistaken for enlightenment, and even more seriously, to the complete undoing of deserving patients neurotically tortured and psychoanalytically crucified.

One such tale in my correspondence will suffice: The writer is a woman who had had tragic marital troubles and had procured a divorce from her husband. She writes: "My physician in whom I had implicit confidence, persuaded me to try analysis. I felt no need for it, but not knowing anything about mental troubles I accepted his suggestion to my lasting despair. I was analyzed over a period of a year. It not only cost my family thousands of dollars, but as a result I became extremely ill; in fact one of the shocks which resulted from the analysis so unbalanced my mind that I became suicidal."

"To revert to the patter of the analyst, why should the discovery of a 'psychic trauma' be considered beneficial in a depression case? They tell you that depression is a 'flight from reality' and then proceed to make reality worse than it had ever been."

It is indeed difficult to distinguish the sheep from the goats when what under the theories of sex frustration is considered legitimate advice is often, considering the social circumstances of the patient, as preposterous as grossly insulting. It would be unjust to put the

* Dr. Tannenbaum has printed an instance, which, if reprinted here, might bring upon my publisher embarrassing censorship.

burden of quack psychoanalysts or even of foolish and
unprincipled practitioners upon the creditable disciples; but when there is so much irresponsible statement
and sexual distortion among leaders, they cannot be
held innocent of the consequences of their extravagances. There is "wild analysis" in abundance in all
grades and shades of the profession. What reason is
there to expect greater wisdom in practice than in principle? "The surgical crudities perpetrated by the average analyst [show] that his procedure is capable of an
illimitable mischief." The citation is from Schmalhausen, whose general position is psycho-diagnostic in
the critical sense, and who will not be accused of reticence in discussing matters of sex. He continues:

> "In sober truth, as a result of the vast harm per-
> petrated by some of the crude surgeons of the soul
> who call themselves orthodox psychoanalysts, it has
> become a matter of the first importance, practically
> and theoretically, to inquire into the mind's capacity
> for enduring the exploratory operations which it
> must undergo, at whatever costs to personal harmony
> that the analyst, in his infinitely dogmatic certainty
> decides to inflict upon a mind already suffering tor-
> tures beyond its reasonable endurance.
>
> If the practicing experts could summon the philo-
> sophic courage to report upon the cases which they
> have mismanaged or misunderstood (an analyst is
> a man for a' that), the new and very promising
> science of re-education would profit enormously by
> their clean confessional."

The charge is reënforced by the argument which underlies so much of my distrust of the technique, paralleling the protest against the principles as logically

unsound and psychologically unnatural, which is thus pointedly put:

"In the orthodox analytic technique there are modes of procedure that defeat these highly desirable ends: the patient's self-respect is tampered with, his confidence undermined, his courage thwarted. No wonder the analysis often becomes so horribly entangled and bungled that the patient, outraged and bullied in relation to his most sensitive feelings and thoughts, comes away actually much worse off than he was at the beginning."

"There is a delicacy in the handling of psychoneurotics which is frequently enough absent from the procedure of analysts. Dogmatism, magic authoritarianism, smart-Aleck interpretation, bullying, irritating silence, windly wordiness, the slinging around of Freudian jargon that means nothing in particular, are some of the unsweet facts that reduce the therapeutic potency of the psychoanalytic procedure." [SCHMALHAUSEN.]

In balancing the account of psychoanalytic therapy, the debit side requires close consideration; it is glossed over or not even recognized by reason of the fanatical absorption in doctrines—so many of them fictions—and of the undiscriminating and unrefined attitudes of analysts, who no more than any other profession can rise above their cultural and temperamental level. Yet if any calling ever required the maximum of tact and conscience, it is that of the mender of souls and the healer of infected minds. At present much of it proceeds without psychic aseptic precautions and in a temper that rebuffs sensitive and reflective minds. Since the avowed purpose is to bring peace and adjustment, it would seem axiomatic that the analyst should assure himself of the hygienic quality of his methods. It may well be that the protection that nature gives to the inner life is the condition of true sublimation. Digging at roots is dangerous, and in crude hands fatal.

It is the temper of psychoanalytic practice as well as the lack of warrant for its procedures, and the growing recognition of these entirely practical and social considerations, that leads me to anticipate its rapid decline, unless redeemed by a thorough reformation of its objectionable features. That it will decline because of its unwillingness to make cooperative contacts with the professional group to which it belongs, is an equally vital consideration. By all the signs applicable to the rise and wane of similar movements, psychoanalysis is running for a fall; its unwise temper has quickened its disfavor.

Nor can I overlook another charge which tends to make the analyst unpopular and a *persona non grata* in the profession: a presumption, unfortunately characteristic of his prevalent temper. His dogmatic insistence issues from ignoring most decidedly, from ignorance no less guiltily. That the best of them are free from these defects my own experience gladly testifies. The didactic manner of the initiate, superiorly instructing the uninformed, appears in print, upon the platform, even in conferences with medical colleagues. A repeated phrase: *"We analysts know"* violates the considerations of controversy among equals. There may be a touch of naiveté as well as insolence, or, more charitably, an insusceptibility to the courtesies of argument—in this attitude of presumption—of which the offender is seemingly unaware. It is reflected in the factions and frictions of the schools, as well as in the embarrassment of a hostess who had invited two distinguished analysts of opposing sects to dinner, only to find that neither would accept if the other were present; which complication if extended generally—let us say to Presbyterians and Episcopalians or to free-traders and protectionists—suggests unexpected possibilities in psycho-diagnosis. As a propagandist or missionary, the analyst lacks diplomacy.

The presumption of originality and "discovery" appears throughout the presentations. Dunlap comments upon it.

"The great importance of sex in human life is something which is held to have been entirely unknown until pointed out by Freud. It is a constant surprise to disciples of the Vienna physician that a psychologist may recognize, and even emphasize, the fundamental rôle which sex ideas and sex activities play in mind and conduct and yet not be a Freudian. Even the principles of the association of ideas, are, by frequent implication, products of psychoanalysis. The fact that all the details of conscious conduct are causally directed by the results of previous experience was, according to psychoanalysis, never surmised until Freud's *Psychopathology of Everyday Life* appeared. Students unacquainted with psychology, who get their first knowledge of commonplace psychological facts from Freudian sources, necessarily look upon Freud as the founder of modern mental science."

Even so fundamental a conclusion, so fundamental that it finds universal acceptance, may be found in the words of a distinguished American, a geologist * by profession, a humanist by the virtues of his character

* Nathaniel Shaler: The Neighbor.

and temperament, but completely unacquainted with Freud.

"It is hardly too much to say that all the important errors of conduct, all the burdens of men and societies are caused by the inadequacies in the association of the primal animal emotions with those mental powers which have been so rapidly developed in mankind." There is the gist of conflict.

As a further instance of presumption in another direction, I cite the statement of a representative analyst * who speaks of the "discovery of symbolism" by psychoanalysis; who ascribes to psychoanalysis the first recognition of the psycho-sexual constitution of man; who even holds that it has "inaugurated the application of the principle of evolution to the explanation of mental processes"; that "instead of indulging in idle metaphysical speculations as heretofore, we are learning to apply the standpoint of natural science to the investigation of the problems of the mind-body relationship."

This claim for psychoanalysis must overlook a goodly share of psychology that knew not Freud, must explain in what sense a "metapsychology" is an expression of the naturalistic standpoint; nor is it quite clear why "we psychoanalysts who witness day by day the warfare which rages between man's primordial instincts and his higher trends" should be exclusively capable of that insight. The presentation includes a four-page eulogium by H. G. Wells on the value of *psychology* and its *applications* for the progress of men, in which that writer not once refers to psychoanalysis or uses the term, which concludes that this popular writer expresses himself "enthusi-

* Van Teslaar: in "An Outline of Psychoanalysis." 1925.

astically on the subject of psychoanalysis and its promise for human welfare."

It is this strident and grating note, that offends the proprieties of argument as clearly as it contradicts the facts in the case. The challenge of the rest of psychology should hardly extend to its disdain.

Though I leave but a paragraph for the cultist temper of Freudian analysis, its effect upon the reception of the movement has been and remains marked. A single citation from a disciple: "Nothing formulated by Professor Freud from the beginning has had to be rejected" carries the attitude of papal reverence unseemly in a scientific venture of admittedly tentative nature. My experience with the temper of cults is fairly extensive. This tendency to join in the refrain when the leader sets the text, is characteristic; then continuous repetition is mistaken for added evidence. Cults form schisms and factions; each sees nothing but futile heresy in the other, from the days of Homoousian and Homoiousian on. Cults estrange and secede from the growing nuclei of progress. I have heard the remark by an analyst that Freudians may presently be limited to fellow-Freudians for their social as well as professional intercourse; the rest of the world will not understand them, nor their outlook and language. That there is a sound core of science in the Freudian formulation has been repeatedly indicated; it is almost lost in the cultist excrescences. It is the "cult" in psychoanalysis that betokens the fall of the house of Freud.

JUDGMENTS

The judgments rendered by the competent form another basis for prognosis. I shall assemble a variety of approaches and angles of observation. Psychoanalysis presents itself as one solution of certain major problems in psychology; and psychology, as a naturalist sees it, is a province within the broader empire of the life-science of biology. If that foundation-course is neglected or wrongly laid, the flaw in any construction within the "biological" domain is basic. Haldane, physiologist, holds it to be so for psychoanalysis:

> "The sort of organism which Freud imagines is a mere product of his imagination. . . . Of the characteristic features of conscious activity, his conception gives no account at all. . . . The whole structure of any such psychology rests on bad physics and bad physiology, besides being hopelessly inadequate from the special standpoint of psychology. It misrepresents our actions, because it misrepresents both our perceptions and our passions."

Dunlap, psychologist, is still more drastic in his rejection. Lacking the naturalistic basis, psychoanalysis "becomes an assault on the very life of the biological sciences. Psychoanalysis attempts to creep in wearing the uniform of science, and to strangle it from the inside." It is not the persistently speculative course alone that offends the experimental-minded. A tolerant psychologist, Dodge, freely admits that

"Facts without hypotheses are dead"; but adds that "hypotheses which cannot be verified might as well be."

The Freudian invasion of the house of science seems an intrusion and a violation; just how or why it is not easy to say. Psychoanalysis just does not seem to belong there; it carries an alien atmosphere. Trotter, sociologist, expresses the out-of-placeness skillfully.

"However much one may be impressed by the greatness of the edifice which Freud has built up, one can scarcely fail, on coming into it from the bracing atmosphere of the biological sciences, to be oppressed by the odour of humanity with which it is pervaded. One finds everywhere a tendency to the acceptance of human standards and even sometimes of human pretensions, which cannot fail to produce a certain uneasiness as to the validity, if not of his doctrines, at any rate of the forms in which they are expounded. The quality I am trying to describe is extremely difficult to express in concrete terms without exaggeration or distortion."

Turning from rejection to endorsement, there is the opinion of Holt,* psychologist. Writing in 1915, he calls Freud's contribution epoch-making in that it gave to the science of mind a causal category. He continues:

"It is the first key which psychology has ever had which fitted, and moreover I believe it is the only one that psychology will ever need. Although of course these two statements would be savagely disputed by the comfortably established professors of an earlier school, who are a bit mystified by Freud and suffer from the uncomfortable apprehension that he is doing something to them; they know not quite what. And in fact he is, for he is making them look hopelessly incompetent."

Much water has flowed under the Freudian bridge since then. In reply to my inquiry whether he would still hold this opinion, the reply is generally affirmative and specifically negative.

* E. B. Holt: The Freudian Wish. 1915.

The "wish and the conflict of wishes and their mutual reenforcement," he upholds and makes the essence of the acceptable Freudian emendations. "On the other hand, I feel little interest in psychoanalysis as a therapy; and I believe that the concepts of the 'libido' and 'sublimation' are erroneous and misleading" which means: as actually employed. Holt concludes: Freud "deserves neither the furious dispraise nor the frantic worship which has been accorded him."

I dwell upon this opinion as an early constructive criticism of importance; for Holt even then saw the need of reinterpreting Freud. He sketches the bridge that might have been built upon the Freudian piers. Holt's "Freudian wish" would have fused "purpose or project for a *course of action,* whether it is being merely entertained by the mind or is being actually executed— a distinction which is really of little importance," important, indeed, pragmatically or socially, but not as shaping attitude; it would have fused purpose, intention, inclination, prejudices for and against, desires, attractions and repulsions, and the instinctual urges, whether their dynamic energy flows mainly above or below the undulating surface of consciousness.

This concept is fundamental to a psychology of conflict, from petty domestic squabbles to Leagues of Nations deliberations. Had Freudianism developed along Holtian lines, its future—which is now its past—might well have been of a wholly different content and temper. The concept of "conflict" would have broadened into a give-and-take of human relations in all its myriad phases, its cleavages and harmonies, its zests and aversions; and the Freudian factors would have been incorporated into the dynamics of depth psychology. "Back to Holt" would be an appropriate cry at the present juncture.

But it was not to be. Speaking of a more specific issue, he is obliged to state that:

> "Freud has never raised this question in so explicit form." And again: "What I shall say . . . is confessedly more than Freud has said; it is, however, as I believe, the inevitable almost immediate deduction from what he has said."

It is not only "more"; it is, alas! quite different, from what Freud since then has said. The anticipation of my position from a different approach is peculiarly welcome. There is a kindred note on the clinical side in the advocacy of Freudian views by J. J. Putnam.* His is a sympathetic statement of the valid purpose of the psychoanalytic procedure and its merits. What Dr. Putnam's opinion would be, had he lived to witness the growth of the movement farther away from the therapeutic mission which won his adherence, is a matter of conjecture. I infer that he would have aligned himself with the more conservative Freudians.

I turn to the critical view as it appears in Germany.† The question is raised as to which will prevail:

> "the present many-sided and established new knowledge of man's mental life, within which psychoanalysis as a method and a theory will find a place along with others all relatively valid: or a one-sided psychoanalytic doctrine adhering to a single point of view, and making that absolute?"

* Reprinted in Van Teslaar: above cited. It is an expression brought forward by the visit of Freud and Jung to America.
† Prinzhorn: Die Krisis in der Psychoanalyse. 1929.

Many analysts deplore the extravagances that have crept into theory and practice, and the popular preoccupation with them. They hold these to be "excrescences" which do not affect the vital core of truth. Again citing a German view:

> "the shell compasses and covers the doctrine which thus takes on more and more the appearance of an occult science, and specifically with regard to dream interpretation. The extravagances, past and current, are indeed so vast as to condemn the entire product as untenable; but all this is in the foreground and determines the impress it makes, but is not its essence."

On the other hand Kraepelin confesses "that with the best will I am not able to follow the lines of thought of this 'metapsychiatry' which like a complex soaks up the sober method of clinical observation." And there is Bleuler, favorable to many of Freud's doctrines but questioning or rejecting so many of them that Freud says: "I have been puzzled to know what remains of his tribute." And Rieger, speaking of the more extreme derivations: "I have always regarded this sort of thing as frightful nonsense." Bumke * maintains that if psychoanalysis stands, "then what until now has stood as science will disappear, and naturally my modest career as a psychiatrist ends."

Rivers, whose corrections are also restatements of the Freudian doctrines, is generous in his verdict:

> "His followers, however, and to a large extent Freud himself, have become so engrossed with the

---

* Oswald Bumke: *Die Psychoanalyse: Eine Kritik.* Berlin, 1931. An important recent critique by a distinguished psychiatrist. It is reviewed by Dr. Sachs in the Journal of Mental Hygiene, 1932.

cruder side of sexual life that their works might often be taken for contributions to pornography rather than to medicine. In some of Freud's followers this absorption in the sexual has gone to such lengths that perverse tendencies and prurient ideas are scented in every thought, waking or sleeping, of the patients who come under their care." . . . "The mistake which is now being made by many is to regard this excess as a necessary part of the Freudian scheme instead of an unfortunate excrescence, probably due in large measure to the social environment in which the theory had its origin."

"To me it is only such an hypothesis designed, like all hypotheses, to stimulate inquiry and help us in our practice, while we are groping our way towards the truth concerning the nature of mental disorder. Are we to reject a helping hand with contumely because it sometimes leads us to discover unpleasant aspects of human nature and because it comes from Vienna?"

Among American psychiatrists who write in the same strain, there is Moss, who says: "Nothing could be more deadening to future progress and true scientific understanding of mental disorders than the general acceptance of a theory which explains the mental diseases in terms of mysterious psychogenic causes resulting from the suppressed memories of infantile sexual experiences." And Myerson: "One of the strangest things in the history of science is the rise into dominance of some scientific theory which becomes established as a dogma, checking the free growth of knowledge."

Among recent critical views of psychoanalysis, the presentation of Leary * is important. It is a consistent and constructive attempt to bring psychoanalysis into the realm of a rational, naturalistic interpretation.

"Psychoanalysis is at present and has been for some time, in a state of almost hopeless confusion, due to misunderstandings, insufficient knowledge, prejudice and rivalry, plus . . . a tremendous public, popular interest . . . with a resultant further confusion."

"Much of the logic of the psychoanalytic movement is of the very type which its own teachings call dereistic, autistic, primitive, pre-logical, or non-logical; it is in terms of wishes, chance associations, analogies, purpose and desire, rather than in terms of fact, observation, correlation, experiment and congruity with other findings."

Hollingworth † disposes of the matter more simply by heading his section introducing psychoanalysis: *Freudian Fictions,* and sweepingly designates all the attempts to frame explanations upon hypothetical constructions *the psychoanalogical,* "sometimes meaning-

* Daniel Bell Leary: Modern Psychology: Normal and Abnormal. 1928. As Leary comes to such closely similar judgments as my own, including prophecies and redemptions, it is proper to state that my own views were formulated without knowledge of his. His chapter on Psychoanalysis is cordially recommended.

† Abnormal Psychology: Its Concepts and Theories. By H. H. Hollingworth, 1930. This is by far the most critical survey of all the concepts underlying the entire range of problems in the field where Psychology and Psychiatry have mutual interests. Hollingworth shows in detail how Freud's psychology repeats that of Herbart, with its diagrams of forces, but in dynamic, quasi- or pseudo-"biological" terms.

lessly called the psychoanalytical approach." Leary agrees that the "censor," "catharsis," "dream- inter- pretation," "libido," "sublimation," "unconscious" are either fictions or non-logical assumptions; but that they all contain a nuclear core of fact which can be fitted into a naturalistic, even into a behavioristic scheme of realities.

The complete illogicallity of the Freudian interpreta- tions, even on their own premises, and the far better established explanations of the same phenomena pre- sented by Freudians, is convincingly presented by Hol- lingworth. Hollingworth's analysis demonstrates the complete inadequacy of Freud's explanations all along the line of march, alike historically from the first analy- sis to the last, and seriatim in the several stages and phrases of the Freudian repertory, which range from "fairly simple assumptions" to "extravagant doctrines marked by the most extraordinary imaginative free- dom."

"We can dispense with the 'unconscious' and the 'Oedipus complex' and 'projection' as easily as we can dispense with fairies, demons and 'Santa Claus.' . . . The 'psychoanalogy' is all in the explanation, in the theory of the analyst, not in the material of the case. This indeed is quite opposed to the as- sumptions and quite explicable without them. . . . All these 'literary analogies' are dangerous. The un- sophisticated may take them to be accounts of some- thing supposed really to happen. . . . Rational ex- planations with simpler concepts may take the place of the mysticism and demonology of psychoanaly- sis."

The details are just as false. "The concept of *con- version* of an emotion into a tic, for example, or into a stiff leg, presents a picture of the transmutation of the elements before which even the most recent students of radium must retreat." Commonplace facts of opposed emotions are made over into a portentous *ambivalence*. . . . "A child may admire his mother's beauty and kindliness, but feel nothing but disrespect for her timidity and physical weakness. The cook's muffins may be wonderful, but her temper abominable." In terms of applications: if as Freud says, "hysteria is the caricature of an artistic creation, a compulsion neurosis the caricature of a religion, and paranoia a caricature of a philosophical system, Freud's explanation of compulsion neurosis is a caricature of Aesop's fables."

The note of prognosis, duplicating my own adventure in prophecy, appears in Leary:

"New, not so much as regards the isolated and separate facts involved, as new in its dynamic, genetic and unitary point of view in regarding the behavior of the personality, bringing into consideration, in this unified point of view, factors which have ordinarily been slighted, not known or even deliberately discounted. In order, however, to attain to the restatement of psychoanalysis which will put it in line with other knowledge of human nature it will be necessary, first, to summarize the history and growth of psychoanalysis, and then to begin the process of evaluating the various assumptions and conclusions ordinarily contained within its limits in terms of the general point of view we have been developing."

As for the practical effect of the movement, even so uncompromising an antagonist as Dunlap admits that "the final result of the Freudian movement may be beneficial, although the immediate effects are the deluding of many persons and the temporary checking of psychological research. Just as Christian Science has tremendously accelerated the progress of Scientific Medicine, so Psychoanalysis, by compelling psychology to put its house in order, will eventually help in the development of the Scientific Psychology it aims to thrust aside."

"Putting the psychological house in order" is far more than an apt phrase. It indicates an active occupation. The Freudian invasion has compelled attention to just those vital problems of motivation and personlity which were out of reach of the early experimental interests. Yet psychology was independently moving towards this completion. Freud may both have goaded it and stimulated it, have pushed it on and held it back. All in all, there has been no more enlivening episode in the altogether too academic drama of the science of mind than that associated with the name of Freud.

Let this eclectic sample suffice to reflect the sharp disagreements within the fold of psychology and affiliated sciences, and the clear emergence of the critical temper in appraising the validities and the violations of the Freudian concepts. They seem to me to confirm the widespread distrust, to reënforce the growing repudiation, to betoken the rapid decline of the Freudian movement in its present line of advance.

The Freudians, I am well aware, will read it all differently; though they rarely leave the more congenial occupation of adding to untested hypotheses more weakly attested interpretations, except for the equally congenial occupation of contemplating their growing literature, and confidently instructing the uninformed and ignoring or at best shrugging enigmatical shoulders at the resisting reactionaries. They should be reminded firmly yet with unreciprocated tolerance that they are on the defensive; that the crisis in psychoanalysis can be met only by recognizing the extent and intensity of the protests of sympathetic critics. Psychoanalysis must either come within the fold of psychology and psychiatry, or risk the fate of estrangement from the currents of progress.

PROSPECT

The signs of the times converge; they compose the writing on the wall. The decisive verdict cannot but be influenced by the violations of the fundamentals of psychology and the rules of logic, at all stages of construction, from foundation to finish. So considered, the house that Freud built is built upon sand, and with crumbly cement. There is, say those who have lifted psychology from an uncertain discipline to a secure position among the sciences, no place in the psychology of the future for a house of fictions, myths, and dreams. Should this conviction prevail, my attempt to forecast the future, like many another, will come to naught. Psychoanalysis will be declared an outlaw, a pretender, a usurper; when the upheaval which it has produced, subsides, there will be no trace of its sway in the succession. If such is the ultimate decree, Freudianism may come to be regarded as the most glamorous delusion of a scientific age, a modern mirage among the clear-visioned crowded occupations of men.

For my own faith in a different outcome, my belief in the salvaging of what is of value in this encyclopedic survey from a new vista of man and his works, I can cite no parallel among the comparable intellectual movements of the past. Phrenology, after a flash in the pan, is dead and gone; it never truly lived, not in a scientifically minded world. There remains no trace of "animal magnetism" in either hypnotism, suggestion or dissociation, any more than there is a trace of homeopathy in modern medicine. Such movements are not stepping-stones but futile detours; and history is full of them. Neither in management nor in knowledge do men proceed by the direct path; the road to progress is tortuous, meandering and confused. Admittedly my anticipation can cite no precedent. But the status of Freudianism is in many aspect unique; so, I believe, will be its fate. In my analysis it carries some of the earmarks of a genuine progress, an authentic insight; it appears to me a great idea turned into a great delusion through a disparity of qualities in the leading mind that evolved the scheme. Sensing this moment in the core and course of psychoanalysis, I spoke of it fifteen years ago as a great discovery made by the wrong man.

The ground for that conclusion itself forms an interesting application of a psychological finding: the unequal development of the creative and the critical qualities of mind. It is a case in point in the distribution of high-grade special abilities, which have become more and more decisive in a specialized age. Master minds are indeed able in many respects, but their mastery limited to few. To interchange the employments of creators and critics would spell disaster in the affairs of the intellect; each would be dumb at the other's task. Yet the converse is still truer and as definitely recognized; that the requirement of high intellectual endowment applies to both. In the mind of Freud, the uneven development of the two requisite qualities is extreme. I am led to the strange conclusion that "Psychoanalysis" is in no small measure the result of the chromosomes and the intellectual traditions of one brilliant Austrian, which made him exceptionally creative and as exceptionally uncritical. Disaster is imminent when a creative mind undertakes a task that requires creative insight to see it and plan it, and equally critical aptitudes to execute it. It may be a helpful parallel to reflect what what might have been the course of evolution, had the creative mind of Darwin been far more boldly speculative and far less exactingly critical.

Whatever the source of the discrepancy—for mind is mind with all its contradictions, as man is man with all his —the effect of it upon the acceptance of Freud's ideas has been marked. My anticipation that the essential values of psychoanalysis will be salvaged and its misconceptions corrected, may prove to be wrong not for the reason cited, that the scheme will fall into oblivion, but for the very opposite, that it will be acclaimed for its intrinsic worth, and its errors forgiven and forgotten. Such is the view of Stefan Zweig,* whose pen-portrait of Freud conveys a fine appreciation of an admiring friend. He looks upon the advent of Freud as itself the fulfillment of a prophecy, citing Schiller's none too definite allusion: "If there should arise a Linnaeus to classify impulses and inclinations, he would greatly astonish mankind"; or Nietzsche's more enigmatic: *"Alles was tief ist liebt die Maske."* Zweig is confident that the Freudian renaissance will be recognized for all time. "Freud's discovery of the dynamics of the mind," his "introduction of a new investigatory technique"; the recognition of the "unconscious"—"a supreme act of genius": these, as Zweig sees it, assure the future of Freud. If so, "what do the details matter?"

* Stefan Zweig: Mental Healers. 1932. An engaging account of the person of Freud and his life work.

I suspect that they matter enormously. They mattered to Darwin so much that they became his life work; they remain a monument of the critical pursuit of a master idea. We may endorse the summary of Wells, Huxley and Wells: "Sigmund Freud's name is as cardinal in the history of human thought as Charles Darwin's," yet recognize that the course of his contribution, for reasons of which this book is an expression, must proceed otherwise.

"Let not our criticisms," say the authors of *The Science of Life*, "seem to be a depreciation of their work, or above all, "a belittlement of Freud"; and in prophetic vein: "we may confidently expect . . . twenty-five years hence, that the whole controversy between Freudian, Jungian, Alderian and other brands of psychologists will have been relegated to the attics of scientific history. . . . Each party is making its contributions to truth; and less partisan psychologists are already drawing impartially on all those divergent explorers in the field of psychological exploration for a more solid edifice of theory."

Whatever the verdict twenty-five years hence, the interest of the here and now is in the redemption of the Freudian values for the guidance of our thinking, the management of our practice. Attempting to see Freud steadily and to see him whole, we gratefully record that the nuclear core of the construction that places Freud among the master psychologists of all time is the envisagement of man's total psychic activity under a unifying aspect of motivation. That dynamic conception of mental behavior might well have become current as the Freudian "wish"; for this there is no comprehensive term, as the concept though implicit in the modern approach, was lacking. From urge to rational plan its repertory runs. The emphasis upon urge, vague and groping as well as focused, is its distinctive accent, complementing the older over-emphasis upon reflection. The emphasis upon urge carries with it the primacy of all that is primitive, instinctive, ancient, affective, early to appear, feebly, immaturely conscious; the special emphasis converges upon libidinal urges—its focus in sexual libido—on the affective side, upon the "subconscious" in all its phases on the intellectual side. That the false reading of libido and its extreme sexualization, the varied misinterpretation of subconscious activities, the introduction of wrongly oriented genetic relations, and the failure to follow the biological clue, are jointly responsible for the errors of the total scheme, must be included in the picture, even as the high lights of its merits are registered. Thus emerges the Freudian urge psychology, with an original, comprehensive, illuminating perspective. It presents the human psyche in a restored completion, dynamic, vital, significant.

It complements the absorption in intellectualist detail; it corrects the limitations of the behavioristic approach, which is a stimulus psychology. In lowlier functions the stimulus dominates and proposes, though the organism disposes; in highly developed functions, the increasing complications of the urging "wish" determine behavior. Goal psychology appears in the implications of the wish.

The Freudian view-point envisages all behavior under the aspect of primary and secondary function, sees in their conflict the source of maladjustment, slight and grave, and in their reconciliation the clue to therapy and the art of control. It is congenial to an integration psychology which results from the fusion of the two orders of function, pointedly indicated in the pleasure principle and the reality principle. It directs the search-light of this unifying illumination upon the products of the human psyche, past and present, casual and momentous, at play and at work. It sees the whole of human personality and the total march of human enterprise as the embodiment and expression of this basic play of forces, in conflict and in sublimation. It gives a clue to much that was meaningless, reconstructs the perspective of significance, holds out the promise of a franker, freer, wiser management. Such is the enduring house that Freud built.

And yet in the very planning and building, he withdrew the prop from under the structure.

> "The present development of mankind seems to me to demand no other explanation than that of the animals; and what appears in a minority of individuals as a restless drive for further perfection is intelligible as a consequence of frustrated instincts on which the things of highest value in human culture have been built."

Precisely that which gives strength and significance to the Freudian complications in the human scheme is reduced to a moment in its source, thus repudiating the very sublimation which makes culture possible. The philosophy that Freud has erected upon the magnificent survey is a despairing one: "the core of our being consists of wishes that are unattainable, yet cannot be checked." Our bondage to urges, to the sexual dominance particularly, is the obstacle; denying this, we sicken; avoiding it, we soar into delusion. Each man's philosophy is his own version of the trials and hopes of living. A future Freud may build upon much the same foundation a philosophy of sublimation, a program of release through a stronger faith in goals and the integration of urges. The penetration of psychoanalysis has become a clue to the modern temper as well as a guide to philosophy. The influence of Freud is as wide as the reach of current thought.

It is the lack of reciprocity in the Freudian movement, its exclusive detachment, its ignoring of other laborers in the psychological vineyard that has brought about the present situation. This impedes the recognition of the ideas which the psychoanalytic approach could best contribute; it is this that makes a salvaging and a redemption the necessary course. It is not merely a Neo-Freudian correction, but a new post-Freudian reinterpretation that is needed. We may have to await as able a mind as Freud's, yet one of different make-up, to accomplish that consummation.

Because the Freudian method and temper is a temptation to arbitrary and prejudiced interpretation, does its redemption lie in a circumspect balance and discriminating insight—both unfortunately rare in the records of the contentious Freudian movement. No movement of this order, in these days, can proceed by disregarding the more convincing and better established conclusions which progressive psychiatrists and psychologists have elaborated upon a less biassed study of the total clinical experience. Both these groups were ready to move along what we now must call Freudian lines; they found stimulation in what will remain by historical fact the Freudian renaissance. The future of Freud depends upon the adoption of its key-note ideas by responsible psychiatrists and psychologists, divested of the extravagant implications and speculations that for the time have obscured and discredited it. A safe and sane Freudianism is not only possible but imperative.

The Freudian temper has forsaken a redeeming principle of its own doctrine, that of sublimation: that the wise management of the native urges and their redemption consists in their direction to useful, constructive employment, and still more pertinently in their refinement. This becomes physiologically a discharge of lowly organic energy along highly organized psychological outlets; it is hitching the organic wagon to a psychic, even a spiritual star. The psychiatrist above all practitioners of the ministering art should be a humanist; humanism and cultism are not congenial.

The history of psychology shows all too plainly that prejudiced speculation has been its undoing, and that psychologists have erected again and again as the statue on the altar of their temple of learning a god made in their own image, as the mind of the day envisaged it. However imperfect his insight, man cannot but make the attempt to see himself rightly, to see himself whole. What we know of the human psyche is a torso; we feel the urge to restore it to its full human completion. The Freudian attempt, however ambitious and logically inadequate, is yet itself the expression of an urge for completion of understanding, that harks back to the first great intellectual awakening and the classic precept: Man, know thyself! It is a far cry from the academic groves of ancient Athens to the psychoanalytic clinic of modern Vienna. How far the Freudian temper has brought order into the human cosmos, how far it has enhanced or clarified, how far distorted or degraded human values, are questions of large moment for future generations.

Considering both theory and practice, the historian of psychology in the future may well regard the great mass of present-day psychoanalytic literature as one of the strangest anomalies and fantastic vagaries of the early twentieth century. And yet if he is tolerant, he may equally find in the same movement one of the truly notable moments in the understanding of the perpetual enigma—the human psyche.

As to Freud's own view of his construction, these are the modest closing words of his autobiography:

"Looking back, then, over the patch-work of my life's labours, I can say that I have made many beginnings and thrown out many suggestions. Something will come of them in the future. But I cannot tell myself whether it will be much or little."

The citation from Freud which brings me greatest satisfaction, I have reserved for the *finis coronat opus:*

"One might ask me whether and how far I am convinced of the correctness of the assumptions here developed. My answer would read that I am neither myself convinced nor do I ask that others shall believe them; or, better stated, I don't know how far I believe them."

THE END

INDEX

1158